THE WORLD IS YOUR LOBSTER

LEE MOUNTFORD

Wooden Horse Press

First published in 2019 by Wooden Horse Press
Wooden Horse Press
www.woodenhorsepress.com

Cataloguing-in-Publication data is available from the National Library of Australia.

The World Is Your Lobster
ISBN 978-0-6485632-1-1

Cover image by Mr Paterson (www.scottpaterson.art)
Editing by Mrs Mounty

Disclaimer

Woster
This is a record of one of the most amazing experiences a guy could have with the perfect travel, and life partner.
Love you more than White Maltesers

Friends
To our all our friends that supported us during this adventure, and everyone who we met along the way, you know who you are. We couldn't have done it without you, it just wouldn't have been the same. To those who knew I was writing this and kept prodding and enabling me, thank you.

Families
Along with the laughter, came tears. Your support not only helped us to continue, but has been a constant ever since. Thank you.

Mum & Dad
I hope you've been watching all this!

CHAPTER 1

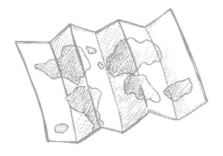

Location: Melbourne

The Exciting Introduction

The sweat was dripping from our brows as the armed policeman debated our refusal to give him a bribe. I was convinced that with his melodic glances up and down, shifting his gaze between our eyes, and the passports he held in his hands, he was mentally pulling leaves from a daisy and reciting 'let them go', pluck, 'lock them up', pluck, 'let them go'. Our only crime was an invalid visa after all, we were not drug runners or anything serious, but I had just refused point blank to give him a US$200 bribe. I've seen those TV shows where innocent people get banged up abroad. How many petals do daisies have in Vietnam anyway?

Nic: 'Dun Dun Dun!'

Lee: 'What?'

Nic: 'Well that sounded like it needed some dramatic music. Anyway, I thought you were writing a book about our trip, and you've started months into it?'

Lee: 'I'm trying to entice people in with some excitement so they will stay with us for the journey.'

Nic: 'Isn't it going to confuse people, jumping around like that? With your mix of past and present tense, they are probably going to feel like *Dr Who* as it is. Shouldn't you at least have introduced us first?'

Lee: 'Face it hun, we are boring people. I fell asleep twice writing about us. If I picked up a book and started reading about us, it wouldn't be long before I'd get distracted and start Googling funny aardvark videos on YouTube.'

Nic: 'Well that's the point isn't it. We're average people who didn't believe they could ever complete a trip like this, it just wasn't in our upbringing. It's a story of achievement, of relationships, of adventure.'

Lee: 'Yes, but other people complete trips like this on unicycles or with a donkey in tow, or circumnavigate the globe doing a *Monty Python* funny walk. Who is going to want to read about normal people?'

Nic: 'We completed a 77,000km trip through 27 countries, 60% of which was completed without flying, a distance of more than the Earth's circumference. That's an achievement in anyone's book (excuse the pun). There were certainly some exciting moments, like nearly being stranded in Siberia; numerous near-death experiences on various modes of transport; and of course that moment in Vietnam, which I'm still trying to forget. Anyway, it's not all about the excitement, you're not Jason Bourne despite what you think.

What about the laughs? What about the moments of heartache?'

Lee: 'To be honest this will mainly be about the fun and laughs, and less about Bear Grylls moments, although I did eat those insects in Thailand.'

Nic: 'How about you just start with us and if people like us, they will hopefully stay along for the ride.'

Lee: 'Fair enough, back to the beginning.'

The Beginning

Let me introduce ourselves to those who don't know us, we are your common or garden average couple in our 40's. Not too boring, not too exciting, socially awkward, reserved as only the English can be. We are certainly not too tall, one of us has a good sense of humour, the other travels with a first aid kit that's the size of a house. Get the picture? Oh yes, our names – Lee & Nicki.

We were brought up in the North West of England, and although we had some limited experience of travelling with family, we were undoubtedly late bloomers as far as being a tourist. At the end of 2002, three months after we were eventually married, we decided to embark on a pretty scary (for us) mini-migration to Australia. Planning to start off in Melbourne 'for a few months', before moving to the next city, and so on, for a total of 12 months before returning to the UK. I'm sure you're thinking that this was a big step for newlyweds, but don't worry we'd just completed a 10 year 'try before you buy' scheme so knew what we were getting into.

So how did our plan go? Well, 10 years after landing in Melbourne, we still hadn't managed to move onward (or return home). Writing that down certainly makes it sounds like we were pretty damn lazy at this travel malarkey. The problem was, we immediately felt at home in Melbourne. Within days of landing we were directing tourists around this beautiful city. On one hand, it was great that we'd built up the courage to travel and we were finally putting ourselves out there. However, when your first stop regularly tops the rankings as one of the world's most liveable cities, the urge to move on, suddenly becomes quite flaccid.

Because of the city's status, you'll often meet travellers in Melbourne who are generally much better at escaping the lure of the city. This gave us the chance to meet many people that have travelled much more extensively than us. Even with the locals, it seemed like most Australians were kicked out of the country to travel the world in some kind of drunken national service/rite of passage. Now I'm sure that this also happens by their UK counterparts but for our age group, the area we grew up in, and our socio-economic backgrounds, it was rare. Even though we had 'upped sticks' and moved across the world, we didn't feel brave enough for any serious travelling. The more people we talked to about their experiences, the less scary and more obtainable travelling seemed. When we initially landed in Melbourne, we felt akin to Lindenberg and Earhart for completing such an adventure, even though the process was actually pretty damn easy. We thought it would be our globe-trotting pinnacle and we'd be able to ride the coattails of this endeavour for the rest of time. This was not to be so.

A couple of years after we arrived, we were introduced to Tim and Moira, a couple who were passing through on a global journey. They had become frustrated with their working life in London, decided to quit their jobs, buy two round-the-world airline tickets, and go travelling for a year. To us, this made them real heroes. We were awe inspired, hearing their stories about different cities and countries over a few glasses of wine, thinking how boring our migration story was. After they moved on from Melbourne, we would often continue to talk of their adventure. Their trip finally came to an end, and they decided that, from all the places they'd visited, Melbourne was the place they wanted to live. They eventually returned, and we became good friends.

Surely this seemed like further validation that we should be more than happy where we were, shouldn't we?

Over the next year, they introduced us to something we fell in love with, scuba diving. This new passion opened up some great dive trips and our first foray into the joys of South East Asia with mini trips to Thailand and Malaysia. We were protected from the potential culture shock of these exotic locations by having these experienced travellers with us, and the fact that we were mostly underwater so oblivious to it. Did we think we could do it by ourselves? No, not really.

Despite getting away regularly for these underwater adventures, it still didn't seem to calm down a brewing wanderlust. The more trips we took, the shorter the gap we wanted until the next one, like an addiction, we just didn't seem to get enough. The general rule was that we had to have the next trip at least planned, if not booked, within a week of returning from the current holiday. Don't get us wrong, we knew we were absolutely blessed to be in such a situation and really appreciated our lifestyle. We both had good jobs, worked hard, and the fact that we are unable to keep a goldfish alive for more than a fortnight has made us refrain from producing our own little travel bugs. Since arriving in Australia with nothing more than our suitcases, we'd naturally accumulated some 'stuff', but not enough to mean we weren't comfortable in a smaller, and therefore cheaper, apartment. All this enabled us to maximise our disposable income.

Working in Australia provided a much-improved lifestyle for us, especially with some of the employee benefits we both received from working in the government health industry. For instance, the use of salary packaging enables employees to pay their rent and eat out in restaurants using pre-tax salary. Where else in the world would you get something called 'leave loading', a mechanism where you get paid a little extra during your annual leave to help you enjoy yourself? One of the key benefits that will often secure a jaw drop when telling folks back home is long service leave. In Nic's case, this rewarded her after 10 years of continuous service, with 17 weeks of paid leave. She is also given the option to take this at half pay for double the time, giving her a reduced income for 34 weeks. As you may have just twigged, this benefit is quite pertinent to the future of this book.

This feeling to travel kept growing within. Apparently, there is a condition called Dromomania which gives people the uncontrolled psychological urge to wander. I much prefer the thought that we were inflicted with this disorder, rather than just being spoilt brats with a 'because I want to' mentality. Either way, we knew something was coming….

A big trip shaped lightbulb

The way things generally work in our relationship is that Nic will spurt out a harebrained idea and I have the bad cop duties of reeling that idea in with practicality, or dash her dreams with the phrase 'We'll see' which we both understand is the non-confrontational code for saying 'No!'. Case in point, one rainy Melbourne afternoon, we were walking through the backpacker section of a travel expo, and she hit me with a real humdinger, 'let's travel from Sydney to London on a bus!'. A typical Nic statement, and a trait that's one of the three reasons I married her. Now, the thought of spending twelve weeks sharing low-cost transportation and dorm accommodation with the great unwashed didn't appeal. I'm way too short to be some kind of father figure, and way too old to spend eleven of those weeks too drunk to remember a thing. I think this idea even bypassed the 'We'll see' response and went straight to 'Not on your nelly, luv', as I made a beeline for a cruise ship stand which funnily enough didn't have any dreadlocks within 20 feet of it. That would be the end of that!

As the years rolled on, Nic's long service leave approached, we thought we should take advantage of this fantastic opportunity and do some form of a trip to celebrate. Not just any trip, one of those big-ticket items like the Grand Canyon or Machu Picchu, but how would we choose which one, and what were the chances of us agreeing on the same place? No problem, we could each pick a location and take an extended holiday. Then, you pull out a map, and you notice; if you go there, then look how close that place is; if we are going there, then it would be silly not to see this place. Just like a dodgy 80's 'made for TV' film, we'd get regular flashbacks to the wine infused fireside stories from Tim and Moira. One thing led to another, bucket list items were added, introducing more countries, the knee bone connected to a cross continent rail trip and the hip bone connected to a trans-ocean boat crossing. There you have it. A one year adventure right around the globe.

Surely we couldn't, it was just little ol' us, on our own without the protection of our regular travel buddies. Could we?

The World is your Lobster

It was time to start getting serious about the route, so we pulled out a large world map and laid it out on the floor. Nic was first to speak, 'Where do we start?', 'Well look, the world is your lobster!', was my reply. I'd used this saying for years with the context that you shouldn't settle for an oyster when you can have lobster[1]. With a little research, I found out that the phrase was coined by a real gem of classic British comedy. A character called Arthur Daley, played by the late great George Cole, in the TV series *Minder*. This made the saying even more endearing, and it quickly became the catchphrase for the whole trip.

So it was now set in stone, it would be a Round the World trip, and we needed to make a complete loop, out from one direction and in from the other. I think Nic's crazy idea of the Sydney to London bus trip had taken a subliminal toll, it just seemed appropriate that we should head west. This meant it certainly wouldn't be a 'follow the sun' trip, but we didn't seem to mind at the time. Between our dive trips and stopovers to the UK, we'd

---

[1] *this probably also explains my dramatically poor cash flow over the years*

previously visited Singapore, Thailand, and Malaysia so liked the idea of starting the tour on familiar ground.

After that, places just appeared from everywhere. It's always been my ambition to visit Moscow, and as we wandered around the next travel expo to hit town, we came across a stand advertising the Trans-Mongolian Railway. Based on the view that if it didn't kill us, it would make us stronger, it was added to the list.

One of the ideas we liked most about the trip was that we wouldn't plan it too much, and just see where things would take us. The romantic thought of just turning up at the airport and deciding where to go today made us very excited, although it never did actually eventuate. The train trip was ideal, it was something we had to book in advance, locking in a deadline of reaching Beijing around five months after setting off. That way, we wouldn't just find an idyllic tropical island and stay there for a year.

The well-trodden 'Banana Pancake' route through South East Asia was looking like a sensible option, but there was another country we had on our radar. My father was based in wartime Burma and told us stories about its temples, especially one he'd seen with a giant reclining Buddha. It seemed like quite a scary place to go, but if we can add Russia to the list then, why not?

Things were starting to fall into place. As we were embarking on our Aussie traveller rite of passage, we would begin in Bali, Australian's Benidorm. It seemed only right that we should hit this hot spot for partying Australians first. From there, we had a rough plan mapped out that took us through Singapore, Malaysia, Thailand, Burma, Laos, Cambodia, Vietnam, Hong Kong, and China. I did say we weren't going to run by an itinerary but figured we needed to have an idea of what a route might look like. That way, if we stopped somewhere longer, or went off at a tangent, we would know what other areas might be missed. Secretly, I created a spreadsheet.

The train would get us all the way to Europe, then what? Surely, it was about time for one of Nic's harebrained ideas. Her timing was perfect. 'Let's buy an old VW campervan like the one dad had when I was 8, and tour in that!'. You already know what my reply was, but as the words 'we'll see' were rolling off my tongue, the voices in my head were saying, 'how cool would that be'. By this point in the journey, we should have taken a few trains and buses, it might be nice to do something different and be more flexible. When we first started to think about having a year out, we initially conjured up an image of living in a French village for a few months and becoming a local. As we'd decided to conquer the world instead, this wasn't looking likely, but the thought of a slow meander through France sounded good. Back when we called the UK home, we loved nipping across the channel and driving our old car through the French countryside to Le Mans, where we would camp and watch the 24 hour motor race. It holds great memories. More and more, I was sold on the idea. The plan was to buy an old cheap campervan that we would use for the trip and sell as soon as we finished. We would start looking for one as we approached Europe. I'm afraid you will have to wait and see how that turns out. For the rest of the route back to Australia, surely we would have time to research that as we travelled.

Big Trip Preparation

It's all a bit vague, but I would say we started planning in earnest about 18 months before we left. First things first, money. We needed to sort out a budgeting plan and ensure we had enough saved, so we quickly opened a high-interest saving account. We chose one that had a website with a nice graph to see the money going up for added saving motivation. I think it's fair to say that we had never been able to save for anything in our life before, financially speaking, we (mainly me) were experts at clearly understanding our means, then living just outside them. This was the first challenge we had to overcome, how could the minimum payment Mountfords get enough dosh together to take a whole year off?

I'm pretty sure it's not just me, but how many of you when faced with a financial situation, find that the dark recesses of your brain suddenly wake up, and from nowhere, out pops: 'I could rob a bank or a petrol station'. How all of a sudden this can become a viable solution in a normally rational brain, I'm not sure. Nic promptly reminded me that I have never looked good in either stripes or orange, so it was back to the drawing board.

Maybe it was time for one of those 'Get Rich' self-help books. I've always been quite sceptical about such things, and the real reason these authors get rich is because of suckers like us buying their books. I'm positive that if I knew the secret of getting rich, I'd be sipping Margaritas in a posh resort somewhere, certainly not encouraging riffraff to get rich and join me. The book (loaned from the library for free, no Margarita for you) did resonate with some sound advice. It talked about the cumulative effect of how we waste money on small things, like buying a latte, and by saving the cost of just one of these each day, makes a difference long term. This made us look at the little things that add up to big things, and we tweaked our lifestyle just a little to accommodate. I suppose we started with baby steps as it's all very well and good to say you're going to stop buying a Latte a day, but what about the fact that without coffee we are unable to perform even the most basic of functions. So we started our holiday saving regime by spending $300[1] on a Nespresso coffee maker. It seemed wrong, but our morning coffees were now a tenth of the cost of what they were. It actually did make a difference, and we didn't really feel any worse off. Probably one of the best bits of advice was to have a salary paid into the savings account and then taking out what you need, much more productive than just transferring what you haven't spent at the end of the month into your savings (which often doesn't happen).

Week by week, we'd watch the graph grow but still never quite believed we would ever reach our target amount. The balance

---

[1] *throughout the book, $ refers to Australian Dollars unless identified otherwise (US$)*

took the occasional hit, but after a while, it did actually look like we just might be able to pull it off. I backed this up with various spreadsheets, they are like comfort pillows to me. They've come to the rescue of many a household crisis, ranging from choosing a wedding location to finding solace when we were thousands in debt.

The wedding location exercise, wasn't so much working out the cheapest venue, it was the fact that we kept fudging the figures to make one particular location rise up the list. We knew, then and there, that this was the one. In a similar fashion, we would later take an antique coin on our journey that would be used to make decisions. Not necessarily to leave it up to fate, but to check that your heart didn't drop a little when the wrong side came up, informing us what we really wanted to do.

Adjusting mental baggage to reduce our travel baggage

Having never done anything like this before we really had no idea what we might need with us on a journey that would take us around the world. One benefit was that we were used to packing for dive holidays. Where, 80% of your baggage allowance is taken up with dive gear, leaving you to live in a pair of shorts and a couple of t-shirts. This meant that we couldn't afford to be precious about our wardrobe. However, these trips never lasted more than two weeks in a warm beach setting, compared to a year in pretty much every environment you can think of. Your first thought is to try and list everything you possess that you might want to use in a year. Then when you realise there is no magic spell to shrink it all into a backpack, you are forced to reassess.

Probably one of the most stressful aspects of packing was making the decision on which backpack to choose. Now is perhaps a good time to delve a little into our psyche to explain the significance of this. We are the opposite of those personality types that just look at something and decide to buy it (or do it), without a single worry about whether it's the right decision. They just go through life looking, deciding, and doing, without any fear of the consequences, and a mind as unburdened as a babe in arms. In our house, they are referred to as, 'lucky, lucky bastards'. We, on the other hand, are deeply troubled by making the right choice after researching all the facts and alternatives, not to mention getting the best possible value. You can understand how significantly different planning a trip like this would be between us and them. To them, it would be like popping down the shops to buy milk, and a spanner set (because they saw it). For us, it's like planning a trip to Mars.

It's a bit of a double edged sword as we are chained down by this inbuilt responsibility to make sensible, informed decisions, and it certainly limits the spontaneous and free-living aspect of our lives. However, it's slightly made up for by the fact that our diligence can give us a faint underlying smugness. We know that any spanner set we buy will be the best it could be, and years later we can turn to each other and comment on, 'how good a decision we'd made on that'. Something that now, post the trip, we are regularly saying about our backpacks.

Given the lack of any magic spell, it seemed that we would need a bag at least twice the size of us, and maybe come with wheels, and a sherpa to carry it. We started reading many forums (of course we did) which all disagreed with this notion. The first big mistake was the wheels, they add weight, bulk and are only suitable on certain surfaces. Next was the size, the consistent advice was that we should get something less than half the size of what we thought, that surely couldn't be right could it?

Luckily, we found a wonderful shop in the centre of Melbourne called Backpacking Light. Much as the name implies, it stocks lightweight products for serious travellers. In the 12 months leading up to the trip, we would visit most Saturdays, scaring ourselves silly about what we were getting into. This place made the trip seem very real.

Nick, one of their experienced staff members, came over as we were looking at a 75-litre behemoth backpack and we got chatting about our plans. He pointed out that his choice would be a 38-litre backpack at which we scoffed in disbelief, how could we manage with so little space for a year? We left without making a purchase that day, imagining how many times Nick must use the old trick of turning undies inside out to reduce the amount he needed to pack. Compared to us, he was a big unit as well, surely just one of his t-shirts would take up the space of three of mine. After regular visits to Backpacking Light to chat with Nick and Tim (the owner), supplemented by more forum searching and YouTube watching, we finally came round to their way of thinking. We were lucky to find such helpful staff, and I would highly recommend building up a rapport with your local specialist shop, so that they understand your plans, and can give you the best advice. Including the advice that you didn't think you needed.

After half an hour of walking around the shop with a bag weighted up to test its comfort, we both decided on the Osprey FarPoint 55. This was actually a 38-litre backpack with a detachable daypack. The backpack has a couple of wings that enclose around the daypack, making it look fairly presentable when arriving anywhere a little bit fancy. One of the hardest parts was convincing Nick to sell both of us the same colour, something he initially flatly refused for our own coolness (or lack thereof). This was an epic moment in our preparations. It had been a long hard decision with lots of research, these bags were after all our home for the next year. From memory, it's previously only been the design of our wedding invitations that have caused as much heated discussion and general indecision. Thankfully, in this case, we came to an agreement without the need for me to sleep on the sofa. So, now we had his 'n' hers backpacks in matching olive green, what the hell do we put in them?

Let me start with one piece of great advice (of course it was passed onto us by Tim and Nick). Packing Sacks, Packing Sacks, Packing Sacks! They are little miracle workers, and each tiny little Tardis compacts your belongings into easy to find sections, meaning you can easily access what you are looking for. You can choose different sizes and colours to help differentiate the contents. Another one of my favourites items, despite being warned that you can look a bit of a knob in them, were zip off trousers. You know, the ones that have a zip around the knee to remove the legs. They're shorts, no they're trousers, no wait they're shorts again. 'Crikey, I'm getting hot in these trousers', 'zzzzzzzip-zzzzzzip', 'Ah that's better!'. Knob or not, they will always be on my essential list, I packed two pairs. The final clothes list was now significantly reduced from our first draft.

It was great fun putting together our travel belongings and finding quirky travel items, such as peg-less washing lines, duct tape, a Shewee, and flat rubber sink plugs (some budget lodgings don't have them). One essential for all travelling Australians is a supply of mini Koala toys, the ones that you squeeze and the hands open up to clip on something. These would be used as gifts on our journey. We even took a washing machine, but I'll tell you about that later. Some items would work a treat and became essential, but for others, we would realise early on in the trip that we didn't need them, and either post home or donate. Obviously, we made sure that we wouldn't take anything we were precious about and couldn't be replaced.

Magic Shirt

I included one clothes item that didn't require any thought and that was the Magic Shirt. I say magic as it's the stuff of fables. In the early '90s a Greek God (Gusset, The God of Needlework) decided that he would use his magical powers to create a shirt to suit all occasions and would never ever crease. He hated being late to a cocktail evening with the other Gods, only to realise he should have ironed. Zeus and Athena would point and make fun as always. The shirt he created could be scrunched up into a ball at the bottom of his bag and then be pulled out looking like new. He made it in a timeless style that could be worn for decades to come. To top it off, he decided to make it available in the River Island clothes store where it would be heavily discounted in the New Year sales to only £6.

The shirt and I have had a faithful relationship for twenty five years now, I've not come across anything else like it and it will be indispensable on this trip.

Sitting on the dock of the eBay

Historically, we are serial hoarders. When we left the UK, we rented our house out and put all the things we couldn't live without in a storage container, we were only going to be away for a year after all. 13 years later, we are still paying the monthly storage fees for those things that we can't live without, whatever they were, we really can't remember.

We were determined not to do the same this time around, no siree bob! This time we would make much more of a concerted effort to minimise our belongings. One saving grace was the fact that our relatively short time in the country meant we hadn't had the chance to build up a lot of sentimental belongings. Most of our Australian possessions had been bought on the cheap as there were only supposed to last a year. Also, our small apartment lifestyle meant that we just didn't have the room to accumulate much.

eBay was our friend and helped to bolster our funds a little too, although because of the urgency of the matter there were good (a.k.a heartbreaking) deals to be had by others. We even managed to sell some memory foam pillows. Now I know they are not cheap to purchase new, and these were a good deal, but to buy secondhand pillows seems a bit weird in my book, especially ones that have a memory. A good friend of ours, Susan, won't even borrow books from the library at the thought of someone previously having a good read while squeezing one out on the big white throne (potentially me). You can bet your bottom dollar that it wasn't Susan that bought the pillows. We were quite lucky with our sales, especially as some larger items were sold with perfect timing, such as the fridge heading to its new owners on the day before we moved out.

Of course, we were then left with, you know, the stuff we can't live without. We found the smallest size storage unit that would fit our essentials, a 2m x 2m x 3m room in a nice new facility nearby. One of the last things we sold was Sherman, a devoted member of the family, a Land Rover Discovery Series 1 (it was a big green tank, hence the name). Before we said our goodbyes, we did as many runs as we could to the storage unit. The last big load was transported using a hire van with the large items such as the bed, TV, sofa, not to mention another member of the family, Big Ted, a huge Costco teddy bear that was bigger than me. He was excellent for hug therapy, but not the most practical possession in a small apartment. We placed him high on top of the storage room to oversee our belongings and hopefully scare the crap out of any would-be burglars.

After a very sweaty day, we finally finished, and vowed next time to pay someone for help. We looked up to see Big Ted staring down at us with sad eyes as we closed the door on our Melbourne life. It felt quite symbolic and would have been an emotional moment if we didn't smell so badly, in some sadistic competition to see who could make the other faint. Only one thing for it, a treat. We'd booked ourselves into a nearby hotel for a well deserved relax and a nice soak in the bath (our apartment didn't have one). That was it, the only things left in the apartment were the bags we were going travelling with.

The following day, having learnt our lesson, we paid someone to clean the apartment before handing back the keys to the estate agent. We were now suddenly homeless. One aspect of this really hit home, we had no keys. None, even our backpack padlocks had a combination lock. Since you've been old enough to be trusted with a copy of the front door key, when do you ever have no keys in your life?

The previous two months before leaving was a whirlwind as we were very focused on our preparation plan. Each day, jobs were ticked off, and affairs were put in order. The enormity of the workload was detracting us from thinking about the actual journey, and helping suppress the worry about what we were about to embark on. As each job was scratched from the list, there were fewer things to distract us, and then on the 22nd of December we reach the last item on the list, 'Get to the airport on time'.

CHAPTER 2

Location: Still Melbourne
Days 1, Countries 1, Kilometers 0, Beds 0
Trains 0, Planes 0, Automobiles 0, Boats 0
Beers 0

And we're off!

Now that we were homeless, our friends, Craig and Susan graciously put us up and offered to drop us off at the airport. We'd all decided that they would just pull into the drop-off zone to avoid lengthy emotional goodbyes. The ride to the airport was quieter than usual as Craig followed a stream of taxis to the drop-off point. We quickly barrel rolled out of the car, which I'm not sure actually came to a halt. I was hoping that this wasn't a reflection of them wanting to get rid of us. We waved goodbye to the back of their car, as they sped off. Then all of a sudden, there we were, the last item on the list crossed off.

We found a nice quiet area in the airport, looking out over the runway, and sat down. Both exhausted, we just stared at each other for about an hour. What the hell were we doing? Yes, we are great at organising, and there's none better when it comes to ticking off lists, but to wander off and travel the globe, seriously!?

We took comfort in the fact that at this very same airport, almost exactly 11 years previously, we emerged from a plane after a similar 3 months of frantically ticking lists, with precisely the same feeling in the pits of our stomachs. Back then, one of the first things we were greeted with on our walk towards the baggage claim was a large Vodafone poster aimed at encouraging tourists to phone home. It showed the biggest crocodile you've ever seen with a giant arrow pointing into its open mouth, the caption reading 'Your family think you are here - phone home!'. Seriously Vodafone, you were really not helping our already delicate bowels at the time. Anyway, as months went by without any reptile decapitation incidents in the Melbourne Metro area, the feeling passed, and that particular adventure turned out alright, so why shouldn't this?

Over some sugar sweets and a celebratory glass of early morning bubbly, we were already working out a plan B, just in case. Basically, it was my Dad's sofa in the UK. Apart from it being the house I was brought up in, it was one of those places that just the thought of, made you relax. A typical front room in a UK council house with a comfy sofa, packed with ornaments, being provided copious amounts of tea, and a complete lack of commitment to any conversation because everyone was happily engrossed in the TV. This would be our 'pull cord to eject' plan. If ever we realised we were not cut out for this life, we would jump on the first flight to the UK, find the bus to Birkenhead and put the kettle on.

This was all we needed to settle our nerves, and now we really started to feel excited. First though, sleep. The thought of travelling on an aeroplane is still so exciting for us, we typically get to the airport in plenty of time, just to hang out. In our early days of courtship, I'd even taken Nic on a date to Heathrow. We got tipsy in a bar, watching the planes take off while I drew diagrams on a napkin to explain the aerodynamic theory of how a wing worked. What a catch I was. The staff at the airport caught wind of what I was doing and offered to have a whip round so that we could go to the cinema instead. Today, even the preflight instructions couldn't keep us awake as we were busy dreaming of what was to come (and snoring a little) before the 737 pulled back from the gate.

1st stop – Australia (wait, isn't that where we left from?)

You must be all wondering, where on earth would this first stop be? The world is our lobster after all, what delights will we get to first. It was Darwin. Well, Darwin was the only major Australian city that we'd not visited, so stopping over on the way to Bali was a great way to address this. We woke to hear the captain's announcement as we descended into Darwin and realised for the first time that our pilot was female. In all my previous flights, this was the first female commercial pilot I'd come across, and it was unusual not to hear that posh middle-class male English accent that you normally hear. I'm pretty sure that airlines round up their recently qualified pilots from all ethnical backgrounds and walks of life, forcing them into a movie theatre and play, back-to-back 1950's English movies. Keeping them locked up until they walk out speaking like Alistair Simms or David Niven. Hopefully, David's starring role in *The Battle of Britain* would be left out of the playlist just in case it gave anyone any ideas.

As an ex Aerospace Engineer, I think it's fantastic that we're starting to hear a female voice over the tannoy. I don't know about you, but I immediately get that comfortable feeling that they would have at least stayed awake for the whole journey. What a perfect display of equality in a once male-dominated area. Well done to the pilot and well done to Jetstar (it's not often I get to praise them) and how convenient too that it's in a vehicle that doesn't need to reverse.

Unfortunately, when we arrived in Darwin, it was shut. No-one was in. Even though it was the last shopping day before Christmas, the town was empty apart from a few local residents enjoying a festive eggnog and teaching us a few new phrases which I won't repeat here. The humidity already made it feel like we were a million miles from Melbourne. In a twist on a classic northern saying, I realised that I do 'sweat much for a fat lass'. I could see the look of concern, disdain, or even fear on people's faces as I walked towards them, beads of sweat running down my head and dripping from the tip of my nose. Folks were crossing the road to avoid me, in case I suddenly self combust. I like to think that this was compounded by my current poor fitness level and hoped that exercise and acclimatisation will improve things as we travel. I'll be sure to keep everyone posted on the perspiration perspective.

It turned out that having an Australian stopover worked really well for sorting out last minute jobs. Thankfully the heavy downpours also meant that we felt guilt-free for not exploring the city more. We realised as we were changing our SMS numbers for internet banking that they wouldn't accept our non-Australian travel SIM. Luckily we had time to quickly run around town in search of a decent Australian based SIM that was relatively cost-effective for travel. If we hadn't realised this before we left home soil, we would have been returning much sooner than our estimated 12 months.

We stayed two nights at Darwin's Crown Plaza, and our excitement for the trip was starting to build, manifesting itself in our telling absolutely anyone about it. Unfortunately, ordinary passers-by had just that, the freedom to keep passing by, so we had to target the captive audience, i.e. the hotel staff. Our enthusiasm must have rubbed off, we returned to our room to find a bottle of bubbly and a lovely card from Jenna on reception.

Darwin, I think you will need to win us over next time, but in the meantime, you have served your purpose well. Next stop, somewhere not Australia.

2nd Stop – Somewhere not Australia

As mentioned earlier, the first 'proper' stop was going to be Bali. Being brought up in England, this brings to mind classic images of palm trees, beautiful beaches, and coconut drinks served by either Bob Hope or Bing Crosby. If my mind had fully assimilated into an Australian one, it would probably have been filled with bikinis, drinking cocktails from a bucket, and having my head down a toilet. For once, I much prefer what's going on in my head.

So here we were on flight number two of who knows how many, and I'm just about to endure one of my most embarrassing mid-flight experiences. There is a welcome place for toilet humour in my life, I am British after all. For a bit of relevant backstory, my ancestors, as a clan, are generally bowel challenged. Just as people that have gone to war, look at each other and know the horrors that they have had to endure, we look at each other in a similar way. A few years earlier, during some hospital experimentation, I saw my insides on a computer screen and I swear it was identical to stage 4 of the RAC British Rally. Even Colin McRae and Nicky Grist would struggle on this route, so whatever hope was there for me. A symptom of this is that a trip to the smallest room is never quick. I don't help myself as I do daydream a little. This can hardly be my fault, I come from a nation where half the men can't go unless they have a newspaper with them. In this modern age, I think mobile phone apps should have a separate rating to judge how conducive they are to keeping people regular. Instead of star ratings, they could have little… Okay, I'll leave it there.

So flying to Bali, the excitement of the trip must have been getting to me, I sensed movement down below. I looked around the plane, and everyone looked asleep, so I headed to the WC for a mid-air ablution.

Time lapses.

Before I know it (which sounds quick but it could have been a good 30-40 minutes) I hear loud banging on the door as though there is a real emergency. Thinking that we were heading for disaster, I slide open the lock, still sat down, pants around my ankles. I peered around the door, the pulsating vertical vein still visible down my forehead. The poor steward must have clocked me going in and thought I'd died or something. As I explained to her that I was just fine and dandy, her compassionate face changed to one of scorn as she glanced over her shoulder where I could see a queue of people behind her, desperate to be in the exact same spot that I was now. Jeez, I bet you don't get this in Business Class.

Bali was just what we needed, 5 days of relaxation after the hectic months leading up to the journey. Although we felt guilty for not starting the great adventure with more gusto, it still wasn't quite enough guilt to stop us sleeping most of the day. We'd predicted this would be the case, so paid more than our budget for a nice hotel. This backfired a little as we were disappointed with the Mercure in Sanur, if only we'd known how our standards would slip later on during the year. After arriving at our first room, we found that there was no in-room safe so asked to change rooms. It was, after all, one of the criteria in which we had made our booking. At this point it might have looked better if they had lied and said that of course room 212 has never had a safe, what were we thinking. Instead, a porter turns up with a look of 'I'll show you where the safe is, you idiots', he opened the wardrobe door and looked at where it should have been. He closed the door and opened it again quickly, maybe David Copperfield was in the room next door and was playing tricks on him. No safe. He literally scratched his head, pursed his lips with a look of concern before picking up our bags to take us to our new room. Once there, we took it in turns to ensure that the safe was secure and was not going to get up and join the safe from room 212, wherever that may be.

Our days in Bali were mainly made up of sleeping, walking along the beachfront, and eating. We were very much at the bottom of a steep learning curve in the ways of budget travel and were given lesson No.1 on our very first morning when we wandered, blurry-eyed, into the hotel's restaurant and agreed to sign up for their breakfast buffet. The amount we paid would be our daily budget (including accommodation) in a few weeks time. It was a real newbie error, especially as we soon discovered one of our favourite restaurants in Bali was literally opposite the hotel entrance where breakfast would cost a tenth of the price. I suppose if we wanted to jump in at the deep end of budget travel then our 5-star hotel probably shouldn't have been the way to go. Baby steps. However, between this and long naps in a bed that was as large as the apartment we'd just left in Melbourne, I was starting to worry that we didn't have what it takes to do this backpacker malarkey. At this rate our funds would only last a couple of months, returning to Melbourne with no money, just in time for winter. I found myself needing a distraction from this negative energy and a large cocktail from a bar overlooking the beach certainly did that. We were warm, relaxed, sitting on hammock chairs, gazing out onto a beautiful beach with the silhouette of Lombok on the horizon when that ubiquitous holiday thought popped into my head, 'This was the life'.

Wait a moment, it really was. This was our new job. Our negatively earning career for the next year. It was time to draw a line in the beautiful white sand and ensure that we can last more than a couple of months. One less cocktail tomorrow. For Nic. A perfect time to capture the moment with a Nostril Shot.

Nostril Shots

We have a phrase that might crop up during the book that I should explain up front, the Nostril Shot. I wouldn't go as far as saying we invented the 'Selfie', but we did. For all you youngsters out there, you need to realise that before camera-phones existed you had to stretch your arm out, holding your heavy camera pointing at you with no idea what you were taking. Before that, at a time just post dinosaurs, you had to use an even heavier film camera. There was no checking the shot and trying again with those. No, you'd have to fly home from the Algarve, unpack, head downtown, place the film in for developing. You'd then come back a week later (or next day if you were minted) to find out you had completely missed everything but a zit, mid forehead, that seemed to be smiling back at you.

As Nic and I met before even the internet existed, we had to endure this practice. It never stopped us trying though. Our accuracy is slightly given away by the fact we called them Nostril Shots, as that is generally all you saw. Now, Nic has the smallest of noses (and small ears for that matter), this pleases me greatly as I was once told that they are the only parts of the body that keep growing your entire life. Imagine finding the girl of your dreams at a young age and she already had a huge honk and ears that slowed her down when running. Yes, Yes, I know, beauty is only skin deep, beauty is in the eye of the beholder, and horses for courses, etc. But when you're both 80 and each day your general frame shrinks smaller and smaller, those things are still growing. It's like Benjamin Button meets the *Twilight Zone*. This was definitely one of the three reasons I married Nic. I, on the other hand have nostrils that have been used as sets for two of the *Aliens* movies. It's a family thing, and we are trained early to use their powers. A quick nostril flare can be seen at least twenty feet away and is a passive aggressive delight. Our early holiday memories are mostly made up of snaps where Nic looks like she's just about to be eaten, or fall into a deep ravine.

Anyway, Nostril Shots. We invented them, that's what they are really called. End of.

We spent Christmas Day in Bali, which was a little surreal with staff from the posh Hyatt next door dressed up as Santa giving out presents to the children on the beach. In the hot sun, one Santa had sweat matting together his long white beard, as he tried not to faint over a chubby fat American five-year-old, almost certainly dashing any belief in Father Christmas and ensuring huge therapy bills in future years. Christmas in a hot climate just seems wrong, especially for someone brought up in the northern hemisphere. In our 10 years of being in Melbourne it still never felt right. We would often rebel with other ex-pats and celebrate 'Christmas in July', a time of the year when the nights draw in early, and the weather was miserable enough to make you think of the UK. Lately, even Melbourne shops have picked up on this, some digging out the Chrimbo decorations in July to try and fleece what they can out of similar, non-religious, revellers.

We started our Christmas morning with a scrubba. No, that's not what you are thinking, please get your minds out of the gutter. The Scrubba was a Christmas present from our friends, a travel washing machine designed by a Melbourne entrepreneur[1]. It was basically a dry bag with a transparent plastic window, and the inside was full of knobbly bits. You would put the clothes, travel wash and water in, close it up by wrapping the end so that it captured a little air inside, and then roll it back and forth on the floor. Although a little hard work at first and looked like you were giving your knickers CPR, it worked a charm and would be a godsend on the trip.

We celebrated with a meal at our newly found cheap restaurant, had a foot massage for $5 and splashed out with a cocktail on the beach. No presents or cards, just the two of us and the world at our feet. We both agreed it was probably the best Christmas present ever.

Actually, I did get a little extra present that night (stop it), walking home from the beach I was pooped on by a bat. Holy guano Batman, that really has got to be good luck, hasn't it? To be fair, the poor little blighter may have done it because he thought I was French. I did have a bit of a quiff in my hair and a nonchalant look about me. It was pretty messy, I think he might have been on the same diet as me, or he was a relative. To rub it in, we then retired to the balcony and I could hear his clicks as

---

[1] *www.thescrubba.com.au*

he flew past. My morse code is a bit rusty, but I'm sure I could make out, 'ha, got you mon amie'.

Bali Hai-er or Lower

Even though we were on an adventure to cast away our normal mundane existence and forget about our office life, I guess it was only a matter of time before I got my geek on and created a spreadsheet. As well as the budget and route itinerary (that we aren't following of course), I thought it would be good to start recording some stats from the trip. My plan was to set up a blog to keep people informed of our journey where I could then post some figures. This was initially just going to be details of the distances travelled, broken down by what mode of transport we'd used. This soon expanded to include stats like the number of UNESCO world heritage sites visited; the number of different types of domestic beers for that particular country; and even the number of flip-flops (thongs for you Aussies) that we went through.

One of the obvious statistics would be the number of countries visited. Of course, this trip was never about beating anyone or about hitting some magical figure. Well okay, I confess, even as I write that I know I'm not being totally honest. I knew what had been achieved by a couple of friends who'd been influential to this trip and I wanted to do ourselves proud.

With that in mind, I now needed to address the big white Indonesian elephant in the room. Could I count Bali as a separate country? Nic wasn't playing along, so I decided to reach out to the half-dozen friends and family that were following our blog and set up a quick online poll with arguments for and against.

The arguments for:
- The Travellers Century Club, a pompous club for people who have visited more than 100 countries, list it separately to Java (lumped with Timor as the Lesser Sunda Islands). They do however also class

Jersey as a separate country which doesn't help their credibility.

- Bali has a very high religious majority of Hindu practitioners (92%) rather than the rest of Indonesia which is Islamic. Even the Hindu religion here has certain idiosyncrasies.
- It has its own government.
- A good proportion of Australian tourists that come here are way too drunk to realise that they have even been to Indonesia.

The arguments against:
- It's not a separate country.

The poll was close, but I didn't get the cigar. After five days on this beautiful island (nay, country), it was sadly time to leave, although we weren't sad to leave the hotel. It was a lovely setting in a quiet part of Bali but wasn't particularly friendly, and it's expensive food and beverage setup was at odds to the travellers we were trying to become. It was time to start the journey good and proper. I know, we said that in Darwin didn't we, but this stop turned out to be more of a relaxing beach holiday, and now we were going to start travelling. Apart from walking aimlessly around the local area, our only exploration was to hire a lovely middle-aged taxi driver called Nyoman who drove us around some beautiful temples and took us for a lunch stop in the beautiful artisan village of Ubud. Our day with Nyoman just moved us from holidaymaker to tourist, but we certainly didn't feel like travellers yet. So with some trepidation, we packed for the next leg, exploring Java. All we had to do was check out at 5am and get to the airport for an early flight. No problemo.

Escape from the Mercure

Next morning, we appear at the hotel desk, still asleep but all packed, to hand over our keys and pay for that bloody expensive breakfast. If we looked tired, then the guy behind the desk looked like he'd just emerged from a coma as he started to slide the bill across a ridiculously wide desk. In my usual trusting style, I was already automatically sliding my credit card towards him until the two articles met at the designated Checkpoint Charley somewhere in the middle. This was the last bit of accommodation we'd pre-booked before we started the trip and had been fully paid up in advance through expedia.com. Expedia knew this, we knew this, but it appeared that the hotel didn't.

Now, I'm a bugger for walking away from a till after paying for something, and Nic would ask me about the cost, 'I dunno' is the frequent response. This causes a lovely look from my wife, where at least one eyebrow reaches for the sky as though someone is pointing a gun at it. This time she was prepared for me and had spotted something not quite right on the bill. In super slow motion, her arm reached across, grabbed mine and pulled back my nervous looking credit card from the walking dead sat across from us. A closer look showed that the bill was $500 because it also included the room costs we'd already paid for.

I explained that we had paid, he turned slightly left towards his computer, pressed two keys and with not so humorous dialogue, relayed that the 'computer says no'. Nic whipped out the receipt from Expedia and plonked it in front of him. We saw a slight look of revelation in his eyes as he walked across to another computer. Obviously, they all have different opinions, and ours could have just woken up on the wrong side of the desk this morning. Time was getting on, but at least it felt like we were getting somewhere and we would be zipping off to the airport any moment now. 'No record!', he said as he sat back down. He stared blank faced at us with the odd quick glance to the credit card, we stared blank faced at him with the odd quick glance to the Expedia receipt. And this went on. As dawn started to break and lighten our faces, if not our moods, I encouraged him to phone his head office which he did with a look of reluctance. At least now we knew he was capable of more than one facial expression. It was a quick phone call, so we weren't hopeful. He came back, printed something off from the computer and slid the revised bill towards us. Not one word was spoken, no apology, no explanation, just a look of defeat (adding to his growing repertoire). This time it was my turn to hold Nic's arm back, 'let's just get to the airport hun'.

Amazing Yogyakarta

I'm afraid I can be a bit of a snob about reality TV, given the fact that it sucks the life out of us as a human race. However, I have to put my hand up and say that we have to thank reality TV for one of the best stops of the trip. One series which we do tolerate is *The Amazing Race*, we were avid viewers, especially for the two series leading up to our trip. It made us both scared and excited about what we were getting ourselves into. At least we wouldn't have to contend with watermelon throwing or eating a barrel of tripe in ten minutes like the contestants. Back in Melbourne, just after we had booked the flights to Bali, we excitedly sat down to watch the latest episode where the teams had recently arrived in Java and were climbing over what looked like an incredible temple. Borobudur is the worlds biggest Buddhist temple and looked so magnificent that it should be worthy of world recognition in the same league as the Pyramids or Chichén Itzá.

A quick search on the internet told us that the closest city was Yogyakarta (often shortened to Yogya) and as well as Borobudur there was an impressive Hindu temple complex nearby. Within minutes of the episode finishing a screen opened up on the laptop to show that flights from Bali to Yogya were only $50. We did later find you could get a very cheap 12-hour bus and ferry ride from Bali, but at this point, the emphasis to travel without flying hadn't fully kicked in yet. The next leg had been decided.

Yogyakarta is the 2nd largest city in Java, and reading reviews had a bit of a rep for being noisy and dirty. We set off from Denpasar with a feeling that this would be quite a culture shock, and the stay in Yogya would be a means to an end for the temples, then we'd quickly get out of dodge. This preconception started to erode as soon as we landed at a lovely, clean little airport with excellent directions to baggage claim and the exit. Our research had informed us that you can get a pre-paid taxi voucher for IDR55,000 ($5.50) at an easy to find counter. There were a few taxi-touts around but a sharp, 'No!' (Tidak), is all they needed to move onto their next victim. The taxi ride confirmed expectations that traffic here is similar to Bali, busy and chaotic. I particularly like the way they inform oncoming traffic that they want to turn right by pulling into their lane and stopping. To be fair, he did have his indicator on as well.

As it was leading into New Year, lots of places were booked up, but we found a great hostel called the Ministry of Coffee that had good reviews on both TripAdvisor and Lonely Planet. The room cost $36 which was very different to our last location, so we were feeling a little apprehensive about it (when we weren't fearing for our lives on the taxi ride there). It turned out that our $36 rewarded us with a top floor room, private bathroom, small balcony with views over the area, breakfast each morning, and a free welcome coffee. The rooms were made up each day, and they even folded the corners of the toilet paper, something we weren't expecting from our first venture into cheap travel accommodation. Okay, so the bathroom had no marble in sight, but this place was a gem, we certainly could travel like this. It was a bit of a revelation for us, and we already started to feel a little better about the coming months on the road.

In fact, things only got better at the Ministry. For two out of our three mornings there, we needed an early 4:30am start. The night before, we pre-filled a form to choose what we wanted for breakfast and when we came downstairs the next day, someone was waiting for us with a nice packup box and a lovely hot cup of Java tea. The only downside was that we didn't realise our room had a speaker for the call to prayer pretty close to our window, a pleasant surprise awaited us at 4am. It was, however, a delightful soundtrack to the area and actually never grew old. From the distance sounds of other speakers, I think it would be hard to find anywhere in the area that wasn't in range. Also, the Prawirotamen area we were located in was a good starting point to walk to the Sultans Palace and Sultan's Water garden.

One of the primary modes of transport around town is the becak, a trishaw type vehicle where you sit up front in a double seat under a canopy and your driver pedals from behind. You look a bit like an offering to the gods as you're wheeled out into the busy streets. Even though the seats are made for two, we quite often saw three or four bodies crammed in. Many of the drivers offer you very cheap fares, but we were warned to beware as they'll take you to local art resellers where you receive a hard sell to buy something.

We always prefer walking so ended up exploring the town by foot, but even then you need to be careful, nice friendly guys chat to you before informing you that attractions such as the palace are closed and try to divert you to galleries and gift shops. This, unfortunately, puts you on edge a little and you don't trust anyone or know if they are official.

Trust vs Footwear

Our first stop was the Sultan's Water Garden (Taman Sari), built by the first sultan as a haven to spend time with his concubines. We paid the enormous amount of $0.75 to enter where a guide quickly presented himself to us. We weren't sure whether he actually worked there or not, but he was both informative and funny, so we decided to roll with it, while still being a little on guard.

Just as we start the tour, he offered to take our picture under the entrance. After checking out that he was slightly overweight, looked like he had flip-flops on, I figured I could outrun him and happily handed over the camera. While posing for the photo I glanced down and spotted something on his ankle, it was a strap, they weren't flip-flops, they were sandals! As top quality as my Havaianas thongs were, I wouldn't stand a chance flip-flopping down a cobbled street after him if he decided to leg it with my camera. I started to sweat. Luckily no-one noticed as I had been drenched in the stuff from the moment I walked outside the Ministry's door that morning.

Crisis averted, the camera was returned, and the subsequent photo shows me looking like a coiled spring at the starting blocks of a 100m sprint. Although our guide did take us to some galleries, he was actually a resident of the compound surrounding the site that housed families who work for the Sultan. He was passionate about the area, and his only agenda was to talk about how excited he was to be working with Unesco who aimed to make it into a world heritage site within 2 years. Also, his concern that the current Sultan is pulling down all the worker's houses to make the surroundings more of a touristy revenue earner. The old houses that are being pulled down belong to families that have worked for the sultans for generations, they hold a lot of history and traditional skills so it would be a real shame. The architecture wasn't breathtaking, and without the guide, I think we would have spent less time here, he really brought out the history of the place.

The few locals we spoke to didn't give you the feeling that they are endeared to their current sultan they quite quickly brought up the subject that he doesn't have any sons so the next sultan will be his brother (who seems to be much liked). We also learnt that the capital of the next region is Surakarta (often called Solo) and it was great to hear that they have a similar banter going on as Melbourne and Sydney do. 'Ah, but we have the Harbour bridge (Borobudur) and the Opera House (Prambanan)', 'that's all well and good, but we have the culture, the art and great coffee!'.

The walk home took us down the main strip called Marliobro which is full of shops, malls, hawker stalls, motor traffic, becaks and horse-drawn carriages. It is such an attack on your senses, and a tropical downpour really added to the experience. After spending a bit of time walking around Yogyakarta and attempting to get across zebra crossings, I'm really intrigued about what the green cross code looks like here:

- Look left and see what is supposed to be three lanes of traffic but is really six lanes hurtling towards you with no intention of stopping.
- Look right and see another six lanes from that direction.
- Now raise your hand in the air and step out.
- Don't look back, don't show fear, they can smell it.
- Keep walking with your hand out until you get to the other side.

It was a real experience, and would be be good practice for other countries in South East Asia.

Are you a Flipper or a Flopper?

So, walking around Yogya after the rainstorm, the ground was quite wet, and we suddenly found ourselves presented with a much bigger life-threatening situation than crossing the road. Although our thongs were doing us proud, the main issue was that in many places the pavements were adorned with nice shiny red tiles. Now, to even the elite of thong wearers this might as well have been ice, as soon as we hit one we changed from cool looking funsters, bombing around in our shorts and thongs to awkward first-time skaters with arms outstretched and tongues sticking out. Looking back, I think one of the biggest dangers we ever faced through Asia was the dreaded red tile.

Anyway I digress. As usual, we try to cover a lot of ground and see as much as we can in the small amount of time whenever exploring a new area. We refer to it as a MountyDay where we try and pack into one day what a regular tour group would take 2-3 days to complete. Admittedly, sometimes to the detriment of what we are able to take in and enjoy, but you just don't know when, or if, we'll be back.

After quite a lengthy 12km stroll in our thongs, we return to the hostel. Before entering, we assess our cleanliness to discover Nic had mud splashed up the back of her legs. There was not a milky white bit of her rugged calf to be seen. My legs, on the other hand, were spotless. We thought it weird, but put it down to a random puddle that she must have carelessly stepped in. I hosed her down, and we went inside. We definitely deserved our Bintang beer at the end of this day and clinked our bottles as we declared it, our first MountyDay of the trip.

Coming back to the thongs, as we travelled further and after more days out in similar weather with the same muddy results, we came to the conclusion that we have both been built differently concerning our thong technique. In the UK vernacular, it certainly was the case that I was a flopper and Nic was a flipper, and any amount of concentration or thong training couldn't change her now.

Bradgelina of Borobudur

We finally made it to our target location, Borobudur is a 9th-century Buddhist temple and has been listed as the greatest Buddhist monument in the world. It is a vast construction of nine stacked platforms topped with a central dome and consists of over 500 Buddha statues. It was neglected, lost and overgrown for centuries before being rediscovered and restored. A short drive from here is Prambanan which is a 10th-century Hindu temple complex that has a large 47-metre high central stupa surrounded by other smaller temples. We hadn't seen anything like these before, and the buildings were just amazing to experience.

Travelling through central Java and visiting these magnificent temples in Java makes you feel like Harrison Ford from *'Indiana Jones'* or Angelina Jolie from *'Tombraider'*. It really is such a special place and so removed from our humdrum lives. However, one thing we weren't prepared for was the interest by the local school kids that were also visiting the temple.

We initially noticed them looking at us and whispering to each other, then one would make a break, usually with another in tow, maybe holding hands. They started walking toward us and then, at the last minute, seem to have a mini breakdown and swerve off at 90 degrees, returning to their group. A bit like seagulls homing in on those last few chips, a few iterations of this and they eventually made it all the way to their goal (us) and asked very politely if they can take our photo.

As soon as contact was made the rest of them appeared from nowhere to surround us. Suddenly, hundreds of cameras and phones appear. One by one, each wants their photo taken with us. One group of girls even let out little screams of excitement after they had their snap taken with Nic. I've never seen anything like it, I felt like the fifth Beatle.

I couldn't work out why. Had they just not seen anyone quite our shape before, or someone that sweated so profusely. Maybe it was the flies. I don't know what it is about me, but I attract flies, so much so that the phrase 'it was like flies around Lee' is an actual saying. If flies are about, they will make a beeline for me (see what I did there). This is a blessing for Nic who gets bypassed, I'm like a free lifetime supply of citronella candles to her. Living in Australia, I've become used to it. You soon realise that if the said beast isn't attacking part of your body with a hole in it, leave it alone because if you move it, it soon will. I've actually had people think I'm wearing a t-shirt with a spotty pattern until they get close and they look at us like we should be in the circus. Don't know why Nic gets included in that, it's not like she has a beard or anything (one of the three reasons I married her). If you are ever travelling in the same part of the world as me, you should seek me out and stick close, because whether I like it or not, I will take one (or a thousand) for the team. Although, in any group photos, you'll think you holidayed with Pig Pen from *Charlie Brown*.

It was both relieving and disappointing to see that other, more normal looking, westerners were also getting the same treatment. Maybe they just don't get to see that many westerners or they were all just having fun and making bunny ears behind these self-important intruders. In the next few countries, we'd walk up to a group of people getting their photos taken, and not understanding why on earth they wouldn't want us there.

Tourist or Traveller

Yogyakarta is a fantastic and friendly place. By all accounts, we should have been entirely out of our comfort zone but we weren't, we felt very safe and enjoyed every crazy moment of it. This was huge for us, it was the first place we felt like a traveller rather than a tourist and now took starring roles in the video we'd previously played in our minds about how a tour around the world would look. We were finally doing it, good and proper, we might just get somewhere before crashing on Dad's sofa. This wasn't the first time I'd thought about what the difference might be between the two words, tourist and traveller, and if there really was any difference. Was it just an exercise in one-upmanship to try to get it across that you've had more than the usual 1-2 weeks holiday. Maybe a trip that you'd put much more effort into planning yourself, rather than being handed an itinerary from a travel agent (who probably hadn't travelled anywhere, apart from an all-inclusive bender in Majorca with his mates).

To this day I haven't settled on a clear definition, the internet has plenty of opinions and interpretations, but you just couldn't get past the fact there were days when you felt like a traveller. Maybe a day where you were rewarded by pushing the envelope of your comfort zone; a moment where you help out a fellow traveller; give good advice on a location; be at a point where your normal life is a million miles away; the 4th day without a shower;

or maybe just that overwhelming feeling that you were living the wanderlust dream. I'm sure this subject will pop up again as we journey through this book and, of course, the world.

Asians vs Phlegm

It didn't take long to realise there was a raging battle going on all around us and it doesn't get any mention on the news or TV. I don't know what the Asian nations have done to offend it, but phlegm is continually trying to kill as many of them as possible! It's happening everywhere, just today we were in a coffee shop with someone behind me, regurgitating a huge invader from his throat. Simultaneously, the person in front was fending off, with much noise, an attack to the left nostril. I felt like the famous British wartime reporter, Kate Aidie reporting from Beirut, waiting for a ball of expelled snot to cruise over my head like a Scud missile. It seems the residents have realised the only way to kill it off, is down the toilet. It's quite common to see all cubicles in use as they are deposited in a mucousy 21-gun salute. If we can clone sheep, put a man on the moon, then surely there is something we can do for these poor people.

New Year, New Country

We arrived in Singapore on New Year's Eve in what would be our last flight for a while, just as whatever God you worship decided to put the city through a car wash. It chucked it down. Even though the bus stopped directly opposite the hotel, we had to take cover under a bus stop, staring at our warm and inviting hotel for about 15 minutes before it was safe enough to venture across the road. As usual, I'd deployed my usual bag of tricks when booking to try and convince them to look after us (more on that later). It probably wasn't needed, just walking up to the reception desk looking like drowned rats prompted the staff to upgrade us to the top floor, maybe to hide us from their other guests.

We planned to arrive in Singapore in time for the city's New Year fireworks, a great free way for backpackers to celebrate before returning to their five-star hotel. Well, it was New Year, wasn't it? After the deluge, we thought there'd be a good chance we would just watch the fireworks from our hotel room window, but the rain cleared in time for the show. The firework display and its harbour-front setting were spectacular. There was a really great atmosphere within the packed crowd.

On the way back we decided to see if the famous Long Bar at Raffles was still open, which it was. I've always had a connection with this hotel, my father was based in Singapore during the early fifties with the RAF, and we grew up on stories of the place. In particular, one story where Mum, running late for a party, burst exuberantly through the doors of Raffles before realising that this wasn't in fact the officers club located directly opposite. So whenever we flew between Melbourne and the UK, we would often stop over and try and nip here for a Singapore Sling in her honour. We knew we couldn't afford a Singapore Sling tonight as a round would have cost about 80% of our normal, non-Singapore, daily budget, so we chose just to have a beer.

As you'd expect, the place was buzzing and was obviously at the arse end of a posh Raffles New Years party. People sprawled about with frocks and dinner jackets everywhere, party hats and ticker tape all over the floor, mixed in with the ubiquitous peanut shells. The band was still playing and lots of people still dancing. It felt like a throwback to the good old days (can I say that? Were they good?). I blended in well with the drunken revellers as I fell off my chair when presented with the bill, $58 for two beers! It was worth every penny though, and highlighted a phrase that has long been a mantra in the Mounty household, 'you've got to be in it to win it'. A lovely way to bring in what will be an epic new year and what a great time to start a new chapter in our book.

CHAPTER 3

Location: Singapore
Days 9, Countries 3, Kilometers 6,580, Beds 3
Trains 0, Planes 4, Automobiles 0, Boats 0
Beers 4

Singapore on a budget – it's hard

It was the start of a huge New Year, and money was on our mind. Singapore was going to be a bit of a challenge as we love this city. We'd stopped off here many times before on our way to, or back, from the UK but we've never had to do it on the cheap. In fact, it's usually the opposite, we save up so that we can 'large it up' in posh hotels and have nice food. Even on a good day, the Singapore we know, is not a cheap place so how are we going to manage here for four days. Baby steps, accommodation first. The hotel for New Year was a treat but was only for that one night, the next hotel was challenging as it was just a three-star hotel yet it was still nearly 4 times the price of the Ministry of Coffee in Yogya, with no breakfast. It wasn't bad as such, but looked like we'd just been transported back to the '80s with it's green plastic bathroom suite. We were too cowardly to stay somewhere with shared facilities this early on in the trip, although we did walk past an option we'd shortlisted and immediately regretted not going for it. It looked much better than our hotel and was full of people meeting and enjoying themselves like some club 18-30 TV advert, or an episode of *Friends*.

All we could do was suck it up and search out the free and cheap in Singapore. We did quite well, but the first hurdle was a hard one. No alcohol. Two drinks here would be a meal and accommodation in Indonesia, we just couldn't justify it. Of course, the country did have a couple of domestic beers that we had to taste for the trip stats, so that helped. We did what we usually do, we walked. Everywhere. Concentrating our efforts in the Little India and Chinatown areas which gave us a rich backdrop to our day and also coincided with some cheap hawker food. A Kopitiam (traditional coffee shop) serving cheap dumplings near the hotel provided dinner for around $5 and proved to be a regular hangout.

For something different, we headed to Changi on the east of the island, an area where my father had spent time when based here in the 1950s. It was great to see some of the street names he talked about, and it's not often you have curry for breakfast (the area has a strong Indian influence). Next stop was the small island of Pulau Ubin, a short boat ride and yet a whole world away. Its lush, tranquil setting with very few cars is a welcome break from the city's hustle and bustle. We explored the island by bike for the price of a few dollars and had the best fun.

From one extreme to another, the next day we took the train out to a very different island to the west, the resort island of Sentosa. Full of opulent hotels and shops, there was nothing we could afford but it was still great to look around and people watch. A visit to the island's fantastic aquarium blew the days budget. More window shopping on the way home as we saw how the other half live in the Marina Bay Sands shopping centre, nestled at the foot of this now iconic building. Any thoughts of hitting the hotel's famous Skydeck were out of the question. Instead, we watched the tourists rowing boats through the man-made river that runs through the hotel's shopping centre (yes I did just type that). We ended the day with yet more fee-free walking through the beautiful Gardens by the Bay and finding cheap hawker food on the way home. Singapore, (aquarium aside) maybe we could do this. It was a city that we knew well, but the nature of this trip meant we saw a different part of the city than we usually would.

Exit stage left to Malaysia

Our thriftiness continued even as we exited the country. Our research had told us that the train prices from Singapore to Kuala Lumpur would cost double the amount if we bought them in Singapore, rather than just over the border in Malaysia. Our internet searching also found an incredibly useful blog, describing the best route to obtain the cheap tickets. This involved a local train, a bus, walking through customs, and another bus, to arrive at the correct train station and favourable ticket office. We followed the instructions to the letter, it was a great adventure, and we ended up with VIP train tickets (we upgraded to celebrate the savings, but don't worry it was still much less than the Singapore prices). Result.

Like Singapore, we'd visited KL before, but not as a back-packer. Our budget lead us to a hotel in the Brickfields suburb of the city, a busy Indian community which has lots of history and culture but I'm afraid our little area wasn't particularly pleasant. This was made evident when we saw not one, but two security guards manning the front door to our hotel. The hotel itself was nice enough but after one day exploring the area, including the famous Petaling Street shopping district, we camped down under the duvet for the next as a recovery day, recouping before the next adventure.

Thongs for the Memories

That adventure was in a town called Tanah Rata in the Cameron Highlands, Malaysia's most extensive hill station with a tropical highland climate. It's an area that invokes images of a colonial era.

A lovely hillside region, full of lush tea plantations and cottages that would look at home in the English countryside.

Our budget splurging needed to be put in check and it was about time we returned to travelling cheaply, so this was our first stay in a proper backpacker hostel and it's certainly a different experience than a hotel environment. There are pluses and minuses to this travellers scene. On the plus side, it's only $23 per night for a private double room, with an attached shower, there is free flowing tea and coffee, there is a communal lounge to meet other travellers from all over the world (this has its own pluses and minuses), you have easy access to cheap tours, and fast free WiFi.

The downsides include: the fact that the bed is as hard as bricks; it's very noisy with people coming and going (mostly drunk); the odd faint sound of someone throwing up in their room; there is no safety box, so you have to carry your valuables with you. The thing that topped the list was that on our first night there, one of these great unwashed stole my thongs! There was no footwear allowed in the building with a rack outside the door to house your thongs. I was devastated, only four weeks old, we had already been through numerous adventures together, and I'm sure they've saved my life on more than one occasion. I'd gone through hours of anxiety choosing them from a wall of multicoloured Havaianas in the local Jetty Surf, and now they are gone!

I spent the morning making sweeping unjustified allegations about the thong snatchers possible country of origin. Maybe the assailant had just been introduced to one of the many backpacker book-swap shelves, found in local cafes and thought the same thing applied to sandals. I did have a quick look myself to see if an upgrade was available, but there wasn't anything sans fungus. I needed a couple of beers to commiserate, despite the fact I couldn't afford one, as I was now in the market for new footwear.

We distracted ourselves with an organised tour to something called the Mossy forest, which did what it said on the tin. The tour then went on to visit the large Boh tea plantation. The plantation was in a lovely setting, and the trip was very educational. It was the first plantation in the area, starting in 1929 by British born AJ Russell and is still run by the Russell family today. We stocked up our supplies of tea bags before returning to the hostel. Despite the thong shenanigans, there is a certain charm to this noisy den of thieves, and we enjoyed our 2nd night here in the beautiful Cameron Highlands (shoes locked away inside). Our next stop, however, would be in a hotel at my insistence.

Hi Ho Hi Ho it's off to Ipoh we go

From the Cameron Highlands, we headed towards Ipoh, one of Malaysia's largest cities and the capital of the neighbouring state. Its heyday was in the 1930s, thanks to a thriving tin industry and a natural water source supplied by the bordering Titswangsa mountain range (Yes, I did just include that fact because it's a funny name). I'm not quite sure how Ipoh got onto the list, we'd seen some pictures of its colonial buildings, and it was a natural path towards Penang. We arrived in the evening and were very unprepared as we stepped off the bus in a large suburban depot. Typically, we'd at least have had a map of the area or have memorised the general layout, so knew where we needed to head. In this case, we had no option but to grab a cab to take us to the hotel in an area called the 'new town' (seriously, not a new town). We paid the price for our lack of preparation, it turned out that we actually could have walked. The taxi hadn't had a chance to warm up before it pulled to a stop outside of our hotel. The D'Eastern, looked empty, I think there may have been only two rooms taken in the whole hotel. It was dated but had a '70s kitschy charm and was within our budget.

We hadn't eaten so decided to head out for a walk. It would be fair to say that we didn't take to the place on first looks. It looked a bit rough and run down, westerners didn't seem to be common-place, and we were getting lots of looks. We were searching for somewhere that looked inviting for food but nowhere did until we came across a corner shop (Restoran Ong Kee) near a night market that was opening up. It was full of locals and had tables sprawling out into the street. We skirted past once, and even though we caught the eye of plenty of staff, there was no love coming our way. We came back for a second run and tried to look for menus, there weren't any, but it seemed like everyone was eating the same dish. Still no love and now both really not liking this place. Dejected, we started heading home and got about a block further before we simultaneously turn to each other, and announced: 'fuck it, let's go back and get some bloody food'.

We found a table, sat down and looked our hungriest. After a bit of gesticulation and sniggers between the staff, they sought out the youngest member of the team who could speak a bit of English and pushed him our way. It turned out the dish everyone was having was the famous Ipoh chicken (chicken with bean sprouts). It was delicious, and although probably overcharged we felt like travellers again and had turned the evening around.

The next day things improved as we found some fantastic architecture, including huge colonial style buildings and the city's grand white train station that locals refer to as the Taj Mahal. It's amazing what a difference a day makes, and we were now really enjoying Ipoh. For our second night, we hit a Malay hawker market and devoured enough satay to sink a ship. There was a little bit of excitement that evening back at the hotel when the power across two whole floors suddenly went out. I was probably the first to know of this, as I'd caused it. It involved a failed experiment trying to use a screwdriver to fool a UK socket with a European plug. Thankfully, the only shock I got was when I saw Nic's face after the staff flipped the trip switch and the lights came on. Don't worry though, my payback was to be electrocuted later on in a whole other country.

One thing that kept making me smile in this town was the fact that being an Apple fanboy, whenever I went to write the name of the place I would initially write it with a lower case i (iPoh) as though it was some new fangled high tech toilet released by the Californian based tech giant.

Curiously expensive in Georgetown

Our next leg involved a really comfortable coach service to Penang, and it just so happened that the day we arrived was the 20th Anniversary of when we met. It had also been Nic's 40th birthday five months earlier, and we'd deferred anything too lavish while saving for the trip. Looks like the stars were lining up for a budget explosion again.

From the planning and reading we'd done over the last year there was one hotel that stuck out as a possible treat. The Eastern and Oriental in Georgetown is a beautiful colonial style hotel that even after many refurbishments over the years, still carries the charm and class of its original era. It was created by the Sarkies brothers in 1885, two years before they went on to open Raffles in Singapore (an added connection). I'd been monitoring availability, without any luck, before a room miraculously become free just a day before we arrived. It must have been a sign, now where did I put my credit card.

It was a lot cheaper than Raffles, but you still get the exclusivity, a large bathroom, separate sleeping area, and separate lounge area that looks out over the sea. It included a massive breakfast choice, a nice pool, and not forgetting your own butler! All for the same price that you would pay for a city hotel in Melbourne. We took one look and extended for a second night. I had come down with a bit of a cold as well which made for a great excuse to relax and enjoy the surroundings. We decided to hit Nic's salary packaging expenses that evening to eat in the hotel's posh restaurant, celebrating the twenty years since we first set our eyes on each other.

As alluded to earlier, one thing I do without fail when booking a room online is to use the comments field. I'll always say if it's a special occasion, and say how much we are looking forward to staying there. If it's not a birthday/anniversary, then I explain that it's just a special trip. I've even played on the fact that Nic is a long-suffering nurse, working all hours and it's a special treat for her. I don't generally lie as that's bad juju, although we were on honeymoon for at least two years after getting married. I would say that this has had a positive effect in around 70% of hotel stays and ranges from a room upgrade to bottles of bubbly being delivered. In this modern age of aggregated comparison sites and one-click purchases, I think that the staff appreciate the actual contact and interaction with a human being.

So in true form, I stated that we had met 20 years ago and it was a special treat. That evening, at the end of a lovely meal of Chateaubriand, the restaurant had emptied to just the two of us when all of a sudden we started to hear singing from the next room. The next minute, five staff members appeared and surrounded us with candles singing the Harry Connick Jnr song, 'It had to be you'. While they presented us with a dessert that had chocolate writing over the plate saying 'Happy Wedding Anniversary', one of the ladies was sprinkling rose petals over our table and a man snuck up to my side, handed me a single rose under the table, and whispered 'give it to your wife'. They then took a photo of us in stunned amazement. During the rest of the stay, this photo would be turned into a special card to remember the occasion, and presented to us on checkout.

We were overwhelmed with it all and really couldn't point out that it wasn't an actual wedding anniversary, so we just rolled with it. I'm obviously biased but would recommend this hotel to everyone. The best part of it was that my butler could make sure no-one pinched my thongs!

Phlegm vs Lee (the Revenge)

Okay, so it looked like the big cheeses at Phlegm HQ didn't take kindly to my comments about their venture into world domination and decided to hit me with an all-out attack. Now, even though I only speak English (albeit generally worse than some who speak it as a second language), it really did make me sound more like a local. I was an absolute delight for Nic to live with, but at least it was in the beautiful surroundings of the E&O, I was very thankful we added the extra night.

Nic's nursing training kicked in, and she suddenly seemed empowered with the right to insert a thermometer somewhere into me, carte blanche, with no warning whatsoever. I felt like Inspector Clouseau creeping around the hotel while Cato was ready to pounce at any moment with a $7 Kmart Electrotemp thermometer in her hand.

This snot filled act of war had affected our usual 'every second counts' MountyDay timetable and although we were day three in Georgetown, we'd hardly hit the pavements at all. Unfortunately, our funds dictated it was time to change accommodation, but we knew it would be too much of a shock to go straight back to our allotted budget so we met in the middle with what was Penang's top hotel on Tripadvisor, the Yeng Keng Hotel. It's a fantastic Anglo-Indian historic building with excellent service, in a great location. It housed a smashing little restaurant that served breakfast in a charming courtyard, just off the busy Jalan Chulia.

The next morning I was feeling a bit better, so we decided to have a 'walk around the block' which turned into 8 hours of exploring. MountyDays were back. The town is full of beautiful historic buildings, both Colonial and classic Straits architecture throughout the decades (including some art deco). It houses the enigmatic Little India and Chinatown districts and even a traditional style floating village that's open to tourists. You have to be careful mind you, as there are real communities in nearby floating villages that are family based and only allow access to those with the correct family name. By all accounts, the occupants don't take kindly to randoms walking through. One was occupied by the Lee family name and I thought about it for a second before opting for the tourist village. It was still lovely to walk through, and it's even possible to stay in a homestay there too.

Georgetown is full of eclectic street art, including various wrought iron pieces on street corners that provide a bit of historical information for that particular area. Mix all this with fantastic street food, plenty of temples, truckloads of history, and you've got an absolute gem.

A Buddhy Great Day

Our last day in town was filled with temples. I was now feeling much better, so we tidied a few admin jobs out of the way, like buying our ferry tickets to Langkawi, before hitting the road. We'd been using public transport buses around Penang which are cheap and have good coverage. I'd highly recommend having a good map as they do go around the houses, making it easy to lose your bearings. Also maybe get all your arrangements in order before getting on board as although the buses are modern, the drivers tend to be a bit mental. We took the bus to two Buddhist temples located opposite each other near Jalan Burma, the first was the Wat Chaiya Mangalaram Thai Buddhist temple and the second was the Dhammikarama Burmese temple. The first has potentially the 14th largest reclining Buddha in the world, and the 2nd has a huge (exact height seems to be a secret) standing Buddha.

The grounds of the Burmese temple were pristine and had won awards, it was a very peaceful place although both sites were a bit commercially biased. Most objects, including hundreds of Buddha statues and even roof tiles, have some kind of nameplate to indicate donors.

From there we checked out the new hip area of Gurney drive and the beach resort of Batu Ferringhi. I have to confess it was here that we did the travellers no no, and made a beeline to the nearest McDonalds. It was hot, and we just wanted ice cream, they are cheap, and we are backpackers. Don't judge us! I went up to the counter and asked the assistant, a very petite young girl, the price for two sundaes. She pointed to a plastic menu showing the price. Now here is the thing, between that and me fumbling through my pockets and wallet to find the right money, she fell asleep, standing up.

It took me a while before I realised this, there was only so far I could shove my 50 Ringgit note under her nose without any response. My first thought was that it was true, I really do have a personality that can bore someone to death. Just as I was trying to look up 'code blue, checkout No.1' in my Malaysian phrase book, she made a bit of a head lunge and came round, she looked shocked, realised what had happened and was very apologetic. I was much more relieved than anything that I hadn't actually killed her. That sundae tasted very good indeed.

Refreshed, we jumped onto more supersonic buses to Kek Loc Si temple, Malaysia's largest Buddhist temple nestled in the side of Mount Penang. If we thought the first ones were commercial, this one took the cake (well, sold it anyway). To get there, you need to work your way through narrow paths of souvenir shops and local vendors. After surviving this, you are taken through paths of the official gift shops, it is hard to know what's for sale and what's not. I kept my hands in my pockets in case I tried to give them $5 for an ancient piece of Buddhist history.

It's undoubtedly a fantastic site to visit, housing a seven storey pagoda and the 30.2m high bronze statue of Kuan Yin, a Taoist Goddess of Mercy. Getting to the summit of the temple requires a small funicular train (at a cost of course) and rewards you with great views over Penang. We ended the day back at the city's harbour front with a culinary tour of various hawker foods. A good touristy day, but it was time for a location change and a chance to be a beach bum for a while.

Dream destination or social experiment

The following day, we embarked on a slow three hour boat ride to Langkawi for a very reasonable $18. It wasn't a great start to the day, as we were too early for breakfast in the hotel and hadn't packed any supplies. We also made the fatal beginners mistake of not negotiating the rate with the taxi driver before setting off on the journey to the ferry terminal. This meant that his day started much better as he fleeced us on arrival. Once aboard, the journey was a relaxing enough.

We were looking forward to this location as we've met people that list it as one of their favourite places in the world, returning each year. We thought that we'd find somewhere a little more upmarket to make the most of this popular holiday resort. For once, a resort sounded just fine for a little relaxation. We found the Resort World Langkawi for a reasonable, although over budget, rate. The resort was a long taxi ride from the ferry port, located at the end of a peninsula on Palau Langkawi. Langkawi is actually an archipelago of 99 islands with this being the largest and most popular. We arrived at this huge resort (also known as the Awana) and it looked pretty empty. As we got out of the taxi, we also stepped back into the early '80s.

Feeling optimistic, I figured that by using my wily hotel skills we should easily score an upgrade in this empty heirloom. Our hearts sank a little as we were shown to a room that overlooked the vast empty car park. A non-smoking room, but bizarrely surrounded by smoking rooms. The room opposite would have had the most amazing views of the harbour and lush green hills, but we had to make the most of watching people doing burnouts in golf buggies. We were determined not to be deflated and thought some lovely Malaysian food would cheer us up, surely this place must have some great food options. In fact, it would have, if any of the restaurants were open but we had a choice of precisely one, an Italian bistro. Despite the menu costing half of our daily budget, we sat down and waited, then waited, then waited some more. In yet another conjoined brain moment we looked at each other and immediately knew what approach to take with this predicament. 'This whole place can kiss my friggin arse. Taxi!'.

Our rebellious smugness dwindled in proportion to the increasing taxi fare on our route to civilisation. There was no public transport here, and our island paradise was quite removed (some would argue from this decade let alone from the nearest amenities). As we reached Cenang, we were now fed up and starving. Good old fashioned comfort food was needed, and there she was, the familiar signs of a KFC. Perfect. It turned out that most of Cenang needed comforting at that very moment too, we entered what looked like a Guinness record attempt for the most number of people to squeeze into a KFC. It was a good job the temperature wasn't in the high 30's. No, wait…

It's funny how insignificant and inane that final straw might be when it's looked at in isolation, but when it does happen you are just mentally thrown from a cliff. In Nic's case, it was when the queue that we'd been standing in, sweating up a storm, closed. She turned to me and burst into tears. I sent her outside for some warm fresh air, and with my elbows projected outwards (as though the doors just opened in a Boxing Day sale), I ploughed my way to the front of a queue. I grabbed the life-saving nourishment she needed, and we made a beeline for the one thing that always helps. Standing on the edge of a beach with our feet in the water. The outburst had worked, pressure was released, and Nic was much happier. Not one for outbursts myself (I wish I could) it worked by proxy for me too.

It was another one of those weird Big Trip juxtapositions as we stood on a beautiful beach in a spot that many people could only dream about seeing and we were fed up. The only justification I could muster was that this wasn't a two week holiday where you force your normal tolerance levels a little higher to maximise the enjoyment of a year's worth of annual leave. I'm sure you won't argue with the fact that this trip should be the happiest and best thing that could happen to someone, but you just can't carry that level of perkiness for a whole year. It's impossible, even when you are not brought up in the land of the whinging pom. I would love it if these moments happened when we are in a shithole but you don't get to choose, it's just a case of how you turn the day around. Good job that's one thing we excel at. After an equally expensive taxi ride back and a little nanna nap in our second-hand smoke infused room, we headed to the harbour front with essential supplies brought back from town, beer and chocolate. We sat in comfy recliners watching the most amazing sunset with the resort to ourselves apart from the noise of a distant wedding. It was perfect, normal service had been resumed. It wasn't the first, and won't be the last bout of the fuckums, but we know that when it does happen, it's short-lived, and it's entirely in our control to turn things around.

Return of the Jack, yes it is!

Something that's been great to see in all the locations we've been to so far is the trendiness of the Union Flag. Before we left the UK, it almost felt like raising the Union Jack was for the hard right only, those who'd stand proud with their head shaved, Doc Martins shiny, and bulldog resplendent with studded collar while chewing on next door's poodle.

Over the years, due to landmarks like the Jubilee and various sporting events (accumulating in the Olympics), it seemed like more Union Flags were flying each time we returned. Now as we travel through South East Asia, it's everywhere, on top of Mini roofs driving through Penang, on iPad covers in Singapore, on cups in KL, and T-shirts pretty much anywhere. Although I'm very proud of this, I must admit that when asked, I do tell people I'm from Australia. Maybe it's because they've offended, colonised, or gone to war with, far less people throughout history. Maybe it's because I feel like it's now our home. Maybe it's because my UK passport photo is hideous. Maybe I should mix up my answer.

Smuggled into Thailand

From Langkawi our next location was in a whole other country, we'd decided to take a boat to Koh Lipe in Thailand. We found a company that operates a large four-engined speedboat, making the crossing twice a day. At the cost of $36, it's a door to beach package. This includes, picking you up from your hotel, transport into town to check-in, transfer to the port where you go through immigration, and then finally to the boat. In our case, this meant arriving back to the same hotel we'd left 90 minutes earlier as it's where the jetty is.

The boat trip takes around an hour and in no way will you make the journey and remain dry, don't even contemplate it. It was especially lumpy on our particular day, and so we were soaked. Kids loved it, for the first 10-15 minutes anyway, then sat there with their dripping wet sour faces for the rest of the trip. Only a couple of passengers were ill, but not us so it could have been worse. Once you arrive at Koh Lipe, there isn't a jetty to disembark onto, so they use a floating pontoon where a guy with a hat took everyone's passports. Then you and your luggage are lowered (thrown) into wooden longtail boats that transport you to the beach in a Dunkirk style landing. Longtails are narrow wooden boats that have a large engine pivoted on the top of the stern with a huge propeller shaft (at least 6 feet long) that can be used to steer the boat as well. During all this commotion I tried to keep my beady little eye on the guy with the hat and our passports. He did work for the company, didn't he?

We all wait in a beach front cafe for about 15 minutes while the passports disappear and eventually magically return containing Thailand immigration stamps. It felt like a real clandestine mission, as though we were being illegally smuggled across the Mexican or Cuban border. It was great fun, and we are so glad we did it. On first impressions the island is beautiful, the water is bright blue and clear, the sand is a lovely white and ultra fine. The island is becoming more popular on the tourist radar these days, and the place looked a little busy but had a great vibe. It was probably a bit more expensive than we hoped to pay but for $40 we have found a bamboo bungalow about 20 metres from the beach, with private bathroom/shower (cold water only), no air con but with a fan and a mossie net. Bring it on.

Pirates and Snakes

Well, we might now be in our '40s, but we just made it to our first half moon party. Okay, well strictly speaking the party started at 9pm and we left the bar at 7pm, but that's still pretty rock 'n' roll for us. We stubbled across a little pirate bar with its own beach, it looked more like a little hippy commune with a few tents sprawled around the back, and a small hut where apparently world-class DJs come to perform. Not that I'd know a world-class DJ if I fell over him or her, I'm more experienced with the type of DJs that play weddings with Agadoo in their repertoire. The bar was pretty cool, there were only three staff setting up while we had the beach to ourselves, sitting under a Jolly Rodger and watching the sunset. A quite perfect moment. We even cleared them out of their last beers as the delivery for the party hadn't arrived yet, so again sounded slightly more rock star than the reality of it.

'Let's go the long way back around the island and pop up near the shops to get some water', I can't remember who said it but let's blame Nic. It was now dark, creepy and we only had a dodgy map, but I did have my trusty dive light with me to blind any unsuspecting tuk-tuk driver that came past. Our navigational skills were not too affected by the beers, and we impressively only had to backtrack once. It was during that excursion down a dead end path that my quick reactions stopped Nic from standing on a snake. Yep, a snake. What can I say, I saved her life (for like the umpteenth time). So what if it was only a teeny tiny snake, maybe a half breed between a worm and snake but we weren't to know how cunning this little critter could be. Interestingly though we did find out the hard way that, just like sharks and baseball players, if you point a torch at them they will come, and quickly. Who said you can't run in thongs.

Loopy over Lipe

Koh Lipe was such a great decision, it's a beautiful small island with lovely beaches and crystal clear sea, the scene usually reserved for postcards. We loved it here. Our accommodation was right on the beach and run by an unfriendly bunch of young Italian guys. It was almost funny to see them avoid any inclination towards a smile or polite conversation, it became a game to try and coax it out of them. Their attitude was harmless enough and didn't affect our stay. It was a bit like one of those Italian restaurants where they have an air of aloofness as though you are so lucky to have made it inside.

Each evening they lay out mats and Thai pillows on the sand and dig large holes for fires so you can chill out with a few drinks in front of the water. Other nearby bars along the beach also put on fire dancing shows to keep you both entertained whilst fearful for your eyebrows. This was especially the case when the performer took his dinner break, and a bunch of local school kids jumped in to replace him. The restaurants had great seafood selections laid out in the evenings where you can come and choose what you want, they barbecue it before serving on a plastic beachfront table. We could only afford it one night, so we each had three prawns the size of a baby's arm, sweetcorn the size of said baby's leg, and potatoes that bear no resemblance to any part of the baby. It all came to $33, with the odd Chang beer thrown in, something we would have been overjoyed about on a normal holiday but was a sharp uppercut to the daily budget.

Nevermind, there are no ATMs in coffins (or anywhere on Koh Lipe for that matter).

Not being folk for spending hours lying on the beach we pretty much explored the whole island, it's that small it doesn't take long. The one day we did actually have a lazy beach day, resulted in the expenses taking a hit with copious supplies of Aloe Vera from a local shop the following day. To give you an idea of the size of the island, its few shops were grouped together on a small laneway, called 'Walking Street', the highlight of which was a small banana pancake stall. This wasn't called the 'Banana Pancake' route through South East Asia for nothing, and we made a point of sampling this cheap backpacker delicacy at every opportunity along the way.

Ferry 'cross the Andaman

It was so hard leaving Koh Lipe, but we knew this was a journey and who knows what good things lie ahead. We checked out of our great little guesthouse with one last effort of friendly inter-action with the Italians. Fail. Will try again when we go back one day, we will not be defeated, we will fight them on the beaches....

We caught a longtail taxi to our ferry. After getting drenched in the last speedboat, we decided to take the slower ferry instead, meaning a 5-hour journey to Koh Lanta rather than 3.5-hours. As the boat started to fill, most of the backpackers headed straight to the roof to carry on with their beer drinking and sun worship-ping (it was 9:30am after all). We settled into the comfy seats downstairs where Nic promptly fell asleep.

Looks like we made a good call, initially the slower ferry still generated a lot of spray as it motored along. Pretty soon, most of the great unwashed who were up on the roof appeared downstairs, miraculously now looking very washed. As the seas calmed down they slowly moved up again. The ferry called at a few other islands on the way to Koh Lanta and they all looked beautiful despite not getting much of a mention in the guidebooks. We'd thought we were being brave for getting to Koh Lipe, but in hindsight, we should also have stopped at a few of these on the way.

We both slept a little between watching the beautiful island views. At one of the bigger ports a group of locals jumped onboard selling snacks and drinks, so we grabbed some sliced pineapple on sticks. Fact: All food tastes better when it's on a stick. It was great entertainment watching them jump over the boat carrying their wares and shouting with huge smiles.

On our arrival at Koh Lanta, we were welcomed with a barrage of taxi drivers touting for trade, we'd already arranged a pick up from our hotel so tried to barge our way through them all with a smug wave of a hand. It was probably the most we'd been hassled so far, and 'no' wasn't in their vocabulary. We broke loose to find no-one waiting. I was determined that I wasn't going to head back into the throng with my tail between my legs, so I called the hotel with my unhappy voice. I'll give those who know me a few minutes to stop laughing at that notion. Anyway, after a stern conversation to someone who could barely understand what I was saying, they sent a pickup. While waiting for it, we realised that the ferry was a little late, actually three hours late. It had taken 8 hours, we had slept more than we thought, and the pickup had actually already been and left. I was now much more polite to them once they turned up and already thinking about what a nice hotel this was probably going to be.

(5) Koh Lanta

We finally arrived and our room was on the 2nd storey of a motel type affair in a building that was just outside the resort's main complex, next to some derelict land housing some ill-looking cows. The first thing I noticed were the mattresses laid out in the sun (a known process for getting rid of bedbugs). We are shown the room and I can see that the door has recently been kicked in and someone had attempted to put it back together with a few panel pins. Being the last lodging next to the fire exit I'm sure that I've seen the very same room on a CSI episode referred to as 'murder central'. Just for a change, we burst into a frenzy of perspiration as soon as we closed the door, but couldn't see any remote for the air-con so I headed back to reception. The receptionist was friendly and, bless him, was trying his best as he started to rummage through a box of old remotes. I could see he had a good think about trying to palm me off with a Sharp TV remote but could sense I was onto him. In the end, he offered us a 400baht discount to make up for the inconvenience, so we decided to put up with a fan for the night. He made a point of asking us to come and find him in the morning and let us know if we wanted to extend our stay. Poker face.

We did what our in-depth training and planning has taught us in such situations, we hit the bar to ponder over a beer. We sat down next to an English couple in their 50's, Kev and Ali, who were also not looking the most relaxed to be in this luxurious abode. They were partway through a six-week adventure through Australia and South East Asia. Like us, they had also just checked in and had opted for a pool villa to find that the pool was full of Irish 'lager lout' stereotypes, swimming around and wrestling with large bottles of beer in their hands. We simultaneously hit the world wide web and had a great chat comparing travel tips. They were apparently much better about talking to randoms than us, and always seemed to be getting tips from people about this and that. Certainly something we needed to improve on.

Just as we were parting ways for the night, Kev mentioned that at least the place was quiet in the evening and there was no sign of the lads from earlier. I quipped that they are probably all back in the room next to ours. Bingo! Luckily after having to endure a brief conversation outside our room about which blokes from Eastern Block countries you would or wouldn't get into a fight with, they must have retired with a good novel. We made sure to sleep in our protective silk sleep-sheets that night, the place was horrible. You came out of the shower feeling like you needed a shower. In the morning I bumped into Kev heading out on a hired moped to scour the coast for a better spot. We'd better get on and do the same.

Sliding Doors and Travel Karma

Remember the movie with Gwyneth Paltrow, when not getting through a sliding train door had a significant impact on her life. Well not to her extent, but we've had a couple of those moments recently. They also compounded our belief in the concept that you get in life, what you dish out. You know, the whole Karma thing.

Ever since we started to plan our trip, you would see us stalking backpackers around Melbourne, studying what they were wearing, what make and size backpacks they had. We didn't quite get to the stage where I was following them home to see where they stayed, although I was tempted with the odd Swedish visitor. If ever we saw someone looking a bit lost we would magically appear from behind a bush and help them out with directions. All this with the hope that if we were in the same predicament, in a strange place, someone would do the same for us. So far during this trip, we've also helped out fellow travellers wherever we can (who generally seemed to be Canadian for some reason).

So back to Koh Lanta, we needed to get some new digs after last night's grotty room and started by walking up and down the local beach. The only outcome of which was getting very hot and bothered. We returned to the hotel bar and jumped back onto the internet to find a room on Agoda.com in what looked like a nice hotel. It was expensive, so we decided that we would go in person to try and barter the price down. We bid farewell to the flea pit and bombed it down the road with our bags in a tuk-tuk.

We walked excitedly into a lovely hotel reception to find that they were actually full, even if we'd booked online they wouldn't have accepted the booking. We were now getting tired enough to even think about going back to murder central. But, as we were leaving, one of us decided to turn around and head to the hotel's bar to regroup (okay yes it was me). The bar was actually a separate entity called 'the Koala bar' which sounded perfect for two stranded Aussies. It was run by a guy from Perth called Todd who saw we were a little over it and asked what was up, as I ordered a beer. He said that he might have some tips for accommodation so come and see him after we'd relaxed and cooled down with a drink. Beer finished, I went up to him expecting some directions on the back of a beer mat, so was surprised to see him grab his hat and say follow me. Next minute, he threw me onto the back of his moped, and we shot off down the road. This was the first time I'd been on the back of a motorbike since I was 8 years old and had to quickly work out the right places and appropriate strength to hold on, without him getting the wrong impression. I tried to act as though I was taking it all in my stride, but my voice was at least an octave higher as we dodged traffic without helmets. Then my hat blew off which, although only made of cotton, was all the protection I had. It required a quick double u-turn in front of traffic to kick it out the way and retrieve it.

The first place he took me to was full so onto another which looked okay but just had a very basic room and I felt it was a bit too rustic for our current disposition. When we got back to the bar, I said that I really wasn't expecting the lift and he explained that he'd travelled plenty and if five minutes of his time could make a big difference to someone struggling on their journey, then no worries. Feeling newly invigorated (i.e. glad to be alive) I tried the final recommendation for the hotel next door. It wasn't Todd's first choice because of the price. I headed around for a haggle and secured an absolutely fantastic room for only 200baht more than we were supposed to pay for the last place. Happy days. We repaid Todd's help by giving his bar lots of business, helped by the fact that it also served probably one of my top 5 favourite burgers of all time.

A couple of chilled days later we headed to the nearby port town of Saladan to sort out ferry tickets to Krabi. We were walking around looking for a breakfast spot and spotted an Ocean Divers shop with an attached restaurant, we peeked in but it looked closed, so we turned to leave. Halfway out, we decided to turn back and try anyway. They were open, or at least happy for us to stay, so we sat down near the only other guy in there and started a conversation. He turned out to be Aidan (the owner) and by his accent we were expecting him to teach us more about Cockney rhyming slang than the introduction to Thai breakfasts we received. He talked us into ordering a local Thai breakfast of spicy minced chicken on rice with pickled vegetables and egg. A great choice.

We mentioned that we were looking for tickets and he told us to use a local couple who run a guest house a few doors down. The husband and wife team at the Sincere guesthouse were fantastic and sorted us out with a cheaper, quicker, and more interesting route to Krabi using a minibus and car ferries. They even sorted our onward transport to Bangkok via an overnight bus, you bet your ass you're gonna be hearing more about that.

It had felt that those two quick decisions to change direction and turn back had really turned each of the days around and the help we had from everyone involved really did make us feel like Karma or someone was looking over us. So obviously the important moral of the story is that if you see two short, sweaty, slightly smelly backpackers with a mixed UK/Australian accent on your travels then do everything you possibly can to help them out. It may, in turn, help you in some other way.

Battle of the Tourist Bulges

One thing we regret is that we didn't lose more weight and get fitter before we left Melbourne, but with everything we needed to prepare, it's understandable that this one fell through the creases (see what I did there). Although we didn't have an exercise regime while travelling, the walking, sweating and change of diet was definitely helping us lose weight. In a world with no tape measures or scales, it's hard to keep track, so I came up with an ingenious scale based on a comparison to the various nationalities around us.

First, you have the Asian locals, they always look so thin and super fit. Although they are a similar height to us, I think it would take three of them to make one of me. Coming a close second, are the French. I don't know what it is, but I think this has something to do with a diet that consists of a glass of wine and a croissant for breakfast and then just their three pack of cigarettes a day habit to tide them over till the next breakfast.

Next, there are the young parents who used to be fit but have let themselves go a little, compounded with the fact that parenthood has driven them to drink, so they have little tiny beer bellies. Next is us. A deceptive group that when properly clothed look quite svelte but when naked would scare children and the infirm. Then there is the ex-pat lager louts who have had a few years to develop their large bellies, unless of course their tattoos have plenty of vertical stripes which, as you know, has a thinning effect. Finally, we have the middle-aged German tourists - sausages and sauerkraut, say no more.

With my new found confidence in the order of things, I decided to hit the beach in my Daniel Craig (or Sean Connery, depending on your age) trunks to assess our status on the scale. We quickly walked straight past the naked Swedish, lounging around the pool and hit the beach where all the Germans were hanging out (literally). Score one for the Mounties. However, during my swim, all the sunburn blisters I'd acquired on Koh Lipe filled with seawater. When I walked seductively out of the surf (Ursula Andress styley), rather than James Bond, I resembled a cross between the Singing Detective and the Michelin Man. Nic was a lucky Bond girl that day as I flopped down on the beach bursting the blisters underneath sending squirts of liquid towards her eye. What a catch.

Crazy Crabs in Krabi

Most people we'd spoken to didn't have a lot of praise for Krabi, it seemed like most tourists head to the nearby beaches at Ao Nang or quickly move onto their next destination. We stayed longer on Koh Lanta than we were going to, so only had time for one night in town. The journey there was a quick 2-hour route in a minivan using two car ferries, firstly to get to Koh Lanta Noi, and then across to the mainland. I only found religion twice this journey, so must be mellowing out about the traffic. Although this was our third trip to Thailand, it was the first time we'd set foot on the mainland.

Krabi isn't the most picturesque of towns but has a certain charm, and the people were super friendly. The nearby twin limestone massifs of Khao Khanap Nam offer a great backdrop to one of the best parts of the city, its markets. One of which was right next to our hotel. The food selection was fantastic, we slowly ate our way around the stalls, and our 5 courses only cost around $3 each. Standouts include a chicken massaman and a freshly cut pineapple with sweet chilli sugar.

From there, we headed down to the riverfront, armed with more take-out food to watch the longtails whizzing by, but when we looked down from the promenade, we saw two of the strangest things. The first, hundreds of mud hopper creatures that would walk on sand and reverse into little holes before jumping across the water as though someone had just thrown a round pebble. Next, were tiny crabs with one of its main pincers disproportionally huge, about the size of the rest of its body. I could only guess that they were juvenile males. We did notice that it was right near what looked like a waste outlet leading into the estuary, so I don't know if that had anything to do with it. I was half expecting to see the three-eyed fish that keeps cropping up in the *Simpsons* cartoons.

Early next morning, we hit the indoor Maharaj fresh food market. It was a wonderful photo opportunity, and it's not everyday you get to see a bucket of frogs for sale. Some stalls were actually selling those big arm crabs, but I hope they didn't catch them from where we saw them last night. Suddenly at exactly 8am, the overhead speakers crackled to life, and the national anthem started. What, a minute earlier was a crazy melting pot of people shouting, carrying, chopping, and eating, suddenly stopped and everyone stood bolt upright in silence for the anthem. It was great to experience and when it finished I had to restrain myself not to clap and cheer with a shout of 'play ball!'

Night Bus - Bangkok for your Buck

Our fantastic little tourist agent in Koh Lanta had informed us that the sleeper train from Krabi to Bangkok was full so we had a choice of changing dates or taking the bus. At this point, we only had two things locked in our itinerary, a balloon trip in Myanmar (Burma) about 10 days later, and then not until early May for the Trans-Mongolian in Beijing. We didn't want to delay things or have to take extra unnecessary flights within Myanmar, so we reluctantly decided on the bus.

I say reluctantly as we'd heard lots of bad things about the 820km, 12-hour journey. This included; stories of being thrown out halfway; made to use old dilapidated uncomfortable buses; unsafe drivers; and many reports of theft. We quizzed the agent, and she had said that she puts lots of westerners (farang) on these buses and there has never been any problem. Even in Krabi our hotel receptionist kept stressing to Nic about having her valuables strapped to her, so as you may expect, we were a little nervous. The fact that the whole journey, including pickup from the hotel, only cost $15 did help the budget but didn't help our confidence.

The minivan picked us up and drove us about five kilometres to the outskirts of town before stopping in a paddock with some kiosks. We registered to receive stickers displaying which bus to get on (or potentially to indicate which of our body organs are going to be sold on the black market). The paddock was mostly full of backpackers, as everyone else with any sense was paying a few dollars more to fly, but that's not in our trip edict so here we are. We scanned the crowd to see who's on our bus. I was also checking to see if anyone had my thongs on. There wasn't any allocated seating, so it was a case of identifying the weakest when it came to the mad dash to the bus. Maybe that's why everyone was looking our way and nodding.

Eventually, our bus appeared, a proper coach with comfy seats and air-con. Result. I don't quite know how we managed it, but we ended up at the front of the queue when the doors opened, we legged it upstairs and spread out on the front row. No-one else seemed to be rushing down this way, this might have been down to the massive crack across the glass windscreen in front of us. We ended up sitting next to two Eastern European girls and I used to think Nic could talk, but these girls took the biscuit. After the first two hours without stopping for breath, I was checking them for gills and starting to feel faint due to the lack of oxygen.

The seats were great, we felt very smug with ourselves having great views of the cliff formations leaving Krabi. However, at about 10:30pm, just as we were getting settled in for the night, the coach turned into another dark paddock, and we heard the last thing we wanted to hear, 'Everybody off!'. This was it, the body part harvesting paddock, we were doomed. I was working out how I might be able to offer up Nic to bide myself some extra time. Turned out it was just a bus change, and we lost our great seats. After a 15 minute wait, a much older bus arrived, and this time the rabble were on to us, I blocked as many as I could, fumbling with our backpacks, as Nic clambered upstairs. No pole position this time, in fact, I was lucky enough to pick the special broken seat that didn't recline for our next 8 hour leg.

We'd not long set off again, everyone had just settling down, reading and chatting when the driver turned off all the lights. Pitch darkness. It was apparently time for everyone to sleep. Three hours later, lights blared on again as the bus stopped next to a roadside food outlet with shouts of 'get food! 40 minutes!'. This lamp treatment was probably something taught at Guantanamo Bay, most people were dazed and confused and didn't know what month it was. As we set off again, only the left side of the internal lights went off, in a bizarre continuation of this social experiment.

Sustenance throughout the night was provided by a few packets of fruit Mentos, these sweets have been a staple 'go to' on the journey so far. They are easily available in every country, are cheap, and small to carry. You also know what you're getting yourself into, so it's a safe bet. You'll never find us without a few packets stuffed in different pockets and bags. I didn't sleep but had my broken chair to keep me company, this meant I was a lot more prepared than the other passengers when we got to our final destination. The bus slowly stopped so as not to disturb anyone's slumber before loud screams of 'Bangkok - Wake Up - Get Off!'. Welcome to the madness that is Bangkok for $15.

Khaosan Road - it does what it says on the tin

At least the bus finished its journey just around the corner from where we were staying, so no need for any extra transportation adventures. I'm not quite sure why we chose the area, I think it was due to its location near the Grand Palace, but just by chance, it was at one end of the infamous Khaosan Road.

Khaosan Road has got to be up there in the list of most craziest streets in the world, it's only short, but a lot happens. Our first experience was immediate as we went the wrong direction from the coach, having to walk the whole length of it at 6:30am with our backpacks on. The scene was mostly an aftermath of the previous night's parties, and there were literally people falling out of bars. Some very drunk men with the newly found lady friends (well, maybe) that they'd met during the night. People were clambering in and out of taxis. It was bedlam, then in the middle of it all, we spot a small boy kneeling at the foot of a monk before putting some money in his alms bowl. It was such a contrast and will surely be a lasting memory with a mystical morning mist surrounding them both. I suppose if a monk is brave enough, it has the potential to be quite fortuitous to venture down this street with most people not having any grasp of the cash denomination in their hand. However, I'm sure that at least one alms bowl has been used as an emergency upchuck vessel over the years.

Our well-researched hotel room wasn't ready that early in the morning, so we dumped our bags and went straight into a MountyDay, touring temples and old streets. The hotel was great, although next to a nightclub that went on till 4am, which we'd been prepared for by the hotel's reviews. Other than that, it was a nice quiet little corner and felt far from the madding crowd. Once refreshed, we hit Khaosan road again, this time a little more prepared. During the day, it's buildings are mainly bars, restaurants and hostels with the street-front packed with touristy gift and food stalls. In the small length of the street, four different stalls were openly making any kind of false ID or official document that you could ever want. As we walked past one, we saw someone buying a UK driving license and noticed a degree certificate from Swinburne Uni in Melbourne on display. Don't be surprised if I arrive back in Melbourne as a certified gynaecologist with a pilots license.

Two of the food stalls were dedicated to insects, you can get your teeth into all kinds of different grubs, roaches or scorpions. As we were just about to leave for Myanmar and the guidebooks say, regarding Burmese healthcare, that if you have anything worse than a hangover then get the hell out of the country, Nic refused to let me near their goods.

As you walk down the street during the day, you are regularly stopped by smart young men who want to get you fitted up with made-to-measure suits. It's funny watching them try their hardest sales pitch on German backpackers with bright green hair and wearing half their weight again in piercings. Unless the

Germans were also preparing themselves for an upcoming court appearance, I'm thinking that a pinstripe three-piece isn't on top of their Khaosan experience list.

At night when you return the same guys are there, but this time their signs are much smaller, and they'll only give you a quick glance as you stroll by. I only caught a quick look, but it would seem that this well dressed, mild-mannered group of lads are keen table tennis fans and are pet lovers, especially the reptile/octopus variety. It's quite a refreshing sight in this day and age to see young men with such wholesome hobbies and in such a sordid environment. Good on them.

Foot Massage and the Geneva Convention

One of the great things about South East Asia is the very cheap massages, where $6 will get you an hour (in a reputable joint). We always look forward to getting one and see it as a treat, but I'm not quite sure why.

We usually choose a foot massage as generally we've been on our feet all day and you also get a little neck massage thrown in at the end, so its good value. The first thing I like about getting a massage abroad is that the masseurs often chat with each other and it's great not understanding the language. At home, you might be hearing what Ricky did this time to be thrown out of the house, or what the doctor said about that rash that appeared after the Ibiza trip. Here, you can make up what they are talking about, maybe about the fantastic night of lovemaking that they all had together last night. Me, I imagine that they are talking about how incredible my feet are (it's the favourite of my body parts, and I often feel they should be paying me for the privilege).

You'll get all comfy in a reclining chair with a stool under your feet or sometimes lie on a mattress. They start by using a wet flannel to wash your feet and legs, this feels great, and then they apply some oil to rub in. My internal commentary starts, 'this is great, we should do this every day, I'm going to relax and maybe get some sleep'.

After rubbing the oil in, they start on your feet, one at a time. It's classed as a reflexology massage which should really give you a bit of a warning, but nevertheless, I always seem to be surprised when a knuckle gets inserted firmly into a soft bit of foot between two toes. 'Relax, it will be okay in a second', 'think of something else'. One by one, any part of your foot that can't fight for itself gets a pummeling. 'Don't show pain', 'Smile', 'only 45 minutes to go!'. Then it stops as she turns around and picks up a utensil. Not quite sure what it is, but it feels like a knitting needle, whatever it is I'm sure that it wouldn't get through airport security. It would seem that her boney little knuckles weren't pain inducing enough, so every spot is revisited with this newly brandished weapon. 'Holly crap', 'Sorry little pinky', 'stop frowning and smile', 'show the sadistic cow no pain!'.

That part finishes, and she starts on the ankle and thigh. I'm sure their training is quite complete, but for some reason, she would not rest until she made one of my joints move in a way it shouldn't do. 'What did I do to you?', 'that doesn't go there', 'don't press, don't press', 'no I'm not in pain, it's just some wind'. Thankfully with that leg done, she gently (now with the gently) rests it down and carefully covers it up with a damp cloth as though it's deceased. Onto the next leg, and the commentary repeats. This treatment would not be allowed under the Geneva Convention, and you feel sure there are going to be subsequent photos posted on Facebook of her bending over me, doing a Japanese tourist V sign pose to a camera.

With both feet under submission, she works her way upwards until she has your legs splayed open like a spatchcock, pushing my knees further and further apart. 'Holy Moly'. I'm quite sure that I am now capable of giving birth. Once the pressure on the knees subsides, she moves upwards again, and again. 'Easy tiger', 'don't even think about it, Lee Junior!'. Your priority on facial expressions now quickly changes. 'Now frown, don't look like you're enjoying it'. And it all stops.

You think it's all over until suddenly she thrusts you forward, grabs your right hand, puts it behind your head, and starts twisting. 'Did you hear that? Something cracked! What the hell cracked?!'. Next, the other side, before she leans on your back, pushing your head between your legs 'so this is what it's like to be a dog'. Almost done, she tackles the top of your back and neck. 'Did she just punch me?', 'Why I ought to..'.

Then something very cunning happens, she finds a particular spot on your neck and in a Jedi move, she massages a pressure point, and all memory of what just happened disappears, and you feel lovely and relaxed. You get up, hand over your money feeling amazing and are already working out when you can get the next one.

Anyway, got to go. Massage time.

Burmese Visa run (and they don't even accept visa)

The mission, should we accept it, was to sort out our Myanmar (Burmese) visas. This could have been sorted the easy way before we left by sending it to Canberra, but our passports had already visited the Russian consulate without us, so FOMO directed us to a more adventurous route. This involved a trip to the Myanmar Embassy in Bangkok, bearing in mind that we had flight tickets booked for two days later, we needed it to go smoothly.

We decided to get to the embassy via Bangkok's public riverboats which are an adventure unto themselves. They dart up and down the river with stops on each bank. They're like large long tails but with internal engines and they really don't take prisoners. It felt very James Bondesque; speeding down the Chao Phraya river; past Chinatown; with a package containing passports, money and embassy documents ready for a highly important transaction. As the boat motors quickly up to the jetty they throw it into reverse as a crew member jumps off to tie on a rope, the boat is held in place by the reverse thrust of the engines momentarily. The crew signals to the captain via whistles and once it's 'safe' you hear shouting from all directions informing you to jump off the boat. It felt like a parachute jump, I was muttering 'one thousand and one', 'one thousand and two…' to myself for the first few steps on dry land. These ferry trips are so much fun, and great value as the 30-minute trip only costs 50c.

It's a well-documented routine on lonely planet and back-packer forums about the process of queuing up well before the 9am opening at the Embassy to fill in the appropriate forms and handover two passport photos, money and your passports. There is a handy copy shop around the corner that has developed a little cottage business of supplying the forms before you get inside and you can also get your photos, glue, passport and flight details photocopied here. That way you can fill in the details as you are waiting for the Embassy to open. Nic had researched this part well, and we knew all these tricks and had everything you might possibly need. She ended up helping others around us, directing people to the copy shop. As it seems a bit more of a daunting process compared to other visa applications, there was a great camaraderie within the queue, and everyone was chatty and discussing their trip or previous experiences in Myanmar. Once in, you get your forms checked and receive a number, more waiting until your numbers up, then you pay US$40 each, are given a receipt for your passports, and told to come back at 3:30pm where you queue again. The second part is much more straight forward, you quickly hand over the receipt, and you get your passports back with a full page visa and photo inserted into one of the pages. Result.

The next step is to sort money. At the time we entered the country there weren't any ATMs in Myanmar (there were rumours of the first one being installed while we were there) and no-one accepts credit cards so you couldn't easily access money. Therefore you have to withdraw it in advance and carry the full amount you'll need for your whole trip. You take US$ into the country where you can then change it to the local Kyat. The issue is that it can't be any US$, it has to be at least 2006 edition notes and must be in pristine condition, not a fold or a crease anywhere or they won't be accepted. This meant a journey through town visiting various banks to carefully inspect their dollar bills, holding them up to the light as though they might be a forgery. We rejected many notes and spent many hours on the task, but still ended up with two of our notes refused when we were in-country. This resulted in the best people watching at the departure lounge for the flight to Yangon. Just as in the visa queue, everyone was super excited and chatty with tourist books in one hand, but not surprisingly the other arm was clutching their cash-filled hand luggage as though their lives depended on it.

CHAPTER 4

Location: Yangon
Days 39, Countries 6, Kilometers 9,196, Beds 17
Trains 1, Planes 5, Automobiles 5, Boats 3
Beers 9

Yangon a minute we're going to Burma!

We've been excited about coming to Myanmar (Burma) since we added it to the list, as mentioned previously, I have a bit of family history here. We really wanted to experience it, especially before the tourism boom completely takes off.

Burma (Myanmar) has a population of around 48 million and Yangon (Rangoon) is its biggest city, so you can imagine that it's quite a large bustling location. Most of the streets in the city's centre are laid out in a grid system, thanks to the colonial days. Our small, newish, hotel was located at the centre top of the grid. It was also located right next door to the well known Traders Hotel, a tall building and great reference point for finding our way around or telling taxi drivers where to take you home. The only issue was that the Traders costs six times what we were paying next door, so whenever you mentioned it, the taxi price goes up. We soon got used to saying 'To the Traders, but we are not staying there!'.

Travelling in Myanmar is a bit different to other places we've been to. There was much more of a concerted effort to travel responsibly, especially paying attention to where your money finally ends up. Large hotels, some airlines and big tour companies generate income that often goes to the government (military) as they have a majority ownership of the company. Throughout our trip, we tried to make sure that we worked with smaller Burmese companies and family businesses where the money goes straight to them. We also tried to share the love a little and not frequent the same restaurants.

Things seemed to be changing rapidly in Yangon, and the two-year-old Lonely Planet book we were using already seemed out of date. Where most publications would say that you shouldn't talk about the government with locals, it was great to now have them approaching us and starting conversations. One taxi driver explained after talking about their education system, if we'd had the same conversation two years ago, he would be fearful for the safety of both himself and his family. During our stay we had mixed views from locals about their preference between the name Burma or Myanmar and as you can see we can't make our minds up either.

There were now pictures everywhere of Aung San Suu Kyi, the secretary of the National League for Democracy (NLD) who was famously held under house arrest for 15 years before her release in 2010. The history here is quite complex and very interesting if you get a chance to delve into it; with plenty of regional issues as well as the overall political situation. The plight of the Burmese people has been far more horrendous than just the political prisoners that we generally hear about on the news. Especially for some of the regional ethnic groups such as the Karen and Rakhinc.

By all accounts, the control by the English was no bed of roses either, but it did leave behind some fantastic buildings around the city. Large colonial affairs, some with Roman and French influence. For some time after their independence, these buildings were used by squatters until the military moved them out for government use to then be abandoned again years later when the country's new capital, Naypyidaw, was created. Some are now fully restored, and others are very much overgrown and dishevelled, offering some great photo opportunities. It would be great to see more of these brought back to life again.

The standard of living in this busy city is generally very poor, and it's an educational experience to walk around, which we did lots of. Although walking around is not the easiest here. Most pavements are made of big concrete blocks that cover the drainage system, many of these blocks are loose, broken, misaligned or missing so while looking up at buildings you need to make sure you don't suddenly disappear. Walking through Yangon is such a barrage to your senses that it's like an adrenaline injection, it really makes you feel alive. Despite waking up to the smell of drains and interesting street food instead of roses, I would recommend it to anyone.

Myanmar is fantastic, so beautiful, so friendly and you are treated with its inherent quirkiness as soon as you arrive and have to set your watch to a time zone that is GMT +6:30, one of only a handful of countries that uses a half hour deviation from standard time zones.

The next thing you notice is they drive on the right. However, most of the cars (pretty much all the taxis) are right-hand drive, requiring the driver to sit close to the verge. This doesn't matter too much around busy Yangon, but when you get out to the countryside with nice windy roads, things get interesting. Horns seem to replace sight, they beep for everything. I'm sure they have developed a bat-like sonar system and can formulate 3D images of the surrounding traffic from all the horn noises bouncing around. Some taxis are bare bones inside, you get a loose seat in the back and can check out the road beneath you through the holes in the metal floor. Some cars do have air conditioning, but it's never used. Many buses are fantastic old Hino classics filled with three times as many people as they should carry. A lot of cars and buses turn off their engines at lights to save petrol, and we even saw one Hino ticket inspector jump out at each stop and put a brick behind a wheel as a chock to stop it rolling back.

Other smaller buses are a ute affair where people clamber in the back, and if you're lucky there is a wooden bench down each side to sit on. A sturdy frame structure above your head provides shade. Initially the baggage is thrown on top and then surplus people are added onto that. This layered transport can get quite high and looks like a human pyramid as it bounds towards you on the bumpy roads. Another quirky thing to see is instead of phone boxes you will see a regular house phone sat on a little table at the side of the street with its cable reaching up a tree and across to a nearby building. Somebody mans the phone to charge customers, you can even receive incoming calls. We watched a local man obviously waiting for a call by staring at it as though trying to lift it into the air with his Jedi skills.

The majority of men here wear a skirt, called a longyi. The locals can pull the look off with style, but after seeing how stupid some tourists look wearing one, I refrained until one day its use was compulsory at a Mandalay temple complex (probably to protect Buddha from seeing my scrawny milky white knees). I have to say it actually quite suited me and I enjoyed it, not enough to buy one though, that would be weird.

Here is my favourite quirkiness and it's mainly the men that I've heard do it, the method used by the Burmese to catch someones attention is to make a two kissing sounds. It's great to hear, it's like flirting for the painfully shy - 'Kiss, Kiss', 'Are you asking for a snog?', 'no, could you pass me the ketchup'. I didn't have the nerve to do it in case I ended up engaged to a local family's ugly daughter (actually the women in Myanmar are mostly beautiful). Women and young children are nearly always seen wearing a yellow substance on their cheeks and forehead called Thanakha which protects from the sun as well as being good for complexion. It's made from ground bark and smells like sandalwood. When you first see it, you feel the urge to tap them on the shoulder and explain that 'you've left the house with your face pack still on luv', but after a week in the country it seems quite normal. Different patterns can be used to differentiate themselves and add a bit of style to the process.

As a rule, people here are so friendly, they say 'hi' (Mingala Ba) when you walk past them, or they shout it to you as they speed past on a moped. It's as the world should be and shouldn't stand out as being quirky in any way but nevertheless it's unusual in our normal existence.

Betelmania

As you walk down the street, you'll pass many little stalls that sell strange little packages being prepared by a man sat on a small plastic stool. After a bit of investigation, we found out that they are chopped Betel nuts wrapped in Betel leaves and have been coated in an unknown white liquid. Betel nut is a fruit from the areca palm tree and is the world's fourth most popular psychoactive substance after nicotine, alcohol and caffeine (according to Wikipedia).

Although it looks a plain enough nut when you see it, as someone starts chewing, it becomes very red. Something about it must get quite juicy as their mouth fills with red gunk. You can spot a 'nutter' a mile off as he or she looks like they have just gone ten rounds with Mike Tyson. You can also see a bit of a glaze in their eyes if they've had a few that day. How do they get rid of the excess juices? You guessed it, they spit it out. Some are incredibly proficient at it and would be the envy of the cool kids in any year six playground. You have to be on your guard, especially when cycling, as they can come from any direction at great distance and speed.

Taxi drivers will roll down their windows as they are driving and eject a little bomb onto anything that might be passing. Traffic lights are a popular spot, and a busy junction can look like Tarantino has just shot his latest movie there. The noise involved in this is fantastic, and you just can't get away from it, it seems like half the country is auditioning to be the next Bob Carolgees[1] sidekick.

I eventually decided to try one and plucked up the courage to approach a street vendor who, no matter what I said, just stared at me as though I'd farted violently in his direction. After what seemed to be 10 minutes of this Burmese standoff, I decided to exit stage left leaving my teeth still their traditional English orange-brown colour. This practice didn't really bother us at all, and we put it down to the experiences of a different culture. However, we did struggle one night when our hotel waiter served us our mains with a bright red smile, struggling to keep the red gunk in his mouth before walking to the edge of the verandah and quickly expelling his load, right in front of us. Cheque, please!

The not so safe, safe

Our hotel in Yangon was modern, clean and just what we needed. Although it did have two quirky features to kept us entertained. First, the bedding which was made from the slippyest material known to man. It was almost impossible to climb on the bed without shooting down to the bottom and ending up in a pile on the floor. For our own personal safety, we'd be living like monks for the next nookie-free few days.

Second, was the in-room safe that was sitting on a desk. I noticed that when I closed the door, the whole thing moved slightly. As I walked around the room with it stowed under my

[1] *UK 80s pop culture reference, you may need to Google it*

arm, it became clear that not only wasn't the safe secured to anything, it was as light as a feather. Once we stopped laughing, I was tempted to take it down to breakfast with me to prove a point. I loved the idea of sitting there, eating my noodle broth from the buffet, with one arm leaning on the safe, hugging it a bit closer if anyone approached.

No Spies on Us

In yet another Sarkies hotel fix, we popped into the Strand Hotel and its aptly named Sarkies Bar. Its heyday was at the start of the 20th Century when Rangoon was the third largest harbour in the Indian Empire. Over the years, the hotel has hosted the likes of Coward, Orwell, Kipling, and Welles. It seemed wrong not to splash out on one of their famous *Strand Sour* cocktails as we were passing.

It was here that we caught wind of a soiree at something called the British Club in Yangon which was open to any ex-pats. We worked out that it was a 20 minute walk from our hotel, so headed off in a northerly direction into the dark night. After about 10 minutes we weren't quite sure how safe this area was but became aware of footsteps behind us. I say we, Nic was oblivious as usual, no doubt with her purse out counting through wads of our pristine looking US dollars. Mine, and therefore Nic's, pace sped up a bit, then a bit more, but whatever was behind us didn't drop back.

A shout of 'excuse me!' broke the tension and I turned around to look at a middle-aged man with his wife and daughter. He introduced himself and asked if he could talk to us as we were walking. It felt very much like the start of one of those scam conversations we'd endured in South East Asia. You know that feeling you get when you answer a phone call from an unknown number to quickly realise you are being patched through to a cold call centre. We braced ourselves but ended up being ashamed to admit that the only thing this man was selling was a polite conversation. His wife didn't speak much English, and he would translate a little as we spoke. It was the first time he had spoken to Australians and he seemed quite excited about it.

His opening gambit took us by surprise a little. 'Where are your children this evening?'. So much so that I think both Nic and I looked at each other for a split second with a look of 'Shit, where are the kids!?'. Have we left them somewhere and did we crack the window a little? Next, it was his turn to look shocked when we explained there weren't any. His jaw dropped another inch when we told him our age. We talked a little more but the last thing we heard from him as our paths parted was 'Tonight we will go home and pray to the lord so that he will bring you children, don't you worry it will happen'. Well, if that wasn't a natural contraceptive, I don't know what was. Nic and I made eye contact, it was clearly understood that we would NOT be getting any that night.

Five minutes later we arrived at the British Embassy compound and had it surrounded at least twice before finding the correct entrance. I don't know what I was expecting, but it probably contained Oscar Wilde, Ernest Hemingway, the Queen and a tiger sipping a Martini. Not the case. We signed in, passed through security and were ushered into a bar that had a British Legion/RSL feel where we were presented to a lady in front of a roll of tickets (the type you might see at a raffle). Probably to circumvent licensing or catering laws, we had to purchase tickets which could then be exchanged for drink and food. Expecting to be hobnobbing with the odd spy or foreign ministers, I spent up with about US$40 worth of tickets.

Two pints, two scampi and chips (in a basket) and US$12 worth of vouchers later, we were sat on a patio in a lovely garden near a large swimming pool. Although quiet at first, the place filled slightly as we ate. It mainly consisting of the teenage offspring of government officials who seemed a bit privileged and pompous, and young NGO workers who were there to hit the cheap bar hard. By this point of the journey, we'd become well skilled at talking to absolutely anyone, but we just couldn't connect with anyone this evening, don't really know why. I'm pretty confident I'd spot a spy a mile off, and by my reckoning there were none here tonight, leaving us bored silly with my sweaty hand still clenching US$28 worth of vouchers.

Only one thing for it, I returned to the white-haired lady with the tickets, leaned in and whispered: 'Sorry we have to go, would it be possible to get a refund'. I suspect that the old dear had been doing this honourable duty for the last 20 years and from the look she gave me, this was the first time anyone had asked for a refund. 'Barry', she called to the barman across the other side of the now much busier bar with no reply. 'Barry!' she barked with no reply. 'Barry!!' she shouted, then once again even louder before she got his attention. Her voice was now firmly set on this elevated volume. 'This man wants a refund, what shall I do?'.

As the room suddenly fell silent, everyone turning to face us. A stare and a shrug of the shoulders was the best answer she got from Barry, and after some thought, she decided that she could manage a refund for US$20 worth of vouchers. It wasn't the proudest and far from the classiest moment of our trip, but US$20 is US$20, especially for someone not planning to lift a finger of work for a year. We exited and headed home, wishing that we could once again hear footsteps following us.

Monk-ey Business

I love monks and Burma certainly had a lot of them. I don't know what it is about them, but they do have a certain presence. Over the preceding 10 weeks, we'd seen many and I never seem to get used to it. You don't get many in Melbourne and especially not on the UK council estate that I was brought up on. Most monks we saw didn't interact with us at all but when you are walking down the street, look a monk in the eye and get a little nod, it gives you a very comforting feeling inside. Maybe I'm just jealous of their super smooth heads. If shaved, my 'forceps' head would be a sight you won't forget quickly.

Monks riding mopeds, now that's cool. One weird look is the fact that a lot of moped helmets back in Thailand are modelled on German WWII helmets. Also, in some countries, the swastika is still very much used in Buddhism, so there is potential for a fascinating image indeed if these two concepts combine. One missed photo in Burma involved a large truck-sized bus with a platform on top of the cab to accommodate extra passengers. This one was completely empty apart from a solitary monk riding on top of the cab at the veryfront, facing forward with his legs crossed and wind trying to find some hair to blow through.

Another scene included two monks hurtling past in a wooden speedboat on the Mekong, looking more like secret agents. It's also strange seeing them using modern technology such as mobile phones or Bluetooth earpieces. We spoke to one Monk about it who said that it's not really allowed, but everyone has a phone. He used the phrase 'minimal need' which Nic now tries to remind me about whenever I'm in an electronics store. I was very curious as to where they keep their phones. Do monk robes have pockets? The answer is that they have a utility vest under their robe that would make Batman envious. Obviously, making them even cooler than they were before.

They always look so calm and at peace. Maybe helped by the fact they are confident they aren't having a bad hair day or didn't have to worry about choosing what to wear today. Maybe there is more of a style choice than we realise. A robe wrapped twice around the shoulders and under the arm was so last year.

Some monasteries also offer 'Monk Chat' where you can speak to a monk and ask anything about their lifestyle or Buddhism. At some of the busier temples, young monks may also come up for a chat to improve their English. One night we had a lovely conversation with a 24-year old monk called David at Yangon's magnificent Shwedagon Pagoda. He laughed when I called him handsome and then laughed much louder when I said that I should become a monk after finishing our travels. I think he'd caught sight of my funny shaped head.

I'll Bagan at the Beginning

After Yangon, we flew to Bagan which I know is cheating, but we were a little more cowardly in Burma as we really didn't know what to expect. In hindsight, we would have travelled much differently. We knew a bit about Bagan as it had been on our radar as soon as we added Burma to the itinerary and started researching the country. It's a small area adjacent to the River Irrawaddy that has played a very important and religious role in the country's early history. As a result, this incredible place has a reported number of over 3300 temples and stupas in just 16 square miles. Most were originally built between 900AD and 1300AD, vary greatly in size, and include various forms. Some are not much bigger than a garden shed, and some are tall enough to have many floors inside. This town seems to have a temple per person. They are about as frequent as a coffee shop in Melbourne. Maybe the Pagans who build these temples were ancient-day hipsters, and perhaps that's why modern-day hipsters have the beards, don't wear socks, and ride bikes that think gears haven't been invented yet. Maybe the first reclining Buddha in Bagan had the same reaction from the locals as the first deconstructed frappuccino back home.

Most of our internal flights and hotels were arranged for us by a superb little travel agency in Yangon. At the time, it was hard to arrange even flights online, with tickets being the old school hand-written type. The number of tourists had dramatically increased over the previous year, and there wasn't really the infrastructure to cater for it, so all hotels were getting booked up and charging more than we would typically pay. For Bagan, our friendly agent found us a lovely little hotel that even provided views of temples from our room.

Soon after arriving at the hotel we headed out for a little walk and immediately found a few temples to look at. One memory that will stay with us is of a locked temple that we approached to take a photo. Suddenly, a small boy appeared with a key in his hand and pointed to the entrance. He opened it and walked inside, so we followed and admired the large Buddha statue within. We then realised that we couldn't see the lad anymore until his little head poked around a corner and disappeared. He was leading us to a very tiny, very dusty, staircase that went up to darkness. We pulled out a little torch and followed into what felt like an Indiana Jones movie as we popped up on the roof of the temple where we could walk around the top stupa and see for miles. It was a great spot. Our lasting image was seeing the smile on the boys face as he ran home with a little Australian Koala toy in one hand and a whole 500 Kyat (50c) in the other, glancing between each one, unable to work out which he liked best.

We kept it a low key day as the following morning held something we'd been looking forward to for nearly a year and one of only two activities we had locked in before leaving Melbourne. It was a hot air balloon trip over the temples of Bagan.

Those magnificent temples and a woman in her flying machine

Realising it was going to be something special we decided to pay the extra US$40 to upgrade to the VIP experience. This meant that not only could we feel a bit aloof, but we would have half the number of people in the basket with us. We would also be treated to a champagne breakfast afterwards and given a CD memory album of pictures. We were picked up in a modern taxi at 5am and taken to a sports field in the north of old Bagan town. Our aloofness faded a little when we saw that the rabble in the regular seats had been picked up by the most fantastic classic 1940s buses. They were bright red and very cute.

Next, we met Sue who was going to be our pilot. Like most of the pilots there, she was British and had been flying balloons for over 30 years, including her participation in some well known hot air balloon adverts for the BBC. It was still early, and the balloons were being prepared. There was a real chill in the air with a misty fog covering the field making it very atmospheric and even more exciting. I felt quite at ease with Sue and confident to be in her hands. That was until the tie lines to our balloon broke free while being filled with air by large fans. While the regular balloon passengers started to climb in for take off, we were securing our now deflated one and brushing ourselves clean from masses of hay and grass that had been thrown over us.

It did give us time to meet some of our other passengers including a lovely older couple from the UK, and a foursome of Californians travelling together. Everyone seemed a bit upper-class compared to us, but they were all intrigued by our trip and were very friendly. As the first gaggle of balloons were lifting off from the ground, our balloon was just at the stage where we were ready to climb in (using the exact technique that we'd been trained to). I turned around to ask Nic if she wanted to climb in before or after me and her face looked terrified. I offered assurance, 'Don't worry about the cable thing, they are very professional, and I'm sure we'll be fine'. Her expression didn't improve.

'I need a pee!'.

'Really. Now?'

'Yes really, right now!'

We both looked around, there was no building near and no sign of a toilet, or anything for that matter, except a large bush. With the SheWee packed safely back in the hotel room, Nic had no choice but to leg it around the bush, while I had the job of distracting our fellow passengers by pointing at random objects in the distance to try and ensure they didn't turn around and see my wife's face staring determinedly at them through the shrubbery. Not quite sure how, but we actually pulled it off and

Nic appeared, looking quite pleased with herself, just in time for us to be the last two to climb into the basket. Once inside, Sue turned the burner up to full power which I thought was quite handy as I remembered that old-wives tale about lighting a match to get rid of a bad bathroom smell. If anything could get rid of a smell, this burner could.

We only needed to reach the same height as the treetops surrounding the playing field and already we could see great views of the larger temples dotted around old Bagan. As we passed through the layer of mist, Sue turned off the burner, leaving us in silence with a view of hundreds of temples and the lovely, mirror-like, Irrawaddy reflecting the hills and temples on its other side. It was truly magical. It pains me that I'm not a writer who can depict the scene with any kind of justice. I even look back at our photos and the experience don't seems real, as though we've been superimposed into a National Geographic magazine. Sue brought us lower to pass over some of the more impressive temples, including one with scaffolding that still looked unfinished after 900 years. I figured they'd subcontracted it to a UK company and peered down to see if I could see one of those striped tents that UK tradies stereotypically hide in to read the paper on their many 'cuppa' breaks. There is, in fact, a backstory about it breaking away from the tradition of having four entrances to reflect the four known Buddhas but also had an extra one to welcome the new incoming Buddha. This was deemed to have bad juju which was confirmed when part of it was destroyed by lighting and was left to ruin. Until now that is, as work is underway to repair the temple.

We landed smoothly in the grounds next to our hotel. This was partly expected as we'd seen them land here the previous morning, making the location of our hotel even better. After a quick champagne breakfast, we were taken back to our hotel where we crashed onto the bed with huge grins on our faces. If you ever make the journey to Bagan, make sure that you budget for this.

After seeing plenty of temples by air, that afternoon we decided to hire bikes and explore some close-up. There are a few sealed roads but mostly lots of dusty paths between temples. The guidebooks recommend hiring a bike but unfortunately the ones at our hotel were terrible boneshakers. Even the sealed roads were bad enough, and they really struggled on the sandy tracks. We persevered. It was the type of activity that invokes the involuntary reaction where your tongue appears out of your mouth, trying to touch your cheek as you concentrate hard not to fall off. Nic completed about a third of our journey with a flat tyre, and I had little in the way of brakes. We did come across one of our favourite temples though, and after our experience with the little boy caretaker we were finding all kinds of staircases in the dark to explore (just like looking for the latest cool hipster bar down an alley in Melbourne, I guess).

I'm pretty sure that the phrase 'Mad dogs and Englishmen' was originally written about the two of us. Despite now living in a country that can have 40 degree days, we never fail to forget any sensibility and wander out unprepared at that perfect point where the day is at its most hostile. After a few hours, we'd wrangled the bikes all the way from New to Old Bagan, climbed a few temples, and reached our researched lunch spot. Given that the restaurant name was Be Kind to Animals, it was clear that I would not be ordering anything with meat in it. This was almost irrelevant though, the hot conditions finally took their toll just as I arrived at the restaurant and I nearly passed out. Nic was okay, although her face was so red it looked like she'd been playing the trumpet with Louis Armstrong for the past hour. Maybe just looking at how bad she looked was my tipping point and I slumped into the chair. The staff were too polite to ask, but were obviously keeping a close eye on us. After 15 minutes of shade and plenty of water, I started to feel human again and was able to face some food, which was fantastic. Nic's face slowly returned to a normal colour, and after a long stop, we made our way home with just one major temple to tick off en route.

We put the experience down to an activity that looked better on paper but were glad we gave it a go before a long soak in the bath and a comfy bed.

Life-threatening Flatulence

After the day's Shenanigans, an early night was called for, and I was so looking forward to a good sleep. This wasn't to be as a flock of pigeons took up residence in the metal roof above us. Between their squawking and stomping around (I'm sure each was wearing a pair of jackboots) we both struggled to sleep. Coupled with this, I started to feel ill and my temperature began to rise. You know what that meant. Yep, Nic started prodding me regularly with the thermometer again, and by morning my temperature had hit 38.1 which means nothing to me but made Nic look stressed. When we were researching the trip, so many sources said that it really wouldn't be cool if you needed medical assistance in Cambodia, or Laos, but especially Burma.

I tried to help Nic relax by showing her that we could get a flight from here to Bangkok quickly if needed. She pulled out the house-sized first aid kit to find some paracetamol. We were all out. This didn't help, she started to panic a little and even got a bit teary. Now I have to stress that it takes a lot to perturb my wife (in fact it's one of the three reasons that I married her), but health matters, especially mine will always do it. In a way, it's quite reassuring and I don't feel like she has a secret life insurance policy out on me. I, on the other hand, will always meet such scenarios with levity. I get through life-threatening situations with a joke and a smile. I mean if you're going to go, don't go with a bloody frown on your face. My temperature hit 39. Forgive me if this isn't really serious, I was only going by the grave expression on my better half's face.

Nic decided to hire another dodgy bike and ride into town by herself to find a chemist, which she did with ease. On her return I took the drugs and then suddenly had a rumbling. There was movement inside and a stomach ache that had been slowly building over the last eight hours decided it was time for a spectacular climax. I made my way to the bathroom and waited for something to happen, doubled up in pain. After about twenty minutes of contractions, I finally gave birth to something the size of a small antelope. Immediately I felt better, Nic on the other hand nearly fainted due to the fragrant accompaniment to the proceedings. Within 30 minutes, my temperature was improving and I was feeling much better. How embarrassing would that have been if Nic had talked me into arranging a medivac extraction out of the country to find out all I needed was a good old shit, albeit a Mountford one.

Myanmar Shadow

Walking down the avenue….back to our hotel in Bagan I realised how quickly you adjust to new environments. Burma has real problems with its electricity supply, and there are numerous overnight blackouts. In fact, some areas of the country have mandatory blackout periods through the night. So, we had gone from having a room with a butler in Georgetown to now looking for places that could supply 24-hour electricity.

Throughout the night you'd be lying in bed and hear a *fdumf* as the air-con and everything else switches off. A bit later you hear the beeps as they all come online again. It was funny in Bagan as our room looked out over miles of flat landscape, dotted with numerous temples. Some of the large ones were lit up at night, so just after the electricity went off in the room, the temples also went dark, one by one, only to reappear again later. It was a surreal sight, reminiscent of the clips you see on TV where blocks of Manhattan sequentially go dark in a power cut but instead of modern skyscrapers and office blocks, it was buildings built over a thousand years ago, the skyscrapers of their time.

Bagan, like a lot of Burma, is very earthquake prone and many of the temples have been destroyed and rebuild a few times over the years. UNESCO have it listed as a sight of interest and have provided some assistance to the area but don't count it as a World Heritage site yet (a shame for my stats). This is probably because the repair and rebuilding work on many temples has been pretty dodgy and didn't do the originals justice. There are also electricity pylons and lighting rigs sprinkled around that help light up some temples. Many don't restrict tourists from climbing all over them or protect the buildings adequately. Our favourites though were the 'fixer-uppers' that had trees growing out of them, tilted a little and looked much more original.

For our last day, we discovered a much more enjoyable way to get around than the bikes. For $14 we hired our driver Coco, and his horse and cart for 5 hours to take us around temples and find a nice place for lunch (which might have just been his brother's house). It was a fantastic and relaxed way to get around, very fitting for the environment and a lovely ending to our stay here. I'm sure we will go back to Bagan one day. It really is somewhere you can't believe the whole world doesn't know about, and selfishly you don't want them to find out.

The Road to Mandalay (Irrawaddy there yet?)

There was only one way that we felt we should reach our next destination and that was on the *Road to Mandalay*, the journey up the Irrawaddy river made famous by Kipling's poem. The early start meant that it was still dark as we found our boat positioned near a sandbank (notice I didn't use the term moored as it didn't seem fitting). Once we'd survived a steep, slippery, mud bank with all our bags we boarded via a long narrow wooden gangplank. The gangplank handrails were provided by a person on each side holding a length of bamboo like some crazy game of tug-of-war.

We were one of the first onboard and I think the only people that had to make the mutinous journey carrying all our own luggage.

The boat was much nicer than expected, it had assigned seating inside with AC and included an outside deck with wicker chairs that were available for anyone. The boat wasn't too busy so there was enough room for everyone outside. It was a very sociable and civilised affair as we mingled outback while watching the sunrise over Bagan's stupas. We even bumped into Trevor who we'd met two days earlier. I say met, but he pretty much adopted us.

We were walking past a small brick monastery in Bagan, looking for a nice place to watch sunset, when suddenly we heard a deep booming voice from above. 'Right you two, the entry is round the back to the left up some narrow stairs'. After a few moments, we realised it wasn't God telling us our time was up, but instead it was Trevor (it would have been funnier if his name was Brian). Now, I'd like to think that we wouldn't just obey any old command barked at us, but we did exactly as he said, meeting him on the roof.

Trevor, a fellow Australian, is 78, lives in the Gold Coast, and was travelling to fulfil his bucket list after sadly losing his wife. He was a real tour de force, we hit it off and had a great chat. During the conversation, we discovered that we would both be taking a boat to Mandalay on the same day but didn't know if it was the same one. So back to present day, and here we are on the boat with Trevor by our side. Our plentiful supply of Mentos went down well with fellow passengers and was a great ice-breaker. We started chatting to a Gecko tour group of 10 people, and it was interesting to see the difference between independent travel and being on a tour. The funniest thing was hearing all the gossip about each member after they had spent two weeks with each other. Unfortunately, the two people from the group that were uniformly disliked were from Melbourne. I have to say it only took a short conversation with them, to agree with the consensus.

Despite taking 12 hours, the journey seemed to sail by. The route is significantly lengthened by the fact that the boat needs to zigzag through the river to avoid sandbanks. We'd previously spoken to someone who had been stranded on a bank for four hours, only a few days earlier. We saw a few stranded and partly sunk boats along the way. The route was such a lovely way to see the country and observe life along the river. Fishermen, large transport barges, temporary villages on the sandbanks that must move during the rainy season, small dredgers digging for coal, all kept us occupied as well as the eye-catching golden stupas and temples that dot the green countryside.

Our arrival in Mandalay was a bit frantic with a herd of people surrounding us and shouting transport options as we arrived. We normally walk straight through the crowds to assess the situation on the other side but not this time. We heard a shout and see Trevor clambering into the back of a flatbed ute after throwing his bags on and saying 'we'll share this, it's all sorted!'. It was an 'interesting' ride and a pretty accurate introduction to Mandalay. We met Trevor again for dinner a couple of days later but missed him at our next location of Inle Lake due to a lack of internet access. Good on yer Trevor, it was a pleasure travelling with you, and we hope your bucket list is dwindling.

In love with Inle

The next stop in Burma was Inle Lake and the town of Nyaung Shwe. I know I seemed to skip past Mandalay, but we head back there, so hold your horses. Anywho, Inle Lake is a large inland waterway on a high plain surrounded by mountains. It looked magnificent as we flew past on our descent to the airport. Again in hindsight, we wished we hadn't flown. Even this wasn't exactly playing it safe, a plane from the same airline on the same route crashed about a month earlier. We were more tense than normal during landing, especially as the mountains caused quite a bit of turbulence for the small turboprop, producing our bumpiest landing for quite some time. It's a great way to get all your internal plumbing kick-started into action again. The two companies we used for flights internally (Air Bagan and Air Mandalay) both provided a good service, we'd avoided using Myanmar Airways as they had a bad rep, and were also government run.

Inle is part of the Shan tribal region of Myanmar and feels very different from the other places we've been to in-country. Nyaungshwe is probably the closest to a backpacker village we have come across in Myanmar and has a great laid back vibe. One of the towns best restaurants was next door to our accommodation, and with a three-course meal for $3.50, our waistlines took a hit that we haven't recovered from yet. Access to WiFi here was the hardest to find out of all the places so far, but we did discover a small internet cafe that gave us an hour access and a beer each for $2.70. Although, the owner kept having to run out every few minutes to start up the generator each time the power cut out.

Inle Lake is approximately four miles across by ten miles long and has an abundance of life on it. There are many villages that are basically bungalows suspended over the water. We cycled down one side of the lake where a young lady offered to paddle us through her village on a small wooden canoe, to show us around. This was a great insight into her life, after which we loaded the bikes onto her husband's longtail boat who then ferried us across the lake to start our return trip up the other side, back to town. Although the area does cater for tourists and many locals speak English, you still feel there is a lot of originality to the place. A unique Burmese sight in Inle is the traditional way that the fishermen control their wooden boats. They stand on one end and have one leg wrapped around a paddle which they use to both propel and steer the boat while using both hands to fish with their nets. I lost my balance just watching them.

We really enjoyed Inle, and it was a shame to leave, especially as it meant our time in Burma was coming to an end.

CHAPTER 4

Merry in Mandalay

It was back to Mandalay after Inle Lake, and although it has some great spots to watch how real Burmese people live, it was probably our least favourite place in Burma. In our first stopover here, in a true MountyDay, we covered what we could on foot before jumping on a few local forms of transport to get to the popular temples. Both here and Bagan were very dusty places. Before leaving Melbourne I was looking forward to getting away from the big city air, but our lungs took a pounding here. It certainly brings a new outlook to the toilet humour vernacular 'pebble dashing' and 'shitting a brick'. However, if you need a new garden wall, I'm your man.

On our return from Inle, we were booked into our most expensive hotel in Myanmar, due to poor availability elsewhere. At $76, we were a bit fed up at the price but decided that we'd relax and enjoy it rather than hitting the city again. It was a nice old hotel overlooking the Irrawaddy (our room looked over a grimy backstreet, but was probably the biggest room available with its own separate living area).

The stand out feature was a rooftop terrace with a bar that looked out across the river and up to a large temple on top of Mandalay Hill. Just by chance, we hit the bar at happy hour and were presented with a free cocktail that seemed to be highly laced with Mandalay rum. Happy days. A few minutes later, when that one disappeared, another one turned up, and another, and another. Travelling on a budget means you just can't afford lots of booze. Don't get me wrong, barely a day passes where we don't have a beer, but you certainly can't drink enough to affect your motor function. This generosity wasn't really something we could refuse.

The next day was interesting especially as it was a travel day back to Bangkok, at least the headache distracted us from the fact that we were leaving Burma, somewhere I'm sure we will return and spend longer. We vaguely remembered that at some point during the previous night's shenanigans we had reserved our

Bangkok accommodation, using the rooftop bars WiFi between cocktails. However, when we got there, they had no record of it. Bloody Burmese Internet! I mean, what else could it have been?

Banged up in Bangkok

We seemed to get a bit stuck in the mud and stuck in the city back in Bangkok. I don't know what it was, maybe we were tired after Myanmar and lacked a bit of *oompf*. Partly it was due to the lack of availability of air-conditioned trains to our next destination, we also wanted to do a few touristy things in the area. This time we stayed at Tha Tien, just down the river, next to Wat Pho and near the Grand Palace. Between the disappearance of our online booking, our travel indecisions, and the hotels lack of organisation, we had to change rooms three times during our stay, but it was still a lovely place. Thankfully, they eventually ran out of rooms otherwise we would probably still be there.

Bangkok has some really great sights, and if you can get away from the crowds, there are some lovely quiet places and temples to visit. You have to be careful about the usual scam artists though. At one temple we were approached by a nice friendly guy who started a conversation, he explained he was a teacher and asked where we were going. Teacher, my arse. Fortunately, he wasn't the first teacher that has tried to divert us to a gallery, it was a known scam. As we politely made our exit, he started shouting after us 'Fuck you, I am a teacher!'. Well I never, I hope he doesn't teach that language to the school kids.

Later on that day we saw a sign at the Grand Palace, 'Be careful of wily characters', which I think is a great piece of advice for any point of your life. Just next to the sign was a man in a formal outfit who had been standing by one of the palace guards. He walked up to us and tells us that the palace (probably the biggest tourist attraction in Bangkok) is closed today, but he knows somewhere else that is open. He did this even though there is a loudspeaker system in the background, screaming out that the palace is open every day and don't believe anyone who advises otherwise. In hindsight, I should have retorted that in fact his gallery was closed and tried to lure him back to our guest house to try and sell him some of my old smelly T-Shirts. That evening, we took our first (and last) Bangkok tuk-tuk ride which I believe should be installed in Movie World with height limit and health warnings.

Whilst in town we did succumb to a couple of organised tourist day trips, the floating market and the bridge over the River Kwai. They were great to see, and the soldier's graveyard for the death railway was very emotive, as were the details that 15,000 allied troops died in its construction. What you don't realise is that there were also 100,000 civilians, some of whom signed up for what they thought was a well-paid job. Unfortunately, both places were complete tourist traps, especially the railway museum which was highly disappointing. Maybe we were just getting grumpy. It must be time to hit the road again.

Suffering Sukhothai

We were hoping to get a nice air-conditioned sleeper train from Bangkok all the way up to Chiang Mai but couldn't find any availability, so instead took a 6-hour bus journey north to Sukhothai for a couple of nights. We were glad we did. Sukhothai is a great little town with a historic ancient city nearby. It was originally one of the capitals of Siam and filled with temples. The new town, a bit like Krabi, is full of food stalls and markets. We had a beer in a farang bar on the first night, well two, maybe three. Enough that I'd built up the courage to try a selection of goods from a nearby mobile food stall specialising in insects on the way home. Unlike Bangkok, it was real local food here, and people were rocking up on their mopeds and buying bags of grubs to take home and snack on while watching the footy. From what I remember, they were actually quite nice.

The next day we were transported by a fantastic classic truck with wooden benches to the old city and hired bikes to tour the temples. It's a beautiful place and much quieter than other tourist sites in Bangkok. We cycled up to one temple to sit down for a rest and noticed a couple we'd said hello to in the bar the night before. Dave and Chris were a very well travelled couple from Yorkshire, we chatted and compared scars like a scene from Jaws, except they were mainly emotional or financial scars. They told us about a great guest house in Chiang Mai, the location we were all heading next.

Strangers on a Night Train

Again, we couldn't get availability on an air-conditioned train carriage, so we booked a 2nd class sleeper with a fan from Phitsanulok (a 60km bus ride away) to Chiang Mai. Time for a quick thong (flip flop) update. Previously, I explained that my brand new $25 thongs were stolen in Malaysia, well my replacement $3 pair had done me proud and lasted nearly two months of everyday use. Unfortunately, they were wearing out fast, and I was finding that on any shiny or wet surface I looked more like a star from *Dancing on Ice* than the usual *An Idiot Abroad*. So, after much nagging from Nic, I upgraded to a $2.50 pair from the bus station. Initially not convinced about them, I started leaving them outside the next few rooms in case the blaggard that stole my first pair passed by and felt like a change.

We were quite sure this wasn't going to be the comfiest of rail trips and were a little concerned it would deposit us in an unknown city at 4am (according to the timetable). Firstly let's get things straight about Thai timetables, they mean nothing, not a sausage. The train arrived a punctual hour and a half late, and we climbed on. The cabin was a bunk layout with curtains and felt a bit like an old Bob Hope and Bing Crosby movie, *The Road to Chiang Mai*. The movie where Bing turns up to a ping pong show with a table tennis paddle and Bob gets drunk on

Chang beer before waking up next to a ladyboy with a tattoo of an elephant across his chest.

The bed was cosy (that's me putting a positive spin on things) and they provided a pillow and a blanket. It was all a bit chaotic, but this was mainly due to a few German backpackers who were completely off their faces. They had a keen penchant for pulling back curtains to say 'hi' to people and have a chat. One of them kept a young Chinese kid amused for hours by stomping down the corridor, falling over and making funny noises. Thankfully they eventually succumbed to their vices (the Germans that is, the young kid seemed innocent enough).

It was a hot night, not just hot, but hot hot. The only fan was located in the corridor which meant that as soon as you closed the curtains to your bed (your main line of defence against the Germans), you didn't feel any effect. There was just a small breeze through gaps in the window when the train moved. We soon realised that we were in a Thai budget remake of the Sandra Bullock movie *Speed*, if the train travelled slower than 50km/hr then random passengers would spontaneously combust. I think most of the journey was completed at less than 35km/hr. Nic took the top bunk to avoid having a German fall in on her. I eventually got some sleep, waking at 4:30am absolutely freezing. I thought it was the most insane concept that they gave you a blanket in that heat, but was very glad to find it in the middle of the night. It certainly was a memorable trip (I'm positively spinning again) and thanks to Thai punctuality (now I've reverted to plain ol' sarcasm), we arrived 3-hours late, which was a much more civilised time to reach Chiang Mai.

Trunk call to Chiang Mai

A few people had told us that Chiang Mai was lovely and we felt very much at home straight away. This was helped by the perfect location of our guest house, smack in the middle of the old quarter thanks to great advice from Dave and Chris in Sukhothai, who were also staying there. The old quarter was full of small laneways with restaurants, coffee shops, and massage parlours, it was as though a bunch of hippies had created an alternative South East Asia version of Melbourne. It was very tempting to pull the plug and stop for a month. Just think how even more boring the book would get - 'Had a great meal and coffee today', 'had another massage and a great coffee today'. So just because of you and the other two readers we had to keep moving on.

Something we planned to do in Chiang Mai but didn't sort beforehand was a day being an elephant Mahout (trainer). We managed to get a spot in one of the, reportedly ethical, elephant sanctuaries we'd researched. It happened to fall on the two month anniversary of our travels. What a perfect way to celebrate by being scared witless at the thought of it (they are big you know). Despite reports of elephants getting spooked and running off into the Jungle while screaming tourists hang on (or not) for dear life (or not), we were determined to do it.

We arrived, were introduced to the elephants, spent some time feeding them and getting up close and personal which was fantastic. I could have easily called it quits after that alone. We were told how each one had a different personality and shown a friendly female, next to her was a feisty male called Gangsta. I had a sickening feeling that we would meet again. Next, we were taught how to get on and off. Nic managed really well at this, and I muddled through, although it was noted by most that I looked pretty terrified. Lesson 2, we were taught how to control our assigned ride by tapping the back of their ear with your feet. I did find that mine went sideways a little which I thought was very skilful of me as we weren't taught how to do that yet. After a little circuit, we dismounted and gave our elephants some bananas. As I did the instructor said 'say thanks to Gangsta, he loves bananas'. Now he tells me.

It seemed entirely wrong that a short arse like me would control a beast the size of Hemel Hempstead by prodding it in the back of its head with my foot. Not my first instinct. I would have started with a little friendly reasoning over a cup of tea. Failing that, maybe bribe with food, or arranging a conjugal visit to the pachyderm house at Chester Zoo. Kicking was not something I thought wise to do to anything weighing over a ton and having a foot bigger than my head. Never the less I did, and I backed it up with the firmest voice I could muster, something similar to an 8-year-old girl messing with a helium balloon.[1]

Actually, after surviving Gangsta, I was quite relaxed for the rest of the day, and we had a lovely 1-hour trek through the surrounding jungle. I had a different but bigger elephant (Kam Kua) this time, and we got on fantastically. She laughed at my short memory, and I would take the mickey out of her fear of mice. She took great pleasure in covering me with stuff using her trunk. Initially, she just blew on my feet which I thought was a bit forward but was quite nice that my elephant was fitted with air-con. Next, came water that she'd been saving for me, then soil, then branches. I took it as a sign of affection but ended up looking like I'd been pulled through a hedge backwards. To this day I'm still finding bits of elephant poo between my toes. Everyone else looked pristine.

Next, it was time to get wet and bathe them, which was opportune as I needed a bath myself by then. I got Kam Kua back by throwing water all over her. That showed her. Today was certainly one to add to the 'top days of your life' list.

Prisoner: Cell Block Massage Parlour

Whilst in town we visited a women's prison as, believe it or not, it's one of the top ten attractions in Chiang Mai. In an aim to rehabilitate and retrain inmates, the prison has a cafe and massage parlour where the prisoners can learn new trades. So as

---

[1] *I say kick, but before you get grumpy (as I would), I'm exaggerating for comedic effect, it was really just a slight touch.*

it's for a good cause, because lonely planet told us, and to have a sex-starved Thai criminal fiddling with my feet, we went along.

It's located in quite a pleasant setting and was very popular. In Chiang Mai it seemed like every other shop front is a massage parlour and, in comparison to the prison, most were empty with staff calling after your trade as you walk past. Much to my dismay, none used the phrase 'sexy boy' to lure me in like the highly professional outfits on Phi Phi a few years ago. Okay, I've put on a bit of weight since then, but I have feelings. The inmate massage parlour was so popular that the prison guard/receptionist informed us we had a 2-hour wait so we put our names on a list and had lunch in their prison run cafe. The inmate serving us looked terrified, she didn't speak much English but pointing at things on the menu seemed to work. When my drink arrived it wasn't what I ordered but not knowing what she was sentenced for, I just smiled and said thank you.

Our time came, and we went in. I don't know why but I found I was trying to make myself more presentable in the toilet mirror beforehand. Maybe I figured that they don't get much male contact, so didn't want to disappoint. In my mind, they were all going to have either orange Guantanamo Bay jumpsuits on or those grey outfits with black arrows that you see in silent movies, and we were going to have lengthy discussions about what shower time was like. Like most things, what goes through my head could not be further from the real world.

It was probably the nicest massage parlour setting we'd been to so far. The women were dressed in pretty outfits like every other masseuse in town. We both had our feet washed and were shown to comfy leather chairs. I worked out which two women were going to look after us and decided that one of them still looked a little unhinged so politely showed Nic to that chair first. Mine was very pretty with a lovely face, so much so that you couldn't believe she could have done anything wrong. I do seem to trust people by the shape and look of their face, which I know is a bad thing to do, I'm just so thankful I didn't live back in the day when every other gangster was called babyface this or babyface that. I wouldn't have lasted five minutes.

Next something unprecedented in my foot massage history, she told me to let her know if she was hurting me. Between this and the fact she gave me the softest massage my very handsome feet have ever had, it made me think she immediately had me pegged as a big girl's blouse. Probably worried that any shouts of pain might add time onto her sentence. She also used 'the utensil', and even that was nice and soft. One worry was that between finishing one foot and moving to the other, she lost the utensil and had to get another one. Now I've watched the *Great Escape* with Steve McQueen plenty of times, and I think I'm onto her. I know from previous experience that the utensil is more than capable of digging through concrete and I think potentially there is a tunnel running right under us.

I hope it works out for her and we see a news headline soon about a cunning prison break as I'm sure, with that face, she was innocent.

It's as clear as Black and White, this place is cool

We reluctantly had to leave Chiang Mai. If we hadn't had the target of reaching Beijing for the Trans-Mongolian, we could have easily hung around here for a month or two. The next location was Chiang Rai which was a comfortable journey on a $12 VIP bus that officially had the comfiest coach seats so far and a stewardess that distributed bottles of water halfway through. Our residence in Chiang Rai was at a hostel called The North which had also been recommended by Dave and Chris. They should have been there at the same time, but we didn't cross paths, maybe they'd had enough of our questions and were hiding. All the old cliches are correct about how it's the people you meet that make the journey. It's great to hear stories from others that inspire you and provide useful information on anything from a nice room, a nice meal or even life advice.

Chiang Rai is a little gem of a town with a great market and a bustling evening food scene filled with live music. As well as the common or garden temples, it has two amazing and yet very different attractions, the White Temple and the Black House. The White Temple (Wat Rong Khun) is the mastermind of local artist Chalermchai Kositpipat and has been a work in progress since the start of the millennium. As you approach, it looks like a very impressive bright white and silver compound of buildings, but when you get close, you really start to appreciate the modern twist to this artistic edifice. You enter across a walkway looking down at arms reaching upwards towards you, almost as though they are in pain. When you step inside the main temple building, you immediately look towards a lovely painting of Buddha covering the far wall but then as you look closer you see the side walls are full of murals that include many modern pop culture items such as paintings of the Millennium Falcon. One particularly bizarre area depicted an Angry Bird flying into the twin towers. When I tell people and even when I write this it sounds awful, poor taste, and tacky, but it's not. It is in fact quite amazing. Unfortunately, it's not possible to take photos inside the temple, so now just feels like a weird dream.

One highlight to the day was a little monk interaction, you know how much I love my monk interactions. I turned around to find a young monk in the brightest of orange outfits taking a crafty picture of me on his shiny white Samsung phone so I, in turn, took one of him taking a picture of me. This was just moments before an older monk, obviously supervising the group gave him a perfect clip around the ear. The type you used to get from your mum, or from a policemen in the '50s if you were caught apple scrumping (now extinct in our times of political correctness). We both grinned at each other and moved on.

I was very saddened to hear that since our visit, a lot of this temple was damaged in an earthquake, with its rebuild and further development set to continue till 2070.

The Black House in contrast is not a temple but an area of wooden buildings showing differing architectural styles and features a mix of amazing woodwork and an abundance of animal skeletons. I've probably not sold it have I? Google it and go if you can, a side trip up to Chiang Rai is definitely worth it. Our visit to the Black House was actually part of our exit strategy from this town as we'd arranged for a taxi to drive us to the north of the country and to the border with Laos. It would have been possible to take a bus to Chiang Kong, but with a US$60 taxi, we were able to visit the Black House as well as a meander through the country's north-west. Here, we could explore the golden triangle at the confluence of the Ruak and the Mekong, where the three countries meet.

This included a trip to a very well presented Opium Museum that teaches about the infamous drug trade in the area, including some shameful English history that we certainly were not taught in school. We almost had the museum to ourselves until a coach load of loud Chinese tourists arrived. However, our serenity was hardly interrupted as they passed the displays at double pace without taking anything in, so they could deplete the museum shop before their coach left. A weird comical moment in very serious surroundings.

Time to prepare for our next country, Laos.

CHAPTER 5

Location: Chiang Khong
Days 66, Countries 6, Kilometers 12,356, Beds 31
Trains 2, Planes 9, Automobiles 9, Boats 4
Beers 15

The 'Not So' Mighty Mekong

The trip to the Golden Triangle meant we saw our first sight of the famous Mekong River, we didn't realise it at the time, but this famous river would be our travelling companion for the next 1000km through two countries. We spent our last evening in Thailand on the south bank of the Mekong in Chiang Khong, sat in a family run restaurant watching the local kids playing in the river, their parents tending to the bean sprouts they farmed along the riverbank. Our entry into Laos was on a very civilised two-day slow boat down the Mekong, stopping overnight for safety. The package included, the border crossing from Chiang Khong, the journey to Luang Prabang, and the stopover hotel. We decided to pay a bit more money to get this boat rather than the backpacker alternative as we'd heard stories of boats being overcrowded and uncomfortable. Ours, still one of the same traditional Mekong long wooden boats, had comfy seats, nice toilets, and was only half full. In the scheme of things,

$90 for two days of travel and overnight accommodation was still within budget.

The 21 travellers on board were a great mix of nationalities including Americans, Danish, French, English, German, Austrian, Swiss, and us mongrels. Although we had to traverse the river frequently, avoiding sandbanks and large jagged rocks, it wasn't the furious mighty Mekong that we were expecting. Maybe it was because of how far north we were, or due to the season. However, the scenery was breathtaking with large limestone karsts and fantastic forests bordering the famous waterway.

Along the river you could see locals panning for gold, and growing peanuts on the temporary sandbanks which had been exposed during the dry season. Concrete marker posts gave you an idea of how high the waters can get during the rainy season. You could tell it would be a very different journey at that time of year. Over the two days, we stopped off at a couple of small villages along the river bank, meeting the locals and visiting the schools of each. In the second school, we actually interrupted an English lesson for young teenagers so thought it opportune to disperse throughout the class to practice with the kids. My groups of boys looked petrified which I was hoping wasn't a reflection on my approachability. We struggled through a few things, but it was great to see their look of accomplishment when they did manage to string a few words together. It was probably best not to linger as my English skills and funny accent could set them back a few years.

We stayed the night in a small town called Pak Beng to break up the journey, our accommodation was a small hotel on the waterfront. During our evening in town, we bumped into a Dutch chap that we'd previously met in Chiang Khong, who was looking quite hot and bothered. He explained that he'd just disembarked the backpacker boat, it was overcrowded, had young locals getting drunk on whiskey and then to top it all they hit a rock which damaged the propeller. They managed to get to a jetty just outside of town but then had to carry their luggage for the last kilometre. This fact and the friends we'd already made on our boat, certainly justified the extra expense. The following morning, we all congregated for breakfast in the hotel's dining room where roughly half the contingent chose fried eggs and the other half choosing scrambled eggs for breakfast. You're probably thinking that was a random statistic, even for me. Well, we'll see.

After another beautiful day on the water, part of which Nic and I sat out on the very front of the bow looking like a TV mashup between *Titanic* and *African Queen*. This sedate end to the journey eventually led us to our destination of Luang Prabang (LP to the travelling community). LP is a beautiful UNESCO listed town with a mix of French colonial buildings and ancient temples. You can't help but fall in love with the place as soon as you arrive. Our first hotel was nice and in a good riverfront location, but our room, the last room in the hotel, wasn't great. We found ourselves quickly outnumbered by cockroaches. Not the best of starts but onward and upward, we persevered that first night but moved the following day to a lovely new little hostel above a cafe in a quiet part of town.

Conga-ratulation you've got Luang Prabang Loo

Luang Prabang is one of those towns, like Chiang Mai, that's very easy for tourists to stay in, catering well for visitors with its mix of temples and quaint French influences. It's not a huge place, and so we expected to see the others from the boat around town, but not to the extent that we did. After a few days, it felt like we'd all grown up in the town and knew everyone, constantly waving to people across the street and chatting with our fellow 'boat people'. It felt like Luang Prabang was our town, and there was now quite a bond between us travellers (not tourists). Not long into our stay, we noticed a trend in the conversation. Randomly, some of the team fell ill with quite a grumpy gastro bug. This sparked numerous toilet based discussions over croissants in French bakeries with patients coming and going as they succumbed to the bug. It was too much of a coincidence that so many of us from the same boat were affected. We worked our way back through our eating habits to find the culprit. Two words - scrambled eggs. See, I wasn't just being an anorak by dishing out breakfast stats. I'll bet you're reading this and wondering, what did the Mounties eat that day? Well, the bad news is that only one of us chose the safety of the fried eggs. The good news, it was me.

One of the big tourist draws to LP is its early morning procession of monks accepting alms. It's one of the only places in the world where they join together, en masse, in a long line travelling through town. This produces a highly photogenic event for visiting tourists, even giving them the opportunity to participate if they wish to provide gifts. Unfortunately, some underhanded people pray on this and sell the tourists food offerings at hiked prices and poor quality. So much so that we'd heard about monks becoming ill due to bad food. There were also reports that the monks had threatened to stop forming this procession. They had been told in no uncertain terms, that if they didn't, people would be hired to dress up as monks and perform the ritual for the overseas visitors. As much as I was planning on participating before we arrived, I decided against it and just watched.

Our new guest house was a few streets back from the town centre. A little removed from the tourist throngs but was actually on the inside of a 90-degree turn for the regular monk conga line. A perfect spot to watch, especially for Nic who was now so ill with scrambledeggitus she couldn't leave the room, managing only to sit on the balcony and look down over the procession (trying her best not to inadvertently fill the alms bowl from up high). I spotted some dodgy hawkers trying to sell to the only two tourists on this corner, but they were quickly moved on by the locals. The morning was a touching experience that won't be forgotten soon. You could see the importance of this event for the local shopkeepers and residents. Many women and children would spend hours preparing and waiting patiently until each monk had passed.

Thankfully, just a day later, Nic started feeling a little more human, and we were able to gingerly venture out and about in this city again. Partly thanks to an abundance of dry biscuits that I'd cleared out of the shop below.

LP is quaint, has wonderful historical sites, as well as a great backpacker scene with amazing bars, some perched high on cliff banks and supported by stilts, overlooking the Nam Khan River before it joins the Mekong. You can relax on comfortable pillows watching kids, much braver than I, play in the very fast flowing river. A town market provided the usual tourist wares, but more importantly, awesome fresh fruit smoothies. It also had an adjacent alleyway that hosts a hawkers market with a huge choice of meat and seafood that can be quickly cooked up while you wait. At least having a few days in town meant that the ill could recover enough and have a chance to experience it all.

One of our more memorable comrades from the boat was 'the Austrian guy' (although he himself was memorable, his name, not so much). He was probably in his mid '50s and looked like he could be either an Elvis impersonator or part of a Kiss tribute band. His huge belly and the fact that he chain-smoked from the back of the boat belied his fitness levels. On some of the toughest climbs to caves or lookouts, he'd appear at the top just about the same time we would. He'd be perfectly fine while I'd be looking around for the nearest oxygen tent. True to his form, one evening we plucked up the courage to climb the 355 steps to view Luang Prabang from the top of Mount Phousi and watch the sunset. After a long hot trek, we reached the top just as I was preparing to burst into flames, when there he appeared safe and sound in what would be the only time we saw him in town.

Great Danes

I've already mentioned how you can meet memorable people when travelling and we did just that in Laos. During our boat trip down the Mekong, we met Cecilie and Jannik, a lovely couple from Denmark. We only really got talking towards the end of the trip after Cecilie overheard that we were travelling for a year and was keen to speak to us about it.

From cunning calculations we worked out they were both in their mid '60s, and we discovered they were experienced travellers. Their first ever round-the-world trip took an impressive 18 months during their mid 20's. Travelling was more challenging back then, it even prompted them to get married a week before they left, in case they had problems getting rooms together as an unmarried couple in some countries. Talking about their travels made us realise how lucky and easy it is for us now with ATMs, mobile phones and the internet. They had to arrange in advance to receive mail in places they were heading. During the whole 18 months, they only phoned home once.

In comparison, I think my family have been highly disappointed. They were expecting a bit of peace and quiet from us for the year, yet they've seen our brown faces and crazy hair on Skype more frequently than ever. It really is so easy to travel now, you can't help but think that maybe we aren't doing it right. It's far less challenging than we thought it would be. Jannik and Cecilie have been travelling, off and on, ever since. They quickly became a positive influence and inspiration to us.

After our brief chat on the boat, we were looking forward to meeting with them in town and even performed a stalkerish walk past their hotel without success. They had remained the only illusive people we hadn't bumped into in Luang Prabang. We'd heard from two of the Americans (Dave and Barbara) that the Danes were looking for company in a private van hire to Vientiane. We mentioned that we were interested and would keep an eye out for them. This coincided with the start of Nic's bout of Luang Prabang Loo which, in turn, coincided with a gloomy weather forecast, so we decided on a lazy rest day in bed. Later that morning, there was a knock at the door. Assuming it was housekeeping, I flung open the door to find Cecilie's pretty smile looking back at me. At this point, I quickly regretted not having any trousers on. Thankfully, it didn't seem to phase our visitor. I could only imagine that this was maybe a common way to greet people in Denmark, with clothing having a more optional place in society.

The Americans had passed on our location. Unfortunately, Jannik was suffering the same illness as Nic, so Cecilie had decided to go for a walk and track us down. At least it's a story we will always have. Just like Rick and Ilsa had Paris, Cecilie and I would have me, in my undies, in a Luang Prabang guesthouse hallway. A couple of days later, the four of us met up for our last meal in this wonderful town, pizza was the only thing that the two patients could face. The catchup gave us a chance to plot our onward journey, we would leave early the next morning.

Although the private minibus was a more expensive option, it was a great opportunity to see the countryside on the way down to the capital. We could stop when we wanted, this was ideal as unfortunately it was now Cecilie's turn to become ill, which she pulled off with the style and grace that we'd come to expect from her. At one beautiful lookout, we stopped to take some pictures by a house and met a group of small children playing. They were using rocks to play a kind of 'pick-up sticks' game. Covered in dust and mud, their white school uniforms certainly weren't white anymore, but they were so so happy. Much happier and content with a few rocks than most western kids appear, despite being packed to the hilt with mobiles, iPads, and a PSP. My mind drifted, I was picturing the general meeting at the local school when they met to decide what colour the school uniforms should be:

'I think we should choose white!'

'Great idea, what could go wrong, I'll second that.'

Personally, I would have proposed a dirty water or road surface grey colour, the kids would have looked immaculate.

The journey took us through the town of Vang Vieng which had once been a highlight for the younger backpacking crowd. Infamous for drunken inner tube bar crawls down the river and 'happy' pizzas. Recent laws had quietened the town a little, and it now looked rather quaint with families enjoying kayak trips when we stopped there for lunch. Feeling our age, we had actually made a point of not wanting to include it on our travels, but in hindsight, it looked like it would have been a nice location for a few days. As we continued on our way, it turned out that our minibus driver didn't know the way to Vientiane quite as well as he had promised. Thankfully we'd been prepared with a trusty travel tip. Before leaving Melbourne, we'd expected that in each country, we'd pick up a cheap data SIM. However, once we started, we quickly realised that WiFi was so prevalent we didn't really need to. The only issue was access to maps when moving between the locations that had WiFi. Although there are plenty of offline map apps available these days, we found that just by opening Apple Maps and following the next leg of the route before we left the comfort of WiFi, it would keep the details in its cache. This meant that we could use the blue dot to track our position and guide the driver through the city's one-way system at night to our destination hotel. To this day we don't quite know if the poor bugger found his way home again.

Paris of the East

The capital, Vientiane, was a much bigger and more modern city but still had a very distinct French influence. Our first hotel wasn't a big hit as we had the last room which seemed to be tiny, dirty, and located next to a furnace. The following morning, we decided to use the very handy TripAdvisor app to choose a new guesthouse. The app then directed us to our new home with a moving arrow on the phone, traversing the streets as though we were MI6 tracking down stolen plutonium. Our new room in Hotel Vayakorn will forever be known to us as 'positively palatial'. It was lovely with wooden floors and enough space to lay out our large maps for a trip planning session with a beer or six. The next morning we woke with a sore head and a slight memory that we may have booked some aeroplane flights to somewhere. True enough, we had. Fortunately, it turned out they were good choices and we'd secured a great price from Hanoi to Hong Kong. Although against our mandate it was a much easier way of making it across the Chinese border, especially as time was running out if we were going to get to the train in Beijing.

We blew out the hangover cobwebs by hiring bikes and exploring the city and it's outlying temples and monuments. This included Patuxai, a war monument celebrating the country's independence from France. Although, despite celebrating its independence, it does look very much like the Arc de Triomphe. It is often referred to as 'the vertical runway' as it was cheekily built using funds and cement donated by the Americans in the 1950s to build the city a new airport. Facts like this give you a sense that this place has an underlying coolness about it. Although you'd think that if you were designing a monument to celebrate getting rid of the French, you wouldn't recreate a much loved French landmark but erect something that the French would loathe. Maybe a statue of an Englishman, a female shaving instrument, a no-smoking sign, or a Californian wine.

From the vertical runway, which was much more impressive than it sounded, we cycled to That Luang, a gold painted Buddhist temple. For something regarded as the most important monument in Laos, I have to say, it wasn't that impressive. All in all, we had a great day cycling in this very easy city to get around.

Our last evening in Vientiane was spent back with Cecilie and Jannik, having a lovely meal in an outside courtyard before our paths would separate the following day. It had been an absolute pleasure to spend time with these two, and we now had high aspirations to become them. It was sad to say goodbye, and we both wondered if our paths would cross again in the future.

Don't you know who I am? I'm a VIP

We said au revoir to the very French Vientiane, as we headed towards the south of Laos and to our next stop of Thakhek. We didn't have many transport options so decided that we would take a VIP bus for the supposed 5-6 hour journey. VIP buses had been present in all the South East Asia countries we'd visited so far and are aimed at tourists that have a preference for better odds of getting there alive, or don't want to talk to a chicken for the whole trip. Some of the coaches are very fancy and look like something out of a Sci-Fi movie, often the layout would be two seats then isle then one seat, giving you lots of space. Our previous coach to Chiang Rai had leather seats that reclined right back, as much as we stretched our diminutive legs they couldn't touch the seat in front.

Back to Laos, our VIP tickets cost a whole $14, so we had high expectations. We were picked up on time by a lovely minivan to transport us from our positively palatial guesthouse to the bus station. A good start. Once there I eventually found our correct bus, it was the one already tilting a little bit. I'm sure it might have been quite luxurious in that summer Bryan Adams made famous, but not so much now. As our bags were squeezed into a small compartment on the side, I was trying to work out what else the VIP notation could possibly have meant on this ticket, Vehicle In Poor condition, Vehicle Inspires Perspiration, Vehicle InProbable of getting there, Vehicle In Pre-retirement…. and so on.

The coach started off almost full, but we hadn't finished yet and embarked on a tour of the local area, picking up more passengers. Even though the official seats were full, we continued to pickup fares. Small plastic stools were distributed down the isle, blocking any exit. Let's just hope there were no emergencies during the journey. Even our seats didn't have safety belts, but at least they were attached to the floor. We headed off. I started to relax after a few kilometres, and while Nic was busy reading, I gazed out of the window as we brushed closely past green verges with trees and fields off in the distance. Then something occured to me, I'm sitting on the left and they drive on the right, there should not be a verge anywhere near me! It appears such concepts as lanes are purely notional here, a fact that soon gave the driver a great opportunity to test our brakes as a truck hurtled towards us.

It was also at this point, I realised that the VIP bus status didn't apply to us at all, but to the many mosquito passengers. They had a veritable smorgasbord of international cuisine to feast on. Thankfully there were lots of French onboard which are always popular dining, as are the Italians, especially as it was a bit too warm to go for an Indian. Some liked the Chinese but knew that they would want to go back for more after twenty minutes. I was doing my utmost to look British.

I still had my ticket in my hand and discovered that it was all in Laotian, apart from two lines of English. One line informed me to keep the ticket for inspection and the second line just said, 'Good Luck'. I showed Nic, and we burst into laughter. Moments later, still smiling, we hear a loud *fdumpf!* and the bus started vibrating. We'd blown a tyre and the bus came to an abrupt stop, as the crew of three jumped into action. We could smell burning, and smoke started to fill the back of the cabin when suddenly the emergency exit next to my seat sprang open. I have to admit, I may have expelled a little air myself at this point before realising that it was just a crew member getting his tools. They'd obviously done this many times before, it only took 20-30 minutes before we were back on the road again.

More brake tests ensued, cumulating in one that caused the bus to start skidding at an angle down the road before we hear another *fdumpf!*. The skid produced another flat, just as we missed a minibus. It didn't take long to realise that they only had one spare, but this fact certainly wasn't going to dampen the spirits of the crew who just took the wheel off and ushered us back onboard. Everyone was a bit nervous, especially me as I was sat above the missing wheel. It was a twin axel at the rear, so at least there was one wheel on the ground in my corner. For a short while, the driver seemed to take it easy but quickly forgot about what happened and I soon found my arse whizzing through the Laos countryside with nothing supporting it. The rest of the trip was spent subconsciously leaning to the right because my brain was sure that would help. I looked back down at the ticket in my sweaty hand, 'Good Luck' indeed.

As you can imagine, an eventful trip like this is an ideal way to be thrown together, literally, with new travelling companions and the travel gods were looking down on us as we met Michel and Agmar from the Netherlands. We hadn't spoken on the coach apart from exchanging the odd raised eyebrow, but a frantic experience of getting a tuk-tuk from the coach station, negotiating the fare and surviving the journey soon sorted that. The final nail in their coffin was the fact they inadvertently sat next to us at the town's best restaurant. Their lives would not be the same again.

It wasn't long before we were planning activities together for our stay in Thakhek which included securing a minibus to take the four of us to the Kong Lor Caves, a few hours away. It's a seven kilometre long cave, spanning the width of a mountain with a river running all the way through it. It was a great adventure, as we raced through the bat-filled cave on a longboat. Part way through, we stopped at a small overland walkway to explore the stalagmites and stalactites. A little further on we also had an unplanned out-of-boat section when ours (just ours) didn't clear the bottom for some unknown reason. A little embarrassing as we helped to carry the vessel about five meters to deeper waters with our unimpinged compatriots zipping around us.

Thakhek was a strange place, but we immediately took to it. It was located on a wide stretch of the Mekong and was the start/

finish point for a famous three-day motorbike trip called 'The Loop'. This meant the town was full of bikers, covered in dust, giving it a 'Wild West' feel. Again, the architecture attested to the French influence in the region, but one stand out activity prevalent in the town was more Asian. Karaoke. In this small town we spotted four karaoke bars, and wherever we walked, we could hear people practising in their gardens or through an open window. If China really did have strict training camps for producing world-class gymnasts at the age of six, then Thakhek was the equivalent for budding Karaoke singers.

We hit it off with our new Dutch friends, who also had a wanderlust and had travelled to some interesting places. They had a similar view to us about when you should choose to pay a bit extra to make things easier or to maximise the enjoyment of an experience. Knowing what cost-saving battles are worth fighting for. Our routes overlapped for a while, so we met up when we could, and travelled together when possible which included our next location of Pakse. From there, Michel and Agmar stayed only one night which included a fun evening at a local fairground and rooftop bar. We felt sure we would see them again, somewhere later on in the journey. Nic and I, stayed for another night so we could take a trip to the impressive Vat Phou temple complex in Champassak.

The Italian Hamster

Travelling a well-trodden path through South East Asia has been interesting as you often see the same people crop up here and there. 'Didn't we see that guy with the funny hair about two countries ago?'. Case in point was an upcoming longtail ferry through Lao's Four Thousand Islands where we glanced up at a balcony to see Michel and Agmar eating lunch as we sped off to another island (we had chosen a quieter one, more befitting of our age). Sharing transport with other travellers is also a funny experience, it generally takes the form of a dodgy stand-up comedy routine from the 80s, 'Where are you from?', 'Where are you from?', 'The trouble I had getting here..'. It's always interesting to see who'll engage with you and who has their head shoved a little far up their 'travellers' arse, to speak with mere 'tourists'.

There is always an international dynamic at play even when spoken English isn't a barrier. It's like a cross between the UN and a school disco; the Italians and Spanish dancing up a frenzy in the middle of the room; the French and Germans standing in opposite corners only talking to themselves; the English keeping a stiff upper lip about the poor quality of the buffet food; and the Chinese drowning out the sound of the music with their conversation, even though they are standing RIGHT NEXT TO EACH OTHER! Yes I know it's all sweeping stereotypes and really, we've met many fantastic people from all of those countries, but still, it's funny cos it's true.

Our next journey was a minibus from Pakse to Laos' Thousand Island Region where I ended up sharing a three-person bench seat with a tall Italian gent. You could tell he was Italian as he had a Roman nose, it was Roman all over his face (what did I tell you about the dodgy stand-up). He had huge spindly, hairy legs, and despite being in a confined space, sat with his knees as far apart from each other as possible. I hypothesised that he must have had some body modifications to the inside of each knee where opposing magnets were inserted. They were certainly powerful magnets as no matter how much he might try, his legs just kept defaulting back to a position that I can only describe as 'akimbo'. He was wearing short shorts that were loose, so I was in constant fear of looking down to catch sight of something Italian looking back up at me.

The bus pulled away, turned the corner and immediately stopped again so that the driver could bring his girlfriend along for the journey, making our three-seater bench into a four-seater. The Italian looked quite pleased to have a pretty Lao girl squeeze in next to him, but the knees still didn't close. Fearing he was just about to give birth, I started asking around for some towels and warm water. Just when you thought the knees couldn't get further apart he fell asleep and relaxed, making it now look like I had three legs, one much longer and hairier than the others. I can only describe it as having a hamster with bad alopecia snuggle up next to you. 'Don't look down!' was the journeys mantra. I had thought about moving the appendages together while he was asleep to see if the foliage on each thigh would stick together with a velcro effect, but I just wasn't brave enough to touch them. Eventually, I mustered up the courage and quickly changed position with enough gusto to knock his knee over so that now, the pretty hitchhiker had both knees to contend with. Result.

Anyway, we finally got there in one piece with my sexuality securely confirmed, and gag reflex sufficiently tested. Who will we get next time I wonder? Note, no Italians were harmed in the making of this journey, and we wish him and his baby all the best.

Ripped off again and took it lying down

The Four Thousand Islands province was a good balance between exciting and boring. It turned out to be a perfect choice for us, with hammocks overlooking the Mekong and lots to do, including a day of cycling around the islands, touring beautiful vistas and some amazing waterfalls.

You've probably realised by now that a good percentage of this book's content is related to the travel between places, rather than the actual places themselves. I guess that does tend to be where the action seems to happen and after all, it is a journey. We booked our onward ticket through, what looked like a reliable tourist agency. The guy had a nice face, so you know by now that's all you need to sucker me in. We handed over our $23 each (our most expensive bus journey) which included a VIP bus transfer, the ferry to the mainland, the border crossing to Cambodia, and a 5-hour bus journey to Kratie. Kratie was the first large town you get to in Cambodia, and a good halfway point to Siem Reap.

We took the ferry to the mainland where we assembled with a number of the great unwashed. After 3 months, I'm now starting to include ourselves in that clan, well at least their quirky Aunt and Uncle anyway. We were presented with all the relevant visa forms and arrival cards. Once completed, a perfect stranger collected them up, along with our passports and the visa fee. Since our first entry into Thailand, we were becoming used to this, although still nervous as our passports contained our Russian visa which we consider gold. We were expecting a US$20 fee but were charged US$25 (some reason was produced) then an extra US$5 Laos exit fee was added as well, a few questioned it, but paid up anyway. As we finished and moved to the bus station, Nic spotted the guy working out what cash he really needed and pocketed the rest.

After a short wait, we all got excited when a bus turned up but then noticed it was a sleeper bus so settled down again, as it parked in the far corner of the car park. It was 8am so must have just finished an overnight run. We waited as a few nice VIP buses running other routes came and went. Fifteen minutes later the sleeper bus started up again and pulled up next to us, with an order from the driver, 'everyone get on!'. A bit surprised, we threw our backpacks into the hold and climbed onboard. Now, this wasn't just a sleeper bus with normal seats that recline at night, this bus contained full blown fixed double bunk beds, with a large cosy bed for five along the back, to accommodate the naughty kids.

I'm quite confident that the mattresses and bedcovers hadn't left the bus for cleaning since it was new (during the Reagan administration). Most people started scratching while still walking down the aisle. Nic secured a bottom double for us both, but many solo travellers had an interesting game of Russian Roulette with whom they were about to share their boudoir, without even getting dinner bought for them first. Everyone assumed that this was just to take us the short trip to the border where our VIP coach would be waiting on the Cambodian side. On arrival at the Laos border we expected our extra US$5 to contribute to an extensive exit process, but in actual fact this just involved the driver's assistant getting out and lifting up a barrier himself. SeriousIy, I would have done it for half the price. Next, we were herded to an opportunely placed cafe in no-mans land as our passports are processed, taking nearly an hour.

The funniest part of this was an adorable three-year-old local girl that was in control of the toilets. There was a fee for using them (obviously), and she would rush up with a wad of money in her hand, point to the toilet and shout 'Money! I have change'. She was quite capable of giving customers change although she spotted that I had the exact money, so just walked up and grabbed it out of my hand with a giggle. I guess I must have looked like I really needed to go.

Time to go, we looked around for our upgraded VIP bus. Bollocks. We climbed back into our mobile den of iniquity and speed off (horizontally) with faulty air-con, more mosquitoes than available skin, and just four lovely hours to go. There was a half height toilet onboard that you needed to contort yourself into, but the door wouldn't lock, so if the bus turned right it would fly open mid ablution. Thankfully, after the first few embarrassing moments, a tall Danish guy in the bed opposite would kindly stretch his leg across the aisle and keep it closed for you. I was now very glad to have had my money removed by the kindergarten toilet cop at the border stop. To top things off, this northern stretch of highway was in a state of real disrepair with large potholes and unsealed stretches. It was a ride bumpy enough to remove fillings, which was a worry as my mouth is almost entirely made up of them. There was a distinct chance I could arrive in Cambodia looking like Australia's No.1 gurning champion.

Thankfully, we'd decided not to complete the whole journey to Phnom Penh, a further 6-hours away, that day. Frustratingly though, we had to endure a late lunch stop literally ten minutes before Kratie, probably the driver's brother's restaurant. Just as we restarted, the bus stopped again at an ATM on the outskirts of town because most of the unprepared unwashed didn't have enough dollars to go all the way to the capital. Once they realised that the ATM was out of order they changed their onward route, so threw the Kratie passengers (including us) off, to walk the last bit into town. So we'd arrived in our next country feeling like sheep that had just been fleeced, VIP my sore arse. This wasn't helped by a throng of taxi drivers that appeared to try and tell us that our guesthouse had actually burnt down, but not to worry they could take us to a better one anyway. A scam which was ignored as we walked the last mile or so to our accomodation. Not much fun, but this day was going to get better.

Dolphins in the Mekong

As well as being a good halfway point to Siem Reap, Kratie was more importantly famous for spotting Irrawaddy Dolphins. Let me hand you over to Wikipedia:

'it is not a true river dolphin, but an oceanic dolphin that lives in brackish water near coasts, river mouths and in estuaries. It has established subpopulations in freshwater rivers such as the Mekong'

The Mekong contingent is listed as critically endangered with less than 100 covering a nearly 200km stretch of river. The day before, we were lucky enough to see a couple off in the distance, on a boat trip from Don Khon island. That sighting alone was more than we ever dreamed. Back to today, we arrived in a grumpy mood to the guesthouse in central Kratie, and it was getting late. We asked straight away about the dolphins, the reply was a positive one, but we had to leave immediately. This backpackers guesthouse had its own remork, a tuk-tuk that's basically a trailer carriage strapped to a normal moped. Their young driver appeared momentarily with helmet in hand and beckoned us to get going.

We jumped into the remork like *Starsky and Hutch*, as it sped out of the driveway, tilting as it rounded the corner, straight into a petrol station next door. We had to laugh, it had become an ongoing joke over the last month or so. Whenever we got a bus or tuk-tuk pick up from somewhere we'd often see the vehicle and driver waiting around ahead of time impressing us with their efficiency. As soon as we set off, we would pull straight into a nearby petrol station. Watching the petrol assistant fill us up while mid conversation on an old-school wireless phone handset. I was racking my brains to remember what the outcome of this experiment was on a *Mythbusters* episode but couldn't, so just closed my eyes and hoped for the best.

All good, and we're off again at some speed to chase sunset. The boat landing and the dolphins were about 20 minutes north of the town. This was our first look at life in Cambodia as we drove through some beautiful villages where everyone was smiling and waving. It already seemed quite different from Laos. We got to the entrance, and our driver had a bit of a chat with the ticket seller, we found out later that the entry had closed, but he managed to get us in.

We rushed down a long stairway to the water's edge, met the driver of our longtail and headed out. Within minutes we were near a number of other boats and saw the dolphins, a bit closer than the previous day. After a few teasing appearances they disappeared. One by one, the other boats surrounding us had completed their allotted time and headed to shore. Our captain took us into the middle of the Mekong, to a small island, steering into a bunch of tall rushes where he grabbed hold of a clump to secure us while we waited in silence.

It didn't take long before three dolphins appeared and traversed a section of the river in front of us for the next twenty minutes in search of food. They looked more like Beluga Whales than dolphins and have tiny dorsal fins. Apart from a film crew, we had the river to ourselves watching a beautiful sunset, setting behind these rare animals. If there is one day that had been turned around, it was this one. We smiled all the way home, seeing these rare animals 190km apart in two days certainly made us feel very lucky indeed.

Something Whiffy

We'd only noticed it while travelling in Laos and Cambodia, but there was frequently a comical moment when standing in a guesthouse reception while someone from France, Belgium, or Holland checked in. The conversation would go something like this:

"Here is your key, do you need anything else?"
"Do you have whiffy?"
"Pardon me?"
"Do you have whiffy? To check my emails"
"Oh you mean Wi-Fi"
"Yes, whiffy"

I was constantly holding out for someone asking for a Reum with a Minkey, but it never happened. Ironically, a couple of places did smell a bit Wi-Fi.

Slumber Party in Cambodia

During our stopover in the no-mans land between Laos and Cambodia we noticed that a couple of the women were dressed a bit peculiar, but just thought they were local characters. We didn't think any more about it until we were heading through a couple of villages on the way to the dolphins and noticed that most women were dressed similarly. They were all wearing pyjamas.

Bright orange, red or yellow pyjamas sets with flowery patterns, I even saw an Angry Birds one. Women were running shops, riding mopeds, buying food, cooking, all in pyjamas. It was as though the whole country was having a sleepover. They should have been the ones on the sleeper bus earlier that day, not us. We never really got to the bottom of its origins, but it was everywhere.

In Kratie, I would say around 80% of the women here wore them, becoming a lot less as we travelled to the bigger cities.

Could it have been an overly successful advertising campaign from Peter Alexander, or had a cargo ship full of nightwear ran aground on the Mekong? That would be funny, causing a lingerie version of *Whisky Galore*[1]. It also begs other questions like:

- What do they wear to bed?
- Why aren't the guys joining in and wearing those cotton long johns with button flaps in the bottom like the old western movies?
- How do you know when you are being propositioned by a lady of the night?

Ladies, I think you should all embrace it and give it a go tomorrow at work. Nic would jump at the chance, for the last 10 years, she's been practising most weekends. Flannelette PJ's are the new black.

Cage of Death

At a previous Melbourne Grand Prix we watched a motorcycle display in the cage of death, one of those spheres where the bikes loop the loop. Different bikes going in different directions, moving at speed, only inches away from each other. At the time I thought these guys were heroes, some of the bravest people I've seen. However, after spending time watching the moped drivers in South East Asia, I've come to the conclusion that they are resting on their laurels. To even try to compete with these local performances, I think they need to choose at least two of the following from the list to add into their routine:

- Wear thongs, no helmet and a Bintang t-shirt.
- Text a friend.
- Ride with your foot resting on the bike next to you.

---

[1] *The classic 1949 Ealing comedy*

- Have your wife on the back; the oldest child crammed between you both; and a young child (under three) sat on your lap, holding onto the handlebars.
- Carry any of the following:
    - A dog.
    - Birdcage (with bird).
    - A small food stall.
    - Large gas bottles.
    - 30+ Helium balloons (inflated).
    - 10 double mattresses.

Now there's a show for you.

Angkor's Away

One of Nic's planned highlights on the trip, and a 'must do' location was Siem Reap and the mighty temples of Angkor. We'd heard this was now so popular and should expect many tourists. Indeed Siem Reap was much bigger than we'd thought. For somewhere that's a base for world renowned cultural and historic sites, the town has a lively backpacker feel and even has a street called 'pub street'. It was a nice easy place to get around, but more than anywhere, we were hounded by tuk-tuk drivers. They are all plying to get your business for trips to the temples which is usually worth US$25 per day.

One thing I've not mentioned yet about Cambodia is its strange currency system. Pretty much everything is listed in US$, but only notes and not coins are used. So for anything less than a dollar you use the local Riel, so you'd pay for something in US$ but get change in Riel. A bit confusing at first, but you get used to it. It does, however, lead to some interesting bartering where the salesman will reluctantly reduce the price from US$6 to US$5 plus 4000 Riel (which is US$6). It's also why the majority of tourists needs can be bought for US$1 - water, postcards, gifts, etc.

Our temple tuk-tuk driver was Buntha, who was arranged through our fantastic little guesthouse (Purple Mangosteen).

Buntha was also their night attendant so the poor guy would catch up on sleep whenever he could during any stop. As well as driving us around for three days, he was a great guide for the temples and would either provide some history on a site before we went in, or would join us to show specific points of interest. He was only 30 but knew so much about the temples and was very passionate about it. His aim was to be an official tour guide, and although they call him up whenever a German-speaking guide is needed, he can't get his official license as he didn't have a high school certificate yet.

I have to admit I hadn't done a lot of research about the temples before getting here and was surprised by their number and size. The big drawcard is, of course, Angkor Wat which is what everyone seems to refer to when talking about the temples, but there is so much more. The next two most popular would be Ta Prom (made famous in the movie *Tombraider*) and Bayon with its 216 faces. We ended up visiting at least 10 temples, Nic's favourite was Angkor, mine was either Ta Prom or Preah Khan. The main temple complex starts only about 25 minutes from Siem Reap, with some temples up to a couple of hours away. It was pretty humbling visiting these magnificent Khmer temples that have been around for thousands of years, and some are still so well preserved. Many people have this destination as their ultimate bucket list holiday, and you can see why.

It was a great experience, and Buntha was a Jedi at timing it so we arrived at temples when the tourist buses and the masses were elsewhere. It made us realise how good it was to be travelling independently, rather than on a tour. One of the iconic tourist 'must dos' is to watch sunrise appear behind Angkor Wat, but we felt for many tour groups on the day we were there. The tours are on a tight schedule and many left before the sun actually appeared. Most others left straight after, so we were suddenly almost alone at one of the most famous tourist attractions in the world. It was a beautiful sight, and we then had the freedom to move around and try to get the perfect shots, ideally with a reflection of the complex in the lotus pond out front. As I was wondering how the shot could possibly get any better, a monk appeared for what probably was the monk 'money shot' of the trip.

We were welcomed with the hottest temperatures of the whole trip during our three days in Siem Reap, making us feel like great explorers, or Indiana Jones (I think this is the third time I've felt like Indy so far in this book). After hours of travelling, in what's basically a trailer behind a moped, we'd be covered in dust and windswept at the end of each day. Each temple had its own welcoming party, a gang of young kids trying to sell postcards. The cards were in packs of 10 and the kids, no older than eight or nine, would flick through them like they'd spent the last 5 years as a croupier, reciting the numbers 1-10 in every language they knew. 'one, two, three..', 'un, deux, trois..', 'eins, zwei, drew…', 'ichi, ni, san…'. After about ten minutes of 'no', 'non', 'nein', 'iie' they would move onto the next victim. This was only until they saw you on the way out, where the process would repeat.

The temples were a real mix of style, spanning Hindu and Buddhist eras, including some that had been modified from one to the other. You could also see the damage and destruction from when this controversial area was controlled by the Siam, Chan and Khmer empires over the centuries. You also saw bullet holes left from fighting during the Pol Pot regime. Some temples were not as easily accessible as others, they were designed for Gods to reside in, not for people to worship in, so the steps were not always human-friendly. At one, in particular, I had to send Nic up alone, as I seem to have developed mid-life vertigo. I might still be there to this day if I tried.

The Shower Dance

Climbing through temples all day in mid 40's temperatures took its toll. We were hoping that travelling between them in an open tuk-tuk would deliver some respite, but it just felt like someone was holding a hair-dryer at us with the dial set to 11. Even the lunch locations that we were dropped off at didn't have great air-con. Buntha dropped us off at a restaurant after our extensive tour of the Bayon temple and as soon as we walked in, we burst into flames and were immediately drenched in secondary sweat. It looked like we'd just swam there. We had one weapon in our arsenal that was sure to help, Lychee Iced Tea. As the waiter was still walking towards us, we asked for two cans and more cotton napkins to dry us out.

We'd only recently discovered this delight, it is the most refreshing suger filled drink on the planet. Perfect for this situation. He dropped them off at the table. In unison, we opened and lifted the cans, tilted our heads back, and poured. It didn't hit the sides. The waiter had only made it about two steps before we called him back for another, he made it a whole six steps before the third. I think five cans each over a single lunch is a record we are unlikely to beat.

Between tropical temperatures, high humidity, and covering many miles in your thongs, meant that showers were our friend. An end-of-day shower became mandatory as we were often filthy by that point. It was only after a random conversation that we both realised each of our shower routines contained the same activity. The Shower Dance.

Our feet would be black after transporting us around during the day's adventures. The type of black we thought would never come off, branded for life with the contents of a Cambodian street. Thankfully, most showers had either a rough concrete floor or had lost the enamel from its once smooth surface. Time to step into the shower and press play on your internal playlist.

Different songs led to different dances, different dances were better than others at cleaning various parts of the feet. I'd generally start with a bit of Riverdance, always a good one for your heal, moving onto the odd ballet pirouette, which was great on the bottom of your toes. The best way to finish was always in the

'60s with a twist. The amount of muck would determine how low you'd have to go. I also found out from taking a peak at Nic, that *Shake Your Tail Feather* works wonders. Well it did for me.

Siem Reap was a blur, but a great one. It had such a nice vibe and we even had chance to spend a couple of evenings with Michel and Agmar, as our paths crossed again. Despite packing so many temples into our three full days, we left feeling that there was still so much more to see, and knew we wanted to return one day.

Raffles Backpacker Hostel

Before this trip, we weren't the most adventurous in our accommodation choices for holidays. We do like a bit of pampering and have been known to stay in some nice hotels. So it was with a little trepidation that we started the year knowing we would be pushing the envelope of our comfort zone. Generally, though, this hasn't been a problem at all, our flashpacker budget has meant that we have had some great rooms (mainly in guesthouses) all with private bathrooms and most with air-con, for between $14-$40 per couple.

There have been a few times when we exceeded our normal budget, they generally fall into cities like Singapore where rooms are expensive. Also when we choose a hotel because its history or architecture is such that we want to make it part of our journey (e.g. The Eastern and Oriental, in Georgetown).

After touring the fabulous temples of Angkor for three long days and a long bus ride to Phnom Penh, we decided it was time for a treat again, especially as it coincided with our three month anniversary of travelling. The Le Royal Hotel in Phnom Penh is now a Raffles property, but this great colonial hotel used to be called The Hotel Phnom. It has a fantastic history that included many distinguished guests and was a regular hangout for the western writers and journalists covering the beginnings of the infamous Khmer Rouge regime.

We arrived at Phnom Penh's bus station to the usual welcoming committee of hundreds of tuk-tuk drivers, wanting our business for the hotel transfer. The last thing I wanted to say was the name of our hotel as the price would triple. I tried as many local street names or landmarks that I could remember with no luck. Eventually, we told him our hotel and I swear I've never seen a pair of eyes open so wide, or a smile so big. I'm pretty sure I could see the $ signs in his pupils, just like in the cartoons. I did my best to convince him we were visiting someone there or were the hired help, we eventually agreed a price of US$3 and set off, crammed into the back of a tuk-tuk clutching our bags.

I hadn't thought it through really, the tuk-tuk turned into the hotel's fancy gate and made its way to the entrance where we were met by two uniformed doormen, looking very resplendent with classic pith helmets. We, on the other hand, now covered in dust, looked like rag and bone men. 'Good evening sir, how was your flight?', 'Erm, we came by bus', 'very good sir'. Not the best of impressions. We followed the foot soldiers, who were now carrying our bags, into the foyer to meet the concierge. 'Good evening sir, how was your flight?'. Not again, this would be the 2nd of five people to ask this. We then had to explain that we'd booked using a discount website so that we could use our reward points. You could hear clanging, as a secret button was pressed and the good silver was hidden away around the hotel.

Next, we're presented with an iced tea and a damp, brilliant white, hand towel which by the time we gave ourselves the once over (hands, face, neck, then any crevasse you can quickly find), was returned looking the same colour as the tea. Time to be shown to the room as we follow the concierge who is walking a few steps ahead, probably trying to keep upwind. Now, as you know, I've had my current 'bus station' thongs for two months and about 10,000km, and in that time I've not heard a peep from them. Walking across the shiny marbled floor of Raffles, they start to squeak and then squelch. No matter how I walked, I could not silence them. It was like an alarm, warning the other guests that the hotel had now gone into Defcon 2: Bogan Alert. We eventually reach our fantastic room, handily located at the back of the hotel, requiring the longest squeaky walk known to man (one short squeak for man, one giant leap for backpackerkind). We'd usually be much more comfortable in such a place, it's just that we were only travelling with a 10Kg backpack each, and surprise surprise, my ball gown and Nic's dinner jacket are just not in there.

The other reason that I think people knew we were different was the fact we looked happy. You would not believe how miserable rich people looked at the thought of having to stay in this wonderful hotel. If you even so much as cracked a small grin you were obviously not one of the elite, you'd be ostracised and may not find a partner for baccarat that evening. I broke into a little skip, at one point, walking past the pool just to tease them.

We did have a great stay, including enjoying their more casual restaurant. The cunning use of socks that match the colour of your sandals fooled them, and my trusty Magic Shirt worked wonders. We drank in the famous Writers Bar and had a cocktail made famous from a visit by Jackie Kennedy. Between this, my retro style camera, and hanging out at Phnom Penh's famous Foreign Correspondents Club, I admitted to Nic that I felt like John Malkovich. Now, I know that he's an actor and *The Killing Fields* is a film but figured that I wouldn't dream of feeling like Sydney Schanberg or Al Rockoff. However, comparing myself to someone with strange hair, a funky camera, who was pretending that they were a journalist, now that was me.

Obviously, we could only stay one night in such a pad, so we soaked for hours in their huge bath before filling our backpacks with the free toiletries and checked out the next day. An equal number of staff members enquired about the time of our flight out. Our reply was that we were staying longer in Phnom Penh but were interested in exploring the backpacker district as research for a book, hardly a lie. As we carried our own bags down the steps, the foot soldiers appeared and almost stumbled towards us to try and retrieve them, I don't think many guests make the effort. However, that was probably not what they'd be talking about during their earl grey tea break. It would be the 5-minute argument we had with the tuk-tuk driver as he was trying to charge us US$7. The driver didn't know who he was dealing with, as the doormen slowly and quietly backed away.

Mojo lost and found

We seemed to lose our travel mojo a little in Phnom Penh. I guess there were a few factors involved:

- Leaving a fantastic guesthouse in Siem Reap
- Leaving the majestic temples of Angkor
- Being quite tired after some long journeys and busy days
- Really not connecting with Phnom Penh
- Poor accommodation choice (post Raffles of course)

Especially with the heat and humidity, it is easy to quickly lose spirit. One thing that's very hard to explain is that the constant decision making is tiring. Now wait, before you throw this book down in disgust at more whinging about what should be the best experience of our lives. It really does take its toll.

You'd think it should be one of the best parts of the trip, deciding where to sleep and eat, and it is, really it is. However, when you are moving on average every two days and want to put some kind of quality control over where you lay your head, or what you put in your belly, it takes time and effort. Eventually, you get decision fatigue, especially if you have a bit of a bad run of decisions. You get through it, and just as we did in Langkawi and Bangkok, we knew we would. It was time to turn things around.

This started with trips to the thought-provoking Killing Fields (Choeung Ek) and the S21 (Tuol Sleng) Genocide Museum.

We were glad we did, however, the information and images you see are very disturbing and will stay with us forever, and rightly so. It is a fantastic testament to the people of this nation who are full of joy and hope, despite this very recent history. At S21 we were fortunate enough to meet one of only seven survivors (from over 17,000) inmates of the prison. Bou Meng was an artist whose wife was killed in the prison, but he was spared because he was able to paint good quality likenesses of Pol Pot. I can't comprehend how he could return to this site and found myself overwhelmed to meet him. For the life of me, I couldn't think of one sensible question or meaningful thing to say to him. The right words all came to me hours later, when we were back in our comfy hotel room. I only managed to explain that it was an honour to meet him, and it was. It certainly added even more context to this historic location. So if that isn't a wake-up call, making you realise how little your 1st world problems are, I don't know what is.

Now for some positive and more cheerful Phnom Penh experiences. The Royal Palace complex is a beautiful piece of serenity in the centre of the city's hustle and bustle. The compound is filled with intricate buildings and lovely flower gardens. About two blocks from here is the iconic Foreign Correspondents Club (FCC) which, like the Writers Bar at Raffles, made you feel you've stepped back into history, albeit a modern one. The bar is a perfect spot to chill and looks out over the confluence between the Mekong and Cambodia's famous Tonle Sap.

Turn around complete, I think that if we'd stayed longer, or had arrived at a different time in the journey, we would have come to love the city. Our time here did seem to reinforce our responsibility to make the most of this experience, not to fuck it up, and appreciate how blessed our lives are.

Life is a Beach

After a busy time inland, and a few long bus journeys, it was great to see the coast again, for the first time in over two months. We hit the sea at Sihanoukville, a tourist beach resort on the south coast of Cambodia. We'd heard that the town was a little sleazy and understood why after being offered marijuana for the third time and seeing a bar fight, all within the first few hours. However, having a beer on a comfy lounge chair just meters from the crashing waves made us quickly forget about it. Not enough to stay longer than a night though, we needed to find something a bit more Mountyish (sedate and middle age). A 15-minute tuk-tuk ride later, we were down the coast at Outres beach, the place where it wasn't all happening. We were heading to a hostel made up of bungalows that had a good TripAdvisor rating. Unfortunately, we arrived to find that they were full and weren't even on the beach side of the road. Not to be defeated, I set Nic up with the bags and a fresh banana shake at a beachside bar and hit the pavement (sand) in search of our new home. Sounds like I had my work cut out for me, doesn't it? Basically, I walked next door, asked if they had a room, locked it in, had a chat with the staff, walked back next door looking tired and sweaty. The hero.

Chez Paou was a French/Cambodian run restaurant with about 10 beach bungalows, we scored one facing the beach and only 20 metres from the waters edge. The place was mainly run by a group of young local lads. They worked hard to look after everyone but also had great fun messing around and playing pool on two pristine and professional looking pool tables that appeared very out of place in this setting. The beach here is prone to have rubbish washed ashore, but the staff did a fantastic job of clearing everything up each morning before most guests surfaced. The sea was the warmest I think I've ever been in, it was like slipping into a nice warm bath. The hostel also laid on some of the best sunsets we've seen as well, this really was just what we needed. To top it off, instead of playing *dumf dumf* music to the early hours, they played fantastic mellow jazz covering Sergio Mendez to Louis Armstrong, we really had struck gold.

Okay, so it wasn't perfect, it turned out that our private bungalow was actually a shared one with a few small furry friends. We first realised this when lying on the bed we looked up at the mosquito net to see that it was covered in little mouse dropping. It looked like they'd been having a great time aiming at unsuspecting sleeping victims, wishing the netting wasn't there, hoping for guests who slept with their mouth open.

At first, we were a little anxious about this, spending 30 minutes securing the netting around us, trying to forget the fact that a mouse can easily get through something the diameter of a pencil. We didn't sleep much and planned to leave in the morning. Then we woke up and went outside. The views were spectacular, the breakfast was exquisite and a warm swim topped it off. What the hell, it was only a mouse.

The beach lounge seats saw a steady stream of saleswomen walking by with bracelets, fruit, cooked prawns, and offers of massages and manicures. On the first day at least three came to Nic, rubbed their finger across her not so smooth leg, as though they were checking the top of a door with white gloves on. They would frown, sometimes show friends in disbelief, and offer a 'no pain' hair removal service with a couple of pieces of string. Nic had a cunning plan of shaving that night to deter this banter, but they remembered her and showed their disappointment at the less than perfect job. This wore Nic down, and she finally said yes to a lady offering a manicure. As soon as she said the word, three other young girls appeared from nowhere. It looked like a Formula 1 pitstop as each jumped on an appendage. They pampered Nic for about an hour, having a great chat, and all for a whopping US$5.

Towards the end of the stay, we found out what the pool tables were for, a twice-weekly pool competition that costs US$2 to enter with the winner taking a cash prize. It proved to be very popular with locals and ex-pats. Now, if I can time the alcohol intake just right, I think I'm a half decent player, so signed up. Before the ink had dried, others arrived with their own cues and I discovered that the well-practised staff were also playing, and usually won. Just before it started, a tall, good looking Frenchman appeared and asked to join.

He was so overconfident, his expression looked like we should just save our time and hand over the cash right now. Whatever happened, I had to beat him. For the first round, I drew the bar manager who often wins. It was actually a close game, and I did win, but only because he fouled on the black. Next up, Frenchy. I lost, and in a big way. I was almost whitewashed which didn't really endear me to the guy, especially as he cheated once by knocking a ball. I returned to the bar, plotting my revenge and decided another beer would help. Fate meant that we were drawn together in the next round, now he looked even more smug. Little did he know, I'd just reached my small 10-minute peak playing window as the blood alcohol content reached optimum. I only allowed him to the table three times in a battle not seen since Agincourt. His face now less smug. Of course, I lost the rest of the tournament, but nothing else mattered, even Nic treated me like a hero for the rest of the night.

Kampot Shock Factor

We'd come across some of the dodgiest transport and accommodation on our travels so far; boats that looked like they would sink; coaches with exploding tyres; hotel rooms that had dodgy electric cables hanging from the sockets. By now, it didn't really phase us anymore, you just became used to your surroundings and would pay more attention to such stuff. Things like, working out the fire escape route, or checking plug sockets for burns before using them.

Just as with people, you can't judge a hotel room by its cover. We arrived at a lovely hotel in Kampot, this town has the most amazing French Colonial architecture, and this hotel was made up from a number of old townhouses that had been joined together and lovingly restored. It wasn't too much more expensive than we'd normally pay, but it seemed like a lovely bit of luxury. They assigned us a recently refurbished room with a large TV, desk, rain shower, and a high bed. A little table held the tea/coffee making facilities with a nice cordless kettle, the type that you lift up off the powered base. After a long journey, the English in us will always make a beeline for a nice cup of tea. As I plugged the kettle in, I felt a slight tingle in my hand that was touching the kettle's metal side. Unfortunately, this is where my common sense went completely M.I.A., as I decided to try the kettle in another socket. Nic was busy trying out the fantastic rain shower and was expecting a nice cuppa on her return, so I moved the kettle onto the lovely polished wooden floor and plugged it into a low wall socket.

I guess so far, that doesn't seem too crazy, but it was my next thought that became my downfall, 'How about I touch the side again and see if it has the same effect?'. I leant down to it, so that one foot was in the air, and planted my hand firmly on the side of the kettle before it got too hot (safety first). It didn't quite have the same effect. It was 100 times worse. Now, I'm normally a quiet person. Apart from the odd sinister sounding stomach growls, you would hardly know I'm in the room. Nic's shower was interrupted by an almighty roar as I flew back onto the bed, she'd never heard me make any sound like it and rushed into the room. I was mostly okay, suffering from a mild case of a medical condition that occurs due to the inadequate substrate for aerobic cellular respiration (I was going to say shock, but it seemed like such a cheap gag). I had ringing in my ears, pins and needles throughout my arm and leg, my heart rate was racing, and I felt dizzy. Thankfully, this soon passed. In fact, I think Nic's shock at the noise and finding me, lasted much longer.

On our way out for dinner, we took the kettle down to the reception and told the story in dramatic details, expecting our bill to be wiped or be given a small share of the hotel. The French legacy in this area soon shone through as we were presented with just a shrug of the shoulders. I think there might have even been an 'Ooops!', a quite comical understatement. I guess you can safely say that Cambodia is about as far away from a nanny state as you can get, you quickly realise that any incident that you get to walk away from with just a spiky hairstyle quite rightly deserves only an 'Ooops!'.

Our last few days in Cambodia were quite culinary, we toured the south coast areas between Kampot and Kep, visiting pepper plantations, and trying the famous Kep crab. It's a beautiful part of the country, dotted with great French era architecture, some of which are still showing the scars of war. Our guide and driver joined us for the crab feast, giving us a great insight into his life, including the fact that he was only 16 when he handed over his machine gun to authorities, as it was no longer needed to protect his family. That was only 14 years ago.

It was tough to leave this country, but the journey stops for no one. All in all, I think Cambodia was one of our most favourite countries. The people are so friendly, and we seemed to find a big difference in how people interacted with us, compared to nearby Laos. Aw Kohn Cambodia - we will be back.

CHAPTER 6

Location: Kampot
Days 100, Countries 8, Kilometers 15,252, Beds 48
Trains 2, Planes 9, Automobiles 18, Boats 6
Beers 26

100 Day Update - a word from 'er indoors

Don't know about you, but I think at a milestone like this in our adventure it's only fitting for Nicki to jump in and include a few thoughts:

I know, hold the phone, Mrs Mounty has made an appearance. Lee's been doing an amazing job keeping our travels documented and it must look like he's doing all the work. What the world doesn't know is that I've been doing an equally amazing job of documenting each day in my personal journal. So after 100 days of travelling, what have I learnt?

- That arriving at a new place and being mobbed by waiting taxi drivers is my least favourite part of the journey.

- That I become a different person when the tri-factor of hungry, dehydrated & tired are put together, add crowds to this, and I'm just plain scary!! We avoid this combination at all times after I nearly knocked out a Korean guy at the Grand Palace in Bangkok.
- Not ironing or cooking for three months, I love it. There are moments when I am seriously reconsidering living in a campervan for four months in Europe as I'll have to learn to cook again.
- How easily some things become routine, and others not. For instance, why does washing my underwear in the shower every night not bother me at all, but cleaning my teeth with bottled water still seems such a bind?
- How simple things make me smile, like finding different coloured threads sewn into all our T-shirts, so the laundry lady knows who owns that terrible Thailand top.
- That some of the best things in life really are free:
- Playing football with three young kids in Yangon
- Visiting a school in a Laos hill village and joining their English class
- Watching the sunset on the beach in Cambodia
- Working out how it's possible to get 10 mattresses on the back of a moped
- Hello is the same in every country, when answering the phone. This gets me every time! I think they are about to have a conversation in English, but it only lasts as long as hello!
- Having a private bathroom ranks higher in importance than whether a cockroach or mouse is sharing the room with us.
- I've forgotten how to use a knife when eating, it doesn't come naturally anymore.

- So far, my small bladder has been behaving, and my fear of travelling long distances on a bus without a toilet has been unfounded. Most of the time I think my bladder is frightened into hiding.
- Time has lost its hold on our lives, I haven't worn a watch yet this year. Our clock revolves around; the next meals; the next sleep; and most importantly, is it beer o'clock yet?
- Straightening my hair seems like a whole different world away, what a waste of time. A semi curly mop seems to do just fine here.
- Our flashpacker budget still allows for way too much food, how naive to think we would lose weight travelling. Three meals a day and beer every night, who were we kidding!
- Living out of a 10kg backpack and changing beds on average every second night hasn't phased me at all.

Is there anything I'm missing from our real world? Not a sausage!

Mrs M x

The Joys of Blogging

I'm back again. So far during the trip I'd been keeping everyone back home updated with an online blog, and it won't be a surprise to hear that some of the content in this book originated in the online version. You will also not be surprised to hear that I am not accustomed to writing. Being brought up on a council estate in North-West UK, English is almost a second language to me. I have never written anything before ('we bloody well know!', you scream) but as soon as I started blogging, I immediately enjoyed it. However, now and then you'll either hit a location that doesn't gel or you are just moving and touristing (new word) so much, that you do become quite drained. At this point, the first thing to go is the writing. If it's a choice between a beer at the end of a busy day or to bust out a blog, the malt beverage will win every time. When it started to feel like a chore, I started to wonder why and who I'm doing it for.

Then you look back at what you've written previously. I know we are not spring chickens, and dementia shouldn't have taken its grip on us just yet, but we were already saying, 'I'd forgotten all about that'. You realise then who we were doing it for. Us. Screw you guys (not really, we love you). As Nic just alluded to, she had been doing an absolutely amazing job of recording our everyday activities in a beautiful journal every night without fail, so we've a record of what we did. This narrative is just adding to that with some of those more quirky experiences.

By far the best bit about travel writing is that it affects how you look at things. Especially early on when you are a little bit more precious, clinging to memories of the OH&S rules back in our home 'nanny state' (the phrase OH&S seems to stand for Only Half Survive in some countries we'd travelled through). Whole situations are completely turned on their head:

A coach skidding sideways down the street until its tyre bursts:

Before blogging: 'I'm going to die, and I've not got clean undies on today!'

Blogging: 'I can make a funny blog about this and imply how brave I was.'

A cat and mouse game with an attacking toothbrush (something to look forward to later in the book):

Before blogging: 'WTF is this guy doing!?'
Blogging: 'What a great continuation of the thong theme.'

Some barstool stealing your thongs:
Before blogging: 'Call out the dogs on the unwashed criminal!'

Blogging: 'I'll put my side across in a blog and make him realise his life choices are not conducive with good karma, maybe he will change his ways.'

Being put in excruciating pain during a foot massage:

Before blogging: 'I'm sorry, but this isn't in the brochure, get me the manager!'
Blogging: 'Push harder, this is fantastic material. Now try and twist my leg around my head!'

Two people heaving a motorbike up into the isle of your bus:

Before blogging: 'Now I'm sure this violates at least five safety regulations.'
Blogging: 'Now if you can perch a chicken on top of the seat, this would be perfect blog material.'

Someone local trying to scam you:

Before blogging: 'Well if the world isn't going to play fair then I'm just going to go home.'
Blogging: 'Nice try mate, what else have you got and do you have a pencil so I can write this down?'

I really do think writing has helped immensely with the adjustment of travelling through South East Asia, it's basically a magic bullet for the whinging pom. Between the writing and the photos I'd been posting, my only worry is that it might deprive us of the privilege of boring people stupid by lengthily regaling our adventures at dinner parties for the next ten years. You know what it's like, you have a great trip, return with your holiday snaps and can't wait to meet up with friends to show them. For us, this may now pan out like:
'There was this time when we were crossing the Laos border', 'Yes we know you were put on a sleeping bus weren't you?'. 'Okay, well there was this time my thongs were stolen', 'Yeah, you thought it was the German backpackers didn't you?'. 'Okay, you've just got to see these pics from the fantastic temples of Bagan', 'Seen them'.

Don't be surprised if you see me wandering down Melbourne's Southbank, shouting after random strangers, "One time in Camdodia...."

Good Morning Vietnam

We were a bit apprehensive about the journey into Vietnam using this particular border crossing, we'd read stories about dodgy tour operators that either abandon you or put you onto unsafe and overcrowded buses. We took some advice from our lovely hotel manager in Kampot and the company we used actually turned out to be okay. The border crossing between Cambodia and Vietnam consisted of a no-mans land with a small casino on the Cambodian side. The buildings on the Vietnamese side were much more modern and shiny, it was as though they were pointing out that 'your country is considerably poorer than mine!'.

We changed buses at the border, making our way across no-mans land by foot via a quarantine area where we were checked for our inoculations. Obviously, with Nic on the case, we were veritable pincushions. We'd been bleeding cash, as well as blood before we left Melbourne. If it was preventable, then we had something stuck into us to prevent it. We proudly produced our 'War and Peace' travel inoculation booklets and were waved straight through. The Danish backpacker behind us had no vaccinations and no info. You're probably thinking the same as me, 'I bet they don't let him in the country', 'do they throw his arse back to Cambodia?'. I was feeling quite smug with ourselves about our expensive, and extensive preparations. This smugness quickly dissipated as they charge him US$1, stamped his documents, and waved him through. Quietly, in the background, I could hear my credit card weeping.

Now through the border, we head by bus and ferry to an island off the country's south coast called Phu Quoc (take a couple of minutes to do your own, funny name related gags). We didn't have much time to explore the island so stayed central to visit the market and take a boat out for some squid fishing that night.

The town market was mainly made up of fish restaurants with an amazing display of pretty much anything, even a tank of live sea snakes. Our main regret on Phu Quoc was not eating Eric. I guess I should expand on this. Don't worry, Eric was not a person, but the name given to one of the largest lobsters I think we have ever seen for sale. On enquiry, it would cost $30/Kg, and he would have been a fair weight. We'd also heard rumours that there was great lobster to be had on the beaches further north in mainland Vietnam. At a cost greater than a days budget, we'd only get one bite at an Eric for the whole trip so left it for now and went for the cheaper large prawns instead. Needless to say, to this day, the lobster never did happen, and Eric lived to see another plate. His photo resides, haunting us as to what could have been. Maybe we'd have better luck with squid fishing.

Right from the start, it looked like the squid fishing was never going to produce a bountiful catch. As we boarded, we could see the crew loading a selection of 'pre-caught' critters on board, ensuring we would be fed. The group of Korean men sharing the boat with us, gave up quite early to hit the rice wine down below. We, on the other hand, took the activities very seriously. We'd watched the expert crew closely and mastered the little flick of hand line as we concentrated for the feel of a bite. And concentrated, and concentrated, while everyone else was getting drunk. Our hard work eventually paid off as Nic caught the first squid which tried, unsuccessfully, to spit ink at her for her troubles. It wasn't exactly a beast from a Jules Verne novel, but it was ours. Next, it was my turn before Nic bagged the third and last. We ended up being the only ones on the boat to catch anything, and our three pieces of finger food were the tastiest things on the menu (apart from the rice wine).

To help with the timelines and because we'd heard horror stories about the quality of overland travel from here to Ho Chi

Minh City, we decided to catch a flight from Phu Quoc's newly built airport to arrive into the madness that is Ho Chi Minh City. After spending a whopping $7 on the taxi to the departing airport, we researched a local bus which took us from Ho Chi Minh airport right to the centre of the city's market square for $1. It was a jam-packed locals bus, forcing me to stand all the way and peek through gaps to find our stop.

Crossing roads here was just as terrifying as we'd expected it to be, with hundreds of mopeds hurtling towards you from all directions. Thankfully our experiences so far had instilled some bravery into us, and we soon got the hang of it. For a novice, it could easily have been too intimidating, you risk spending your whole stay trapped on a traffic island. What a shame that would have been as this city, once known as Saigon, was terrific. It reminded us a lot of Melbourne with hidden cafes and a thriving coffee culture; it also had some great architecture, such as its Opera House. It was more modern than most places we'd been to in South East Asia with very upmarket shopping malls.

Trust your Local Tour Agent

At this point in the tour, time was becoming a bit tight as we knew we had to reach Beijing to catch the Trans-Mongolian. Remember back in our 'positively palatial' pad in Vientiane, we booked a flight (while drunk) from Hanoi to Hong Kong to give us some deadlines to work to. We now just needed to work out our route from Ho Chi Minh City in the south to Hanoi in the north. One of the popular backpacker options for getting through Vietnam is to use an open bus ticket. They are available from a few different coach operators that transverse the main cities on the way up or down the country, you can stop off and stay where you want. Our plan was to lock in the whole route to make sure we got to all the places on our hotlist.

As with just about everything, there were conflicting reviews on the best bus company to use, the two main ones had both great reports and some horror stories. While walking through a backpacker hotspot, we thought we'd talk to a few tour agents about them, and get some advice. It soon became apparent that each agent was tied to a particular bus company, so we may not be getting accurate advice. Later that evening, we were taking a pile of laundry to the cheapest place we could find. It was down a small side street, and as we headed down the alley, we spot a tour agent attached to a budget hotel. Walking past the entrance, we were treated to the biggest smile you've ever seen, accompanied by a wave and shout of 'hello' from the bubbly looking girl inside. We found it impossible to walk past and were drawn in like a *Star Wars* tractor beam.

Phuong met us, sat us down and asked what we needed. We briefly mentioned our plan to her while she made quick notes. Within 5 minutes she presented us with a full program, including tickets, accommodation, and two inclusive tours, covering the highlands of Sapa and the islands of Halong Bay. Not wanting to be steamrollered into anything, we took some details away and continued with our laundry. That night we checked TripAdvisor, discovering that a few of the hostels didn't get great reports. We called in again the next day when picking up our $3 worth of immaculately laundered, folded and packaged clothes to discuss our findings. Phuong explained that she didn't know what standard we were looking for, so went for the cheapest options (I must have looked like one of the great unwashed that day). Within two minutes she crossed out the accommodation and started a new list.

I wanted to go away and recheck these, but she knew she was closing in on the sale so whipped out a laptop to search for the new hotels on TripAdvisor. She would turn the screen towards us, quickly scroll to the bottom of the page so we couldn't read any reviews, then turned it back before bursting out laughing. 'Trust me', she explained with her huge smiling face, 'I know what will make you happy and have a great trip'. We already wanted to take her home with us, and you know my theory of nice face = trustworthy person, so we handed over $350 each and walked away with just a slip of handwritten paper as a receipt. As we were leaving, we also asked about our Chinese visa which she could arrange to be sorted once we reached Hanoi, so quickly handed over another $200.

On arrival back at the hotel, I closed the door and immediately started to worry. What on earth had we just done. We'd lost all our power to decide where to stay, but more importantly, we'd just handed over a truckload of our money to a stranger. Did this travel agency really exist or was she busy taking her lovely smile, with our dosh, on her own little holiday somewhere? We couldn't work out if we were being paranoid or the biggest idiots. Our first hurdle was to see if she turned up at her office the following day, where we would be taken to our first bus.

It was a relief to see that this side street office still existed the following morning, but a worry that it was empty. No smiling face to be seen. Fifteen minutes passed and Nic was starting to get a bit tetchy when all of a sudden a moped ploughed its way through the busy side streets, splitting the crowd before stopping in front of us. The helmet flew off to reveal a lovely set of familiar teeth. 'Let's go', and off she marched by foot down the street. The bus stop was only around the corner, and we stood outside as she went into the office, bought our tickets, and told us where to wait before giving us a hug and wishing us a great trip.

A nice looking bus arrives, we board and start moving off, feeling very relieved that we weren't ripped off. However, a couple of hours later, something dawned on us. We don't have any receipts or bus tickets for anything else on our trip, just a typed out itinerary. We were back to mistrust again, except now she'd managed to clear us out of town to boot. We reach our first destination, Da Lat, the transfer to the hotel worked, now it's crunch time. Surprisingly, the hotel was expecting us and put us up in a fantastic top floor room, with a bath and great views, all for $27. Phew!

Delightful Da Lat

Ahh, Da Lat. This is a charming town with strong French influences and some fascinating architecture. We only had one full day here, so it required a big MountyDay. This started with a tour around the craziest of buildings. I guess the clue was in the name, The Crazy House. Hang Nga Guesthouse is a very unorthodox, Gaudiesque work in progress. As far as I'm concerned, this outrageous expressionist fairytale is a must see. You can actually stay in the building which looks like a version of the Disney Castle in a Tim Burton movie. I loved it.

Our walk took us past lovely suburbs, great little French coffee shops, through the grounds of the magnificent Da Lat Palace Hotel, and down to the town's beautiful lake. The lake's edge has lovely pavilion restaurants, but we were there for one reason only, to ride on a big plastic swan pedalo. What fun, and in true Mounty style, we covered the full length of the lake, checking out our next walking route. The following lakeside walk took us through a local flower market before we headed off on a crusade to find a small train station that was still running steam engine rides through the local countryside. After surrounding the very cute station for about an hour, we finally homed in on it to find that we'd missed the last ride for the day. However, a magnificent steam train was parked up for us to climb on and take photos. A taxi back to the hotel and a lovely dinner in a nearby restaurant full of locals, ended a perfect day.

Da Lat seems a bit overlooked on the usual tourist routes which is a shame as it is a lovely, vibrant town with lots of history, and is still intact. Apparently, during the Vietnam War, there was a bit of a gentleman's agreement from both sides that this town would receive a certain amount of protection. This was due to the fact that high up officials from both sides loved the place so much.

Nha Trang's Grumpy Goose

Our travel experiences thus far led us to believe that you should generally read the bus schedule to see how long the trip will take and then add on 2-3 hours to make it more realistic. However, the journey from Da Lat to Nha Trang was not only beautiful but we arrived early, much to our surprise. A free transfer then took us to our next hotel, the Nice Swan. The staff at the Nice Swan were expecting us, but for two nights, not the one that we had on our itinerary. It turned out that the Nice Swan was more of a Grumpy Goose, the staff were really not that friendly or helpful about the change. I'm not sure if we were overly sensitive because of reports about Nha Trang being a bit of a tourist trap and hotspot for scammers. The room was pleasant enough though and was only $28 per night after all.

Once checked in, we headed straight to the beach. It was because of this beach we'd forsaken the pleasure of Eric the Lobster in Phu Quoc. We'd heard of fresh lobsters that were cooked in front of you on portable barbecues, right on the beach. We walked along the beach, found a nice spot, sat down and waited. And waited. Eventually, a saleswoman approached us with a pole across her back, supporting a small barbecue on one side and a basket of seafood on the other. Unfortunately, the basket was full of already cooked seafood that she was just going to warm up. This was one of the things we'd been warned about as the food can be days old and a sure fire way of getting on best terms with the local toilet facilities. We knew firsthand from a friend who was nearly hospitalised in the same town by this suspected source. What had we done? We cuddled up close to each other on the beach, pulled out the phone and stared at a picture of Eric, hoping he'd gone to a good home. Maybe a couple of travellers just like us who didn't feel the grass was greener elsewhere. Instead, we had to amuse ourselves with people watching.

One thing that became apparent as soon as we arrived in town was that this place was full of Russians. Just as the Aussies have Bali, the Americans have Cancun, the UK have Benidorm, the Russians have Nha Trang. All the restaurants had Russian writing in the windows and separate Russian menus. Sat on the beach, we could see a group of the most stereotypical looking young Russian men, drinking vodka, and jumping into the surf as though they'd never seen the sea before. Drinking and swimming is bad enough but today was pretty gusty, bringing a large swell pounding onto the beach. We watched a red face, shaved-headed lad, standing in the surf one minute, waving to his mates before being sucked into oblivion. We watched for what seemed like forever, and just as we were about to rush to help, the sea decided it didn't like the taste of vodka and spat him out, bouncing him along the beach like a scene from *Dambusters*. He stood up, threw his hands in the air, yelled what I'm guessing was an equivalent to 'Aussie, Aussie, Aussie!' (maybe 'Ruskie, Ruskie, Ruskie!') before disappearing again. We decided to exit beach left before our very rusty diver recovery skills were put to the test. We wandered, looking around for a non-Russian centric restaurant and came across a Vietnamese cafe called Morning Glory (well you just have to, don't you).

You'd think an educated man like myself would learn from watching others mistakes but apparently not. At the end of the next day I returned to the room sporting a huge graze just above my arse, where I was also dumped by a wave. My only defence was that at least I was relatively sober. Between, confusion over the lack of bus tickets, checking out a day earlier, and a street-wide power cut, our departure from the Grumpy Goose wasn't the smoothest. We finally boarded a well presented night bus to Hoi An with comfy leather recliners. If Da Lat was a ten, then I'm afraid Nha Trang was only a three.

Historical Hoi An

The lodging supplied by Phuong in Hoi An was a 2km trek from the bus station with our backpacks which was hard work at that time of the morning. It was a lovely little guesthouse, albeit a little more expensive at $37. Hoi An would prove to be our favourite location within Vietnam, it's historic UNESCO listed old town is just beautiful. Although quite busy with visitors, the town hasn't turned completely into a tourist trap and seems able to cater to the masses in a very dignified way. It also has some beautiful restaurants, including the wonderful Miss Ly's, a family run restaurant where on our first evening we sat chatting to Nathan, an American and Miss Ly's husband.

A most memorable eatery would be the Reaching Out Cafe, located in the heart of the old town. We escaped the rainy hustle and bustle, to enter this establishment run by deaf and hearing impaired staff. Immediately, everyone who enters seems to stop talking. You communicate an order with staff by touching wooden blocks and are served with a lovely tea ceremony in silence. Now, I only know two words in sign language, 'thank you' and 'bullshit'. Thankfully, I remembered which one was which as the latter certainly wouldn't be needed. It was a lovely thought-provoking experience.

We were plagued with a few heavy showers in Hoi An, and unfortunately, this included the afternoon we hired bikes to go exploring. The heavens opened as we were cycling through beautiful green rice fields, it was heavy enough to make us pull out our large blue ponchos. They were big enough to cover the baskets containing our picnic, but regularly filled up with air as we cycled along, making it look like we were parasailing. We did however, seem to bring joy to many a local worker as we zoomed past, receiving waves and laughs. Mostly laughs. I wonder if any of them had watched *E.T.*

Easy for you to say Rider

During our various bus journeys through Vietnam, our tickets included transfers from the hotel to the bus station. When you think about it, this is an excellent service as the whole journey could cost less than a McDonalds. You certainly wouldn't get this treatment in Europe. Imagine paying $10 for a bus from Paris to Rome and then getting an air-conditioned minivan to pick you up from your hostel. I think not. As with most things in S.E. Asia, there is always a little variation in the quality of service provided and you never really take anything for granted. As discussed previously, we were never really sure what was happening through our journey north in Vietnam, sometimes it worked as planned, and sometimes not. One of the most memorable transfers was in Hoi An.

We had checked out of the guesthouse and were waiting in the foyer, wondering if anyone was going to turn up as it started to get a little late. All of a sudden, a tiny guy (even by my standards) ran through the door with a bit of a sweat on. The staff pointed him towards us, and he rushed over saying that he was here to take us to the bus. Fantastic I thought, before looking down to see that he had two motorbike helmets in his hands, surely not. We followed him outside and saw his 'VIP' transportation, a tiny moped. 'You first!', he points to me, 'You next, 5 minutes' to Nic and then before I could blink, he perched a helmet on my head. I say perched because it seemed to be a helmet for an 8-year-old and certainly not suited to a long, narrow, forceps head like mine. It wasn't a cool look, I wasn't going to be mistaken for Tom Cruise racing an F14 in *Top Gun* or Steve McQueen as he prepares to jump a fence in *The Great Escape*. I hadn't dismissed however, the fact that we might actually jump a fence on the way.

'What about the bags?' was the only plan I had to try and get him to place us in a taxi, 'OK! OK!' was the reply as he picked up my backpack and walked out. He climbed onto his dented moped, jammed my backpack between his legs, and shouts 'Get on!'. With my daypack on my back, I climb on, holding onto the grips behind me as we speed off into the crazy world that is Vietnam traffic. As soon as we get over 10km/hr, the kid-size helmet strapped under my chin starts acting as a tiny parachute, which although uncomfortable would be a small attempt to slow him down, maybe adding an inch to my height in the process. I looked behind me to see Nic waving goodbye as though I was a soldier heading off into battle. We dodged, zoomed, skimmed and swerved to the bus station (notice I didn't say braked) where I dismount with shaky legs and a long neck.

Our driver heads off again, this time for Nic with the same diminutive helmet in tow. I wait, then I wait, then I wait some more, but there was no sign. Nic had never been on a moped before, she'd already refused to take moped taxis in previous countries, and I was worried that she would be petrified. It seemed like an eternity until I finally see a moped turn the corner with two people on it. Trying to work out if it was them or not, it soon became clear, as all I could see from the passenger was a huge grin that could be spotted 500 metres out. She loved it. At least after that, the terrible bus on this next leg, or any future transport 'experiences' would seem a doddle.

Hue-ever would fall for that scam?

Hue was an interesting place, it didn't start well as the first room we were shown at the randomly named Sports Hotel was pretty dire. Based on the groupings of curly hairs it contained, the bedding had not been replaced in a while. I did feel sorry for the previous tenant as he or she was apparently suffering from some sort of genital alopecia. Not surprisingly, the next room was an upgrade, was bigger, had a balcony, and was pretty much pube free.

As usual, we covered the town by foot, starting off at a local cafe called the Mandarin, locally famous for a free Hue walking guide that they make available to customers. We were now well and truly hooked on the local coffee (served with condensed milk) so didn't need any excuse to stop. Our walk started at the Imperial City, home of the Nguyen dynasty which had been severely damaged by the war but still fabulous to see. From there we strolled through the old town before ending up in a fantastic riverside market. It was a real overload to the senses and great to see. By the time we'd finished walking the length of the market, we were tired and not looking forward to the long walk back around the waterfront. Along the river, at the rear of the market sat a few enterprising old ladies who had the tiniest of wooden canoes. They would ferry passengers across the wide river, to the centre of town where our hotel was waiting for us.

They saw us approach and had a little conflab to set pricing before we arrived, then the battle commenced. With great skill on both sides, plenty of laughter and gamesmanship, the prolonged negotiations ended with an agreeable price for all (about $1 each). I certainly didn't want to pay a lot as there was at best, a 50/50 chance of us making it across alive. Suddenly, an old tune[1] popped into my head and I came up with the idea that we would pay them on the other side. It was a highly memorable trip, and you know what they say, any ferry ride you walk away from (still dry) is a good one, which it was.

Hue is quite a foodie town, so our tour took in some local delicacies such as the famous Hue pancakes (Banh khoai) and of course, more coffee. Our progressive menu through town did get a bit out of hand when at one cafe we realised we'd ran out of cash. Nic had to leave me as a deposit while she found an ATM. The female waitresses were very kind to me while I waited, but I'm sure they were drawing short straws to work out who would have to take me home if Nic never came back. Our interactions with the locals in Hue was a mixed bag, ranging from college girls who wanted to practice their English, to various people trying to sell us drugs, or trying to con us. One optimistic scammer approached us as we were about to cross over the bridge to the market, informing us that the bridge was closed to pedestrians and we should follow him. Even as he was saying it, I was looking over his shoulder, watching pedestrian after pedestrian crossing the bridge. I'm not quite sure what would have happened if we

---

[1] *The 80's Chris de Burgh classic of course*

were more gullible, he'd probably just send us to his mates tourist shop for a hard sell. If it was any kind of plan to sell us to the black market, I figure he knew he'd only make small change.

Our exit out of town wasn't very salubrious either as it looked like our transport had been subcontracted to one of the dodgy bus outfits that we were trying to avoid. Our overnight journey was in a very grubby bus used by locals more than tourists. Once the official passengers were onboard, the driver circled around town for a bit to try to pick up anyone else he could before heading off. Needless to say, we didn't get much sleep.

Thankfully the journey took a few hours longer than billed (surprise surprise). I say thankfully as we should have arrived in the middle of the night, but it was just after daylight when the driver decided to drop everyone off in an outer suburb of Hanoi, rather than drive into the city. By coincidence, the same location that all of is mates were hanging out. 'What did his mates do?', I hear you ask, well they were taxi drivers of course.

We had to use our ninja skills to ensure none of them grabbed our backpacks from the bus, and we started to nudge our way through the usual throng. We made the mistake of trying to convince one guy that they weren't needed as we'd arranged onward transport to Sapa. Another driver overheard this, appearing in front of us to try and convince us that he was here to pick us up for Sapa. It was a shame there were no NFL scouts around to see us plough through the crowd, dispersing the persistent touts. We emerging at the other side, free but with no idea where we were.

Time to whip out the trusty blue dot. With a certain amount of distrust whilst in Vietnam, I'd pre-populated the route on my phone. Between this and a paper map, we were able to walk through a local market area and narrow side streets to find a train station a few kilometres away. This was where the hotel transport was supposed to have picked us up from. By now, hours later, they were unlikely to still be around but to make sure, we circled the station and walked through it twice with no sign of anyone looking for two small sweaty tourists. Again, our preparedness served us well as we had a list provided by Lonely Planet of the more trustworthy taxi companies to use. We found a very helpful lady cab driver who took us directly (as proven by the blue dot) to our hotel. I say hotel but we weren't actually going to be staying here, we were instead booked on a night train to Sapa, a highland area north-west of Hanoi near the border with China.

Phuong had arranged a room for us at one of her company's hotels so that we could shower and freshen up before our journey. It was also where we would once again hand over our passports to a complete stranger, they would hopefully be whisked off to have our Chinese visas inserted. If the process wasn't stressful enough, we received a phone call from Phuong just afterwards, saying that it was going to cost another $20, as though our passports were being held for ransom.

That night we were ferried to the train station. Our sleeper train was a cool, old-school, carriage with wooden bunks. We chose the top bunks in a four berth cabin and were joined by two local tour guides who were on the train to escort a group of American teenagers. Huang, one of the guides was particularly talkative, he even disappeared at one point, returning with beers for us all. We talked into the early hours about his life in Vietnam and ours in Australia. A really lovely experience.

They eat dog here don't they?

Sapa is a quaint little town surrounded by lush hills and valleys. Once again, the room provided by Phuong was perfect. For this location she had also arranged a guide for our two days here, taking us trekking through the nearby rice fields to meet the local Hmong people in their villages. Actually, it was the Hmong that came to meet us in a well-rehearsed routine. They knew the guide, all about the tour, and where we would all meet up. As we walked down to the town's main square, we saw a group of women dressed in their traditional black and bright coloured dresses. I was wondering why these people were staring at us walking down the street, you could see them pointing and whispering to each other. We met our guide in the square and headed off on our walk with no mention of our observers. As we left, they all stood up and moved off with us.

After a while, they started to make conversation, and it became clear they were the female residents of the villages we were heading too. They mostly looked after us, asking if we wanted anything carrying or pointing out any hazardous steps. Each seemed to target a visitor and names were exchanged, it now seemed clear that as we were walking down the road earlier, they were choosing their companions for the day.

My internal dialogue now believing that I was obviously high on the list, my companion probably had to wash down an ox for the privilege of selecting me. As always, I was dubious of our new friends and was waiting for the hard sell, maybe a timeshare in a mud and stone hut with a private well. This scepticism softened when I noticed that one of the women had a sling with a tiny baby on her back. The little tike was so cute, even I found it impossible not to shake his little hand, at which point he grabbed on and wouldn't let go. We walked at least a kilometre with his eyes fixed on me and with a grip of steel. My thoughts that we were obviously kindred spirits were squashed by Nic, explaining that it was just an instinctive muscle reflex by my little buddy. Both days of trekking saw some magnificent scenery in the beautiful countryside and rice plateaus. It was also a fair bit of exercise too.

It looked at times to be a well-trodden route, some villages even touting gifts on stalls as we passed. However, we were quickly reminded that these were still working villages when our passage up a steep path was interrupted as a horn the size of my arm suddenly appeared through someone's hanging washing. This was quickly followed by the rest of a huge grey ox. I hadn't seen any documentation on the Sapa Highway Code but decided to give our fellow traveller the right of way. He was obviously thankful, just as we'd give a quick flash of headlights back home, he gave a quick flick of his tail, sending a few little presents our way.

Our second day ended with a meal in our newfound friend's village. As we finished our food, the women finally showed their flair for sales by presenting each cohort with a range of scarfs and purses, made with a similar pattern to their clothes. Even after spending two days with us and giving us an insight into their lives, this wasn't really a hard sell. We bought a bit more than we had room for and I bid farewell to my little kindred spirit. A magical experience. The rest of our time in Sapa was spent exploring the town and its market, which we were warned would sell dog meat. Thankfully, we didn't see anything but still migrated towards vegetarian dishes when eating out.

Halong to the Bay?

The hot overnight train back to Hanoi was a sleepless affair, and our mood wasn't improved when the promise of a pickup didn't eventuate. After a taxi ride back to the same hotel where we'd changed before Sapa, we were welcomed with no knowledge about who we were. This made us a little anxious, as the last time we were here we handed over our passports. After some discussion and a phone call to Phuong, a gentleman appeared apologising profusely for not picking us up. More importantly, he presented us with our passports that now contained, hopefully legit, Chinese visas. We were happy with this, just greasing a few palms had meant that we didn't need to face another stuck up official in the local Chinese consulate (more on that later). No rest for the wicked, once again we weren't actually staying in this hotel, instead were being whisked four hours away to embark on yet another of our bucket list items for the year. An overnight cruise through Halong Bay.

It would turn out to be a bittersweet day. Unfortunately, during the minibus journey, we were reminded of why it was wise to be hesitant about riding mopeds in Vietnam. At a traffic junction in a small town, a blanket being held up between two locals failed to hide the carnage of a fatal accident that must have only recently happened. It was a sight that hits you with so many feelings, it's something that will never be forgotten.

If you've not heard of Halong Bay, I'm sure you will recognise pictures of it, a beautiful landscape of calm waters, filled with protruding limestone karsts. Our tour actually included staying overnight out on the water in a beautiful old junk. We were served lovely food while cruising through this magnificent region and even had a chance to kayak in one of its bays. It was a much more opulent affair than we were expecting for the money we'd paid Phuong. There was a really friendly vibe amongst the small group of guests onboard. The warm evening air and tranquil surroundings were beautiful and made for a sombre mood, reflecting on the day's events.

Thank Phuong for that

This was the last part of the tour we'd arranged with Phuong back in Ho Chi Minh, and she was true to her word. Not everything worked out smoothly, sometimes we'd have bus tickets waiting for us and sometimes not, sometimes a pickup, sometimes not, some buses were lovely while others were terrible. It was a roller coaster of emotions as we waited for it all to fall into a heap. The hotels were all great, the tours were fantastic, and for $350 each, we had the most amazing 18 days. Sorry for doubting you Phuong, we still want to take you home with us.

Thong Song for Nic's original Havaianas

It's been a while since you've had a thong update. I hadn't really connected with my last pair bought at the coach station, despite the fact they had now taken me through three countries. I fancied a change. Nic on the other hand, was on a mission to make her precious original (not stolen) Havaianas last for the whole duration of South East Asia. They'd actually broken sometime before, and the centre strap would frequently pop out as she was crossing busy roads or generally trying to avoid a life-threatening situation. However, she was determined to make them last. In a city where dodging mopeds is a constant, I had to put my rubber soled foot down. After all we'd reached Hanoi, our last stop in South East Asia. For $4 each, I secured a great deal on designer thongs from a small laneway store. It shows how much I know about fashion though, as I would have spelt Aberconnbie & Fiche much differently.

Also on the thong front was one of Vietnam's funniest experiences. One of the many things that tourists get enthusiastically offered in South East Asia is a streetside shoe shine. Travelling in thongs has meant that this has been the one thing we've been exempt from. Salesmen would generally take one look at us and move on to an unsuspecting American in brogues. Now, picture the two of us having a nice picnic on a bench in a lovely central Saigon park. We'd just been chatting with a local man who we initially thought was going to try and sell us something, it turned out he just wanted to chat. Because of this, we felt a bit guilty about our attitude and our guard was down.

A few minutes later a young guy turned up with a shoe shine kit and looked down at our feet. He made a *harumph* sound, and a submissive roll of the eyes indicated that there was no business to be had. Instead, he sat down next to us for a chat. We felt quite relaxed and fielded the usual questions 'Australia', 'yes kangaroos not mountains' (Austria vs Australia often confused), 'Melbourne'. All of a sudden, I turned towards him to see a toothbrush topped with a white liquid heading towards my left, thong-clad, foot. I quickly moved it two inches sideways, he froze, looked at me, before performing another quick lunge, I was too fast for him with a three inch move backwards. 'It's dirty!', he proclaimed, 'Yes and they will be again after 5 steps in this city! Step away from the thongs mister!'. After trying his best salesmanship lines he finally smiled and gave up, he stayed and chatted a little while longer before moving off. In my book that surely classes as a ten out of ten for effort.

Penalty, Goal !!!

Most of our visa applications and border crossings had gone smoothly, mainly thanks to Nic's planning and hard work preparing forms and relevant information. This skill was, in fact, one of the three reasons I'd married her. In most visa queues, Nic would be helping the people around her who'd come unprepared or didn't know what to do. That being said, we almost had a small diplomatic incident in Phnom Penh's Chinese Embassy when all of Nic's hard work was just dismissed with a wave of a hand. The snotty, embassy official couldn't be bothered processing the application because we were visiting another country before China. The process is not trivial and involved completed forms, full confirmed travel itinerary, letter of invitation, passport photos, and money, all of which we had. I'd be lying if I said I was a model of restraint, Nic extracted me from the embassy before things escalated.

After that experience, we'd decided to get Phuong to help us. We just needed to give her double the standard fee, and our passports. Nothing else, no invitations, no details, nothing. Three days later our passports were returned with all the relevant visas inside, no questions asked. Just goes to show that money certainly does grease the wheels of the visa industry. Anyway, I digress.

In Cambodia we wanted to sort our Vietnam visa in advance, leaving us more time to worry about the Chinese one. We arranged it through our fantastic guesthouse in Siem Reap. What often happens, is that you have 3 months to use the visa, it's activated when you cross the border and is valid for 30 days. Not this one, this was valid from the day it was processed. We didn't realise until a few days after our passports were returned, the last day of our Vietnamese visa was the 21st April, the day before our flight from Hanoi to Hong Kong.

We asked a few people about this and did a bit of googling. All our information pointed to the fact that we should be okay. We'd probably get a stern look, and at worst case a US$5 fine, especially as the discrepancy was less than 24 hours. Even with this information, I think Nic had been dwelling on it over the following few weeks and it had been building up in her mind until the day of our flight.

Although we loved Vietnam much more than we were expecting, we were getting a little exhausted of the scams. Especially in Hanoi, we were overcharged, shortchanged, and messed around, more than anywhere so far. Unfortunately, this didn't stop at the airport. We arrived with three hours to spare so that we would be first in the queue and we waited, the check-in desk didn't open. It wasn't until just one hour before this international flight that the staff opened the counter. This wasn't helping Nic's frame of mind at all. As soon as it opened, we were straight up to the desk, thinking that we'd fly through check-in and then explain our visa situation when we reached immigration.

'I can't check you in, your visa has expired. You need to go to immigration and come back once it's sorted. Make sure you let me know the name of the immigration officer', was our welcome. This last sentence started to set off my scam spider-sense. Just as we walk away, he shouts after us, 'Oh, and I'm closing this desk in 20 minutes'. We run over to the immigration office to find it empty, Nic starts to fidget and sweat a bit, a tell of increasing uneasiness that in my previous experience needs addressing quick sharp. A cleaner sees that we are anxious and disappears behind a door, pops back and gives us a 5 minutes sign. That might just work. Eight minutes later, someone appears.

Wearing a full military uniform, at least one gun, and a grumpy face, he asks for our passports. We explain our predicament as we pass them over and he spends what seems like an hour looking at them. 'Visa expired, you pay penalty', was all he said. I ask how much and after another pause, during which, he looked us both up and down, 'one hundred dollars'. Now it is only five minutes before the gate closes and by this time, my normally worldly wise, experienced, calm, travel partner's nerves have just jumped over a cliff like a lemming. While I'm trying to take a moment to think about how to handle the situation, I hear the following from my right-hand side, 'Each?'. A pause, a little think, a smile and the reply, 'Yes'. Before I can even begin to process this extra information, she's at it again, 'Is there an ATM around here?', 'Lee, show him how much money you have in your pocket!', 'Do you take MasterCard?'.

I was only seconds away from being sold into the sex trade. It was time to say something. Now, the one thing I wasn't expecting to say was, 'No!'. This made Nic stop talking for a moment, giving me chance to get the rest of my words out. 'This fine is US$5, US$10 maximum, everyone knows it. We have asked and know this information. I have US$5 each if you want it. I have no more money'. Poker face.

The sweat was dripping from our brows as the armed policeman debated our refusal to give him a bribe. I was convinced that with his melodic glances up and down, shifting his gaze between our eyes, and the passports he held in his hands, he was mentally pulling leaves from a daisy and reciting 'let them go', pluck, 'lock them up', pluck, 'let them go'. Our only crime was an invalid visa, after all, we were not drug runners or anything serious, but I had just refused point blank to give him a US$200 bribe. I've seen those TV shows where innocent people get banged up abroad. How many petals do daisies have in Vietnam anyway? I don't know about you, but I am also getting a strange deja vu feeling.

He looked down again for a final time, flicking through the passports for what seemed like a lifetime. Expecting a trip to the Hanoi Hilton, he looked up, gave us our passports back and waved us on. No charge.

We check in and pass through immigration, but only after three officials eventually agree that I'm the same person on my passport photo, just with longer hair. We reach the departure lounge where Nic's emotions reach a climax, and a small five-minute meltdown is needed to sort everything out. Once complete, I had my travel buddy back again (she readily admits this was not her finest moment). Deciding she needed some chocolate therapy, I pop into a departure lounge shop where the assistant tries to charge me double the price for a Snickers bar. Get me out of this country!

CHAPTER 7

Location: Hong Kong
Days 121, Countries 10, Kilometers 19,274, Beds 63
Trains 4, Planes 11, Automobiles 28, Boats 8
Beers 37

A load off in Honkers

You can probably sense that although still enjoying ourselves, we were getting a little fatigued travelling through South East Asia. Nic had just calmed down after her mini breakdown, we'd just eaten the 'rip off' chocolate and were heading to one of the most densely populated cities in the world. Did we really want to do this?

Something strange and unexpected happened as we landed at Hong Kong's International Airport, located on Chek Lap Kok island. As soon as we disembarked we felt different, somehow more relaxed. We realised that this wasn't the South East Asia we'd become accustomed to. Yes it was busy, but it was organised, much less chaotic, even downright pleasant. We moved via disciplined queues through immigration, quickly finding our bus into town, which even had free WiFi. The abundance of English signage probably helped our disposition a little. This was just what we needed.

By the time we reached downtown Kowloon, it was about half past midnight, and we meandered our way between high rise blocks, trying to find our accommodation. Once found, we were greeted with a sign on the door saying 'out to lunch'. We looked at each other, and our watches, to confirm that yes, it was the early hours of the morning. Unsure if the note was recent or not, our man suddenly turned up, apologetically wiping the food from his face as he let us in. Our room was tiny, even for us, and despite travelling light we struggled to find space for the bags in the room. Thankfully, we were only here for one night, but you could sense that this was the reality for many in this highly populated city. In our new relaxed state, we slept really well before checking out to move to nicer accommodation.

The Hop Inn couldn't fit us in for the first night, but the reviews looked so good that we didn't mind moving. We arrived and because of its popularity, couldn't check in early, but that was okay. We had a mission to complete and needed to head a few miles north to find the Monkey Shrine office to pick up our Trans-Mongolian tickets. Monkey Shrine was a travel agency that specialised in organising semi-independent travel on the classic rail journeys across Russia. The company was our top choice after a lengthy vetting process (and spreadsheet). Once we returned back to the Hop Inn, we were able to chill in their hipster lounge and rooftop terrace with free WiFi. A excellent opportunity to regroup and touch base with our life back home.

The rooms were on the smaller side but still much more spacious than that of the previous night, they were also quite funky and unique. In fact, we were joined in our room by a statue of giraffe's head (we called it Greg), it's neck protruding down from the ceiling, stopping a little above head height. We loved this place. Once settled in, we went for a 'stroll around the area', which turned into a MountyDay that took us through Kowloon, to the harbour front, then onto one of the iconic ferries to Hong Kong island. From there, we walked up to the base of the Peak and took the funicular (with about 2 million other people) to the top. It's a perfect spot to watch the city's nightly skyscraper light show. A subway took us back to Kowloon where we found a wondrous Peking Duck restaurant (more on that later) before bed. A good day.

The next day we took a ferry to Lantau Island for a day filled with giant Buddha's and a fantastic cable car ride. Back in town, we hit the laneways of Hong Kong island, which included a trip on one of their comically tall trams. This was now turning into a fabulous mid-RTW city break, and we were in our element. The date was the 25th April (Anzac day), so we tracked down the city's war memorial to pay our respects and chatted with the only other person around, who was Australian of course. Next, a walk through a market proved to be exactly as you'd expect from Hong Kong. Stalls full of colour, curious smells, and some sights that were just plain wrong (turtles for sale in plastic bags hanging from a wall). As we returned home to regale our adventures with Greg, we started to realise that soon our epic train journey would begin and both started feeling a little nervous. Greg was neither use nor ornament. Well okay, he was actually the latter.

Honk if we can list Hong Kong as a Country

My cunning plan to get Bali recognised as a separate country, understandingly, died on its arse. I did find out later that my own sister voted against me numerous times in the poll. Yet I'm feeling a little more confident about the latest conundrum. Do we count Hong Kong as a separate country? The arguments for:

- It only became an administrative region of China in 1997.
- Its constitutional document stipulates a 'high degree of autonomy'.
- Hong Kong has a different political system from mainland China.

- The Travellers Century Club (a pompous American club for people who have visited more than 100 countries) list it separately.
- It has its own currency.
- They have their own Olympic team.
- Its primary language is still listed as English.
- We didn't need a visa for Hong Kong but do for China.
- As far as Chinese immigration is concerned, if you travel from mainland China to Hong Kong, then you are leaving China.

The arguments against:

- It's not a separate country.

We loved this city and hanging around in the ex-pat bars of Hong Kong island certainly made us think that we'd like to live there. Despite being action-packed, we felt rejuvenated and ready for the next adventure. From Hong Kong, we would start our epic journey all the way to Helsinki by rail. The first leg of which was a high speed train from Hong Kong to Shanghai. The train had been pre-booked through our Monkey Shrine package, and they spoilt us with a private sleeper cabin which meant our own toilet and shower. The train looked new and was full of friendly staff. This was great, but in the back of our minds, we were conscious that we really shouldn't get used to it. Once the train arrived in our next country (see what I did there), it was just a two-mile walk on a lovely day to our hotel.

Chinese Oxymorons

We weren't sure how we would find China. 'With a map' you cry, but you know that's not what I meant. We'd heard stories from people that had loved it, and others who hated it. It was a polarising country and just like Bangkok, we initially saw it as a necessary evil. We needed to travel there to board the

Trans-Mongolian. Hong Kong had been a bit of a taster, but probably wasn't an accurate indication of mainland China. Right from the start we enjoyed Shanghai. A well-chosen heritage hotel in the historic Bund area certainly helped. Although called a penthouse, it was an attic room that looked across at both the historical and modern sides of the river. The preconceptions we had about China were destroyed both here, and later in Beijing. There were fewer people, less traffic, less smog, everything was clean, and the language barrier was not a big problem in these popular cities.

For our first night in Shanghai, we decided to eat in a cafe local to the hotel as we were quite tired. This was our first mistake. The place looked nice and was cheap, but an understanding of the English language was about as rare as a familiar cut of meat. It was a case of taking a staff member outside and pointing to a picture of a dish on a poster. Unfortunately, the nicest looking picture turned out to be some kind of animals knuckle. On the plus side, it proved good value as we were there for hours in a private treasure hunt for edible meat, eventually being defeated by the fat and gristle.

There were a few cultural differences in China that we were prepared for, but not always tolerant of. It struck me that a raft of common phrases suddenly became oxymorons here:

- Personal space
- Chinese whispers
- Customer service
- Good manners

I understand that other cultures can be very different than ours. The trip has taught me to accept and embrace these idiosyncrasies, but I still struggle when it comes down to what we deem to be basic manners and courtesy. Politeness, especially when queuing, certainly seems to be a sign of weakness here.

Never more than a concept in my head, I plotted sweet revenge by becoming a disgusting individual and blaming it on our cultural differences. For example:

- Farting in a lift is a sign of appreciation for its excellent engineering.
- The nostril game of 'Pick it, roll it, flick it, GOAL!', has been passed down for centuries from elders looking to hone our hunting skills. 'Oh, I hit you did I? Well that is a sign of good luck. It's okay, no need to thank me'.
- Giving a random old person a wedgy is a way of lifting their burdens and lightening their load.
- Spitting in the street randomly without warning or directional skill… Bugger, they already owned that one.

Booty Call

Our hotel had a cosy English stately home feel about it and we were disappointed to only have two nights here. The building included a local institution called The Peacock Room that, when added in 1911, housed the city's first ever ballroom. For each night of our stay, the room was kitted out for an elaborate wedding, but by morning it was returned to normal, ready for breakfast.

During our second night there, the hotel was very busy with two wedding parties and lots of elegantly dressed people milling around. We were upstairs in our penthouse at around 11:30pm, when there was a knock at the door. We knew it would probably be a mistake so ignored the first knock, but it came again. I looked through the door's peephole to see a pretty girl, all dressed up. Assuming she was one of the wedding guests, a little lost after a few celebratory champagnes, I opened the door (on its chain). Hopefully, just the sight of a scruffy westerner with disobedient hair would immediately make her realise the error of her ways. She looked at me, looked down at her phone, looked at me, and said, 'Hello'. The words 'these are not the droids you are looking for' nearly came from my lips as she just stood there, waiting for an invite inside.

I started processing the facts before me. Pretty girl, first meeting, in a hotel, and arranged by phone. It suddenly dawned on me what was occurring. While she stood there quietly, I was working out how to tell her that I was Nicki's Lee and not her John. I went bright red while explaining that she definitely had the wrong room, making funny hand gesticulations to indicate my wife was around the corner. She looked at her phone again, looked at me and said, 'Hello' again. I replied 'Sorry, wrong room' and closed the door slowly. I spied through the peephole again, trying to find out what room she was supposed to be at and am sure I saw a little look of disappointment on her face (yep, still got it). At least we didn't have to worry about keeping the neighbours up.

We woke early and were presented with a beautiful morning to stroll along the waterfront before it got too busy. Many years ago, someone had told me that the Shanghai waterfront was influenced by Liverpool's historic architecture along the banks of the Mersey, a waterfront that included the famous Liver building. Being brought up in Merseyside, I was excited to compare the two and wasn't disappointed. The Bund was indeed lovely, the buildings were magnificent and architecturally diverse. Large groups of people wearing white silk outfits were performing Tai Chi together before work. They were so synchronised and precise with their movements, it looked like a ballet. My imagination matched this against the equivalent back in Liverpool, where the silk outfits were replaced with Adidas shell suits, and the gentle ballet movements were part of an effort to separate a tourist from his wallet.

A little further along were a number of older gentlemen flying kites, ranging in size from large to enormous. One squidgy old guy even encouraged Nic to help him launch his craft into the sky. Both of these waterfront activities seemed to generate such a relaxing environment in this busy, bustling city. The Bund's western-influenced buildings were mostly built around the turn of the 20th century and feature architectural styles that included Neoclassical, Beaux-Arts, Art Deco, and Baroque. We even explored inside some of the buildings, including a perfectly placed rooftop bar. The Bund was such a contradiction to the opposite side of the Huangpu River which is full of glass covered shiny skyscrapers, covered in bright lights, and dominated by the iconic Oriental Pearl TV tower. We had to break up the sightseeing duties and head to the shopping district, looking for warm clothes and supplies, in preparation for Mongolia and Russia.

A new day brought the need to move again. We skilfully navigated the metro to the newly constructed, Hongqiao railway station, where we boarded a bullet train to Beijing. No cabin this time, we sat watching the digital display showing we were travelling at over 300Km/hr, meaning the journey only took five hours. Once we arrived, the Beijing metro was much busier and more complicated to fathom, but we coped well, and our cleverly chosen hotel was immediately outside one of the main stations. Before arriving, I was convinced that between the complicated metro systems of Shanghai and Beijing we would quickly become lost, travelling around these underground worlds for years, a bit like Tom Hanks in the movie *Terminal*. Once again China had surprised us.

One Up, One Down

With the upcoming Trans-Mongolian journey on our minds, we decided to treat ourselves to a comfy hotel before we set rail (that's my train version of the nautical saying. I think it might catch on). Our theory was that it would make up for the potentially arduous 21-day experience ahead. As well as being close to the metro station, our Novotel was also located nearby the Beijing Main Railway station. Our departure point for the adventure.

When booking, we took the usual steps in trying to secure a decent room. This included joining their loyalty program and adding comments in the online form. This clearly had no effect as during check-in we were informed we'd have to move rooms halfway through the stay. Something we really didn't want to do. My first reaction was to rely on my years of English upbringing by letting out a big sigh, making sure everyone knew I wasn't happy. I started to step away from the counter, defeated, but then something came over me and I actually put my foot down. The words 'This isn't good enough' appeared from my mouth, I'm not quite sure who was more surprised. Maybe my time skimming through self-help books in the library was beginning to pay off. I explained, still quite politely of course, that we'd paid for an expensive room, were longtime members of their loyalty program (less than a day, but who's counting), and were just about to be sent to Siberia for God's sake.

Things went quiet for a moment. Then, with a smile, we were handed a key to one of their two-storey club rooms on the top floor. We headed to the elevators at speed before they changed their minds. On entering the suite, you could tell that it was originally two rooms, one above the other, that had been joined together with a spiral staircase, giving us a bath each. This would do just nicely.

Flipping forbidden! Our flopped attempt to see Chairman Mao

The hotel was well placed to visit a few local tourist spots and only a block away from Tiananmen Square. We spent a hot and sweaty day exploring this and the nearby Forbidden Temple before climbing up to the peak of Jingshan Park which gave great views over the two. We weren't well researched here and just winging it, so hadn't realised that the area also contained the mausoleum of Chairman Mao. In Vietnam, we'd popped in to see Ho Chi Min, and were planning to hang out with Lenin in Moscow, so it only seemed fitting to pay our respects. The queue wasn't too long and was moving quickly, so after about five minutes we were just about to enter when we heard a commotion behind. I looked around to find two security guards shouting loudly in Chinese. It wasn't long before I realised that it was me they were shouting at.

I hadn't the foggiest what was going on and had thoughts that maybe my visa was invalid and China now had a dedicated team, scouring Beijing by CCTV to pick me up. My imagination even stretched as far as picturing a new 'tank vs person' incident in Tiananmen Square, but this time it was me in front of the Type 59-IIA tank. Looking down the barrel, in my shorts and thongs with Lonely Planet map in my hand. As I was being bundled out of the queue, it became clear that it was my thongs that were the problem. I just didn't meet the dress code to see Mr Min. I was in too much shock to try and argue that the man himself might have donned the odd sandal back in his day (I would, of course, have had to learn Chinese very quickly to be able to do this as well). It's not often that NOT seeing a dead guy puts a downer on your day.

What goes up must hurt coming down

Although not really keen on organised trips, we were feeling guilty about not properly touring the area, especially to see the Great Wall of China. We decided to take the easy option and arranged a trip through the hotel.

After a pleasant bus ride to the wall, we were dropped off at the base of a middle section, not realising that there would be a substantial set of steps just to get onto the wall itself. Despite being the svelte, athletic types that we are (snigger), we decided to pay extra to take a cable car from ground level to the wall's walkway. Once up, we had a choice of which direction to take along the wall, so headed off towards a hilly section that had less tourists. It was quite surreal being there, one of those places that's so iconic, you know so well, despite never having been there. I have to say that I found it a little underwhelming. I don't mean to sound dismissive, and you should know by now that I'm not one of those tourists who put a negative spin on everything they see (more on those later in the book). The wall really is a fantastic achievement of engineering and ingenuity. Looking back at my photos, they are some of the most impressive nostril shots from the whole trip, but while I was there I just felt 'yep, I'm on a big wall'.

Anyway, we dropped down in elevation for a bit and then started to climb, and climb, and yep you guessed it, climb some more. Vertigo, my long forgotten friend, made an appearance as some sections were very steep without handrails. We spotted one of the main wall turrets at the top of a hill stretching off in the distance, and the more we walked, the more we wanted to reach it. We only had three hours on the wall and time was quickly disappearing. I had no doubts that our driver wouldn't think twice about heading off, leaving anyone that was more than five minutes late back to the coach.

The gauntlet had been set. We looked pale and sweaty, not a great representation of either of our home countries so pretended to be a more believable Scottish. About twenty minutes away from our goal, we noticed someone from our coach bounding towards us from the other direction. He was checking his watch and looking nervous. As he passed he made comment that we needed to be careful of time, before adding that it's much more painful going down and will take longer.

After pondering on this for a split second, I came to the conclusion that this guy was mad. We were in agony and close to cardiac arrest going up, the only thing helping was the thought of the easy jaunt down, smiling, maybe skipping with the wind in our hair. Going down is harder, my arse (ironically I actually did have to go down a bit on my arse due to the vertigo). I feigned concern, ignoring his comments to carry on with the mission.

We finally reached our goal to find a group of locals running a small tuck shop, feeding the unfit tourists, chocolate bars and cola. There was a large picture perfect Chinese flag waving in the corner of the turret, but there was a charge to take a photo of it. We did what two-thirds of all tourists do and took a sneaky picture while facing the other direction. From here, it was a fantastic view down the wall, and you did get the feeling of what an impressive structure it was. We could see for miles, we could even see our coach looking like a small dot in the distance. 'Nic, what time is it?'. Bollocks.

The journey down was interesting. The heavy vibrations of our footsteps made my man-boobs ache so much that the use of my bum to get down steep bits was a nice respite, although not my coolest look. I looked like a dog who'd just found out how to wipe its arse on the carpet for that clean, post ablution feeling. Unfortunately, there was something in what our fellow traveller had said. That's as far as I'll go without admitting he was right. We made it back with about five minutes to spare with red faces and burning thighs. All in all though, a fantastic experience. We slept the entire journey back to the hotel.

Getting our Ducks in a Row

One of our favourite foods in the whole world is Peking Duck. We love it, although the thought of how that might relate to travelling through China hadn't really occurred to us. It was only after we'd landed in Hong Kong that it dawned on us, of course we should try our favourite meal in its own country. This then started a mission to search out the best Peking Duck we could, starting back in Honkers. The internet is a wondrous thing, and we found great reviews for a Hong Kong restaurant, hidden upstairs above a shop near to where we were staying.

It wasn't the most inviting of places, but we were fresh from our escape from Vietnam and feeling brave. Surprisingly for Hong Kong, little English was spoken but there was an English menu. Back home, we were used to Peking Duck portions being quite small, so we also ordered some sweet and sour pork as a starter.

That dish alone was large enough to fill any mere mortal. As we finished the first course, a large man in a chefs outfit pushed a table on wheels to a nearby spot and flamboyantly removed the cover off what was the biggest duck we have ever seen. He then took to it with a massive knife in what was becoming more like dinner theatre.

I felt bad that he didn't get the standing ovation he deserved when he finished, leaving our duck finely sliced and divided up on our own individual plates. This pleased me greatly as I really don't like feeling hard done by about getting my fair share of the duck. I can get quite territorial, which tends to take away the romance in a meal. Each serve was probably bigger than any complete duck portion we'd ever had before and to top it off the pancakes were much thicker than we were used to. We were going to be here for the duration, but were determined not to be beaten. Not only because the thought of leaving duck horrified us, but also that this meal cost much more than we should be spending. Sure enough, by the time we reached for the last pancake, the restaurant was empty and the staff were starting to sweep up around us. Now it felt like we should have received the standing ovation.

It's funny how you trick your mind into justifying expenses, now we had a mission the budget was out of the window. Our research showed that there were two notable locations in Shanghai that we should try. After our knuckle experience on the first night, we chose to 'large it up' at the Hyatt, especially as it was within walking distance from the hotel. We scrubbed up the best we could but still felt a bit out of place, especially as we made one bottle of water last the evening to help with the bill.

Back to Beijing, we had two great duck experiences here that were entirely different. Both in shopping centres but at different ends of the price range. The first was an everyday sort of place. The only staff member with a smidgen of English was assigned to us and looked very nervous about it. The evening almost ended prematurely as Nic threatened to storm out of the restaurant when we discovered that there was turtle soup on the menu. This was compounded by a picture of the dish, showing a little tiny turtle floating in a bowl as though getting a luxury spa treatment. Peking Duck however, is a powerful thing and it had taken us two attempts to actually find the restaurant. Overall, it turned out to be a good effort, probably equalling the Hyatt.

On the last day before our epic train trip started, we decided we should treat ourselves (yep, doesn't take much does it) and travelled to an upmarket shopping centre to find its famous duck restaurant. Here, we really did feel out of place, and were immediately concerned about what we'd just gotten our limited finances into. It was as though Heston Blumenthal had opened a Chinese restaurant. This time, the duck chopper-upper had a plastic face mask that he could lift up and down as though he was about to spot weld our duck to something. His knife was longer, and he spent much more time slicing the duck to produce the smallest most intricately displayed portions. It was presented as a piece of art in what could have been a scene from *A Clockwork Orange*. As well as the duck, we were supplied with a stream of other smaller dishes that we didn't think we'd ordered, cumulating in an extravagant strawberry based dessert.

We had no idea if this food was included or what the bill was going to be. Our concerns about the price would come in waves between each course and quickly forgotten while we were eating. To our relief, it wasn't too bad. I wished I'd known during the meal so that we weren't trying to work out the fastest route to the door and identifying who the slower staff might be. I suppose if it came down to it, I only had to be quicker than Nic.

So I know what you are asking yourselves, with all these restaurants to compare 'Who won?'. Well, we did of course.

Bribing the Prison Guards

It was fast approaching the part of the trip we were equally the most excited, and most anxious about. The Trans-Mongolian.

We'd researched this quite a lot and had an idea of what to expect, but it still didn't seem to help our anxiety. Our last minute shopping list for essentials like plastic mugs for soup and some thermal underwear had been ticked off. We'd completed a dummy run to the station to check timing and make sure not to miss the most expensive train ride we'd ever booked. That would have been a great result wouldn't it, over twelve months in the planning, copious amounts of dollars handed over, numerous visa applications, to then oversleep and miss it.

We checked out from the comfort of our duplex, saddled up the backpacks and walked to the station. As with most of these anxious moments in your life, it was all pretty straight forward really. Once there, it was clear we needed to congregate in an old departure hall where we would wait for news of the train's arrival. Once the platform was confirmed, we took a deep breath and headed off to find our carriage, not knowing what level of comfort or company we were about to get ourselves into.

The carriage wasn't as old as we had expected but wasn't new by any means. Our first obstacle was getting past the two provodnista who stood either side of the door. During our research, we'd heard much about these fabled staffers, but had associated them more with the Russian part of the journey. The stereotypical image of a provodnista is a female wrestler, in uniform, who had bought a job-lot of makeup in the post-Cold War era that she's trying to get through by applying it in a volume not frequently seen. Their hairstyles are something to behold and are highly secured down, allowing for absolutely no movement whatsoever (even when they put their head out of a moving window). The provodnista (or male, provodnik) run the carriage, what they say is law, they will decide for you if the window will be up or down, if your compartment will be locked, and when you are allowed into the toilets.

Apart from being Chinese, our first two were just what you'd expect from a provodnista. They took our tickets, examining them in great detail before parting slightly to clear a path for our entry into the carriage.

We had many options available when booking this epic journey. They varied from a private cabin in the very expensive Golden Eagle service (think Orient Express), all the way down to a 3rd class seat. The choice had been an internal battle for some time. Our default approach would usually be to choose a private room so that we can hide away, but venture out when we felt safe. This didn't seem to fit the spirit of the trip, and we actually did have some serious conversations about a 3rd class adventure. We eventually met in the middle and chose to have two berths in a four berth compartment so that we had a bit of a protective boundary but were forced to meet people.

The cabin had two larger bottom bunks that doubled up as a seat during the day, and two fold down smaller top bunks. A table attached just under the window came almost halfway across the room. As we'd booked the trip months in advance, we'd secured the two large bottom bunks which also had the benefit of having storage underneath them, where we secured our bags.

I needed to ensure we had enough photographs, so politely asked a provodnista if I could get back off the train and take some pictures. I took the slight gesticulation of her head (no smile) to mean that my request was approved and took the obligatory pics of the train. I then decided to push my luck and asked if I could take their photo. They looked at each other, and then blankly at me which didn't really give me an indication of my success or not. I then pulled out my trump card and explained that it was because they looked so beautiful. One obviously knew a little English, and I swear I almost saw the makings of a smile, she informed the other of my comment, and I was awarded a nod. I say nod, but it was done with her eyes, not her head. I figured that it was rehearsed so that anyone watching would not see them approving anything they shouldn't. I took the picture, boarded, and then quickly sent Nic to open the 'provodnista's sweets supplies'. Our research had informed us that this little extra might be the difference between a warm or cold shower. I was hoping that we now had secured a friendly relationship with our guards.

Spotting the Great Wall

We pulled away from the station feeling incredibly excited, we had the cabin to ourselves for the start, and a nice big window to watch the Chinese countryside go by. Despite travelling as light as possible, there was one book that we'd been carrying with us since we'd left Melbourne. It was a route guide to the Trans-Mongolian and Siberian railways. It gave us the exact schedule for all the stops, and also pointed out areas of interest as we went past. The position was plotted against markers alongside the track, small posts showing a kilometer distance from a specific spot. It took us a while to work out what they looked like and you had to be quick to catch the number as it flew past, trying not to crick your neck as you spun around. Possibly because we were so anxious about the trip, we hadn't really looked at the route in detail before starting. We opened the first few pages and both laughed when we spotted one of the primary attractions was the Great Wall of China. After all the expense and long day out, could we have just watched it glide past from our comfy train seats? We were now on a mission, determined not to miss it.

This initial part of the journey was very picturesque. It went through an area of mountains and valleys where the train would be traversing a steep cliff face and then dart through a tunnel to the next valley. We were scanning the horizon for the Wall but nothing so far, expecting that the train would cruise past an iconic view of the wall giving a picture postcard vista. From our previous experience, we knew that the wall's condition varies significantly along its length and actually only a small part was still in good enough shape to walk on. True enough, we eventually did see something that once could have resembled a wall, but if we hadn't had our trusty guidebook, we would have easily missed it and it certainly wasn't a replacement for our thigh burning day out.

A Scottish woman and some Melbournians walked onto a train...

As we were getting on board, we were slightly relieved to find there was another English couple in the next compartment, they were younger than us and embarking on their own adventure. They were returning to the UK after living in Hong Kong and were planning to get the train across Russia before cycling home from Eastern Europe. Unlike us, they'd paid for a full four berth cabin just for themselves, so they also had room to store the bikes safely. We didn't spend a lot of time with them, but it was nice teaming together at the start to work out where things like the boiler and toilets were.

We immediately noticed that there was a disparity between our excitement levels and theirs. It felt like they just saw one of the most famous train journeys in the world as a means to get their bikes across the continent. After a later conversation, we discovered that while Nic and I were glued to the scenery (and our trusty route guide), they'd been busy watching back-to-back episodes of *Only Fools and Horses* on their laptop. I remember being amazed at how different people can be.

In a nearby cabin, was a very friendly Scottish lady who was travelling with her son. She certainly saw this trip as an adventure and was moving between the carriages meeting everyone that she could. She had the superpower of finding out everything about someone, in the shortest time, and committing it to memory. After chatting with us she moved down the train, disappearing for an hour or so, when she came back she told us of a large party of Melbournians down near the food carriage. I reckon she'd be a great person to have at a dinner party, within minutes everyone would know everyone else and be getting on like a house on fire.

Later that afternoon we decided to venture down to the buffet carriage and try our hand at getting some food. We timed it well and took the last seats in a diner car full of the Melbournian crowd. They were a lovely rowdy lot, and we had a bit of a chat but didn't see them much after that. It was great to speak to people from our home town, but at the end of the day, we can do that after the trip. Even before the food options had been depleted by our fellow travellers, the choices were quite limited. We tried some sweet and sour chicken that was surprisingly better than expected. The carriage was run with military precision with the diner stewards giving the provodnistas a run for their money. Feeling proud that we'd survived the experience, we returned to our cabin as it was starting to get dark.

Bogie Woogie on the Trans-Mongolian Choo Choo

As the sun went down, we started to enter the Gobi desert, the view through the window was one of the most amazing sights I've ever seen. During my time on this planet, I thought I'd seen some star-filled skies before, but nothing quite like this. Neither of us had ever seen so many stars of all sizes and brightness, but that wasn't the impressive part. It was the fact they started as soon as the horizon ended and they were as bright on the horizon as they were anywhere else. It was a surreal sight, looking somehow superimposed. A standout experience that would stay with us well after the trip was over. Hopefully, next door weren't too busy watching their laptop to miss it.

Later that night, we reached the border between China and Mongolia where we experienced one of the strangest of procedures. As we slowly rolled into a terminus in the black of night, there was a cold low-lying mist, but you could make out bright neon lettering on a station building as we approached. We could hear some music that we initially thought was coming from one of the other compartments, but then realised dramatic classical music was being piped from the station. Suddenly, it felt like we had just been transported into a Francis Ford Coppola movie. We were already trying to forget the fact that we'd watched the movie *Transsiberian* before the trip. This scene in itself seems pretty dramatic, doesn't it? How about then, having the carriage dismantled while you are still in it?

The railway gauge used in China and Mongolia are different sizes, and the tracks change at the border. Now, I would have thought that the sensible way to solve this would be to have another train waiting at the border and passengers change from one to the other. But no. Years ago, the top brass of the railway companies met to discuss this, maybe around a blackboard. Then someone at the back shouts out 'Let's unhook each carriage, lift it off the ground, change the bogies and put it on the other track'. Maybe it was the stupid nephew of a powerful oligarch who had been given a job in the sticks (sent to Siberia no less) where he couldn't do any harm. To avoid the wrath of his uncle, the others decided it was a dandy idea.

Back to reality, it was possible to get off the train and wait at the station, but with the freezing temperature outside we decided to stay comfy and be willing prisoners to this madness. We were bumped around a bit as the carriages were disconnected and moved, but the process of lifting us up and changing the under-carriage went quite smoothly. I couldn't help thinking that part way through it looked like someone had made the unfortunate decision of parking the train on a council estate back in Liverpool where it had quickly been lifted up onto bricks and the wheels had been pinched.

The whole process took about 8 hours, and we were off again. To me, it just doesn't make sense, but it was a lovely little bit of quirkiness that adds to the magic of this journey.

3 in 1 Goodness

Back in Beijing, we found a local supermarket to stock up on supplies for our trip. Sounds easy enough, doesn't it? However, it is fair to say that a supermarket in China is not quite like popping out to Safeway. Very rarely in our home town are we weighing up whether to get the barbecue flavour Pringles or the vacuum packed pigs head. I manoeuvred Nic around the shop in an effort to hide the live turtles in a holding tank. The last thing we needed was for her to tear off her coat revealing a Sea Shepherd T-shirt, before ramming the tank with her shopping trolley and freeing the shell wearing occupants. It was often hard to know what we were actually picking up, and although we aren't particularly squeamish, we wanted some comfort that our noodles were not sprinkled with the dried liver of a snow leopard, or contain a newborn Pandas little toe.

We ended up being boring and chose plain packets of noodles, an abundance of sweets (the bribes) and the saving grace of our shopping trip, 3-in-1 coffee packets. We'd become hooked on them while travelling through South East Asia as most places we stayed had a kettle, and they were cheap. For those unaccustomed, they are just individual packets (made by one of those well-known companies that own a third of the planet) containing instant coffee, sugar and powdered milk. Now, don't be a snob for just a minute. Don't forget, I live in Melbourne, one of the top coffee capitals of the world (and will arm wrestle anyone who disagrees). We pretty much have a cafe per person in this city, and we can be some of the most obnoxious coffee snobs. In the first few years after arriving, I had gone from happily drinking coffee from a vending machine in the UK, to not tipping if my skinny Latte wasn't placed in front of me with the spoon at the right angle to pick up. However, when you are travelling away from home, and on a budget, you know that a decent flat white may be hundreds of miles away. These little 3-in-1 critters can be incredibly comforting. Even after we returned home, the smell of one of these sachets immediately takes us back to travelling.

Every carriage on the train has a boiler at each end called a semapor. They were once heated with solid fuel but, although didn't look it, are a little bit more modern now. This meant as long as you kept the provodnistas supplied with sweets and smiles, you had constant access to hot water for your packets of noodles and coffee beverages. This rail journey may go down as one of the most enjoyable and memorable experiences of our lives, but it won't be the most gastronomic.

Our Mongolian Doctor

After seeing the stars over the Gobi desert, we were disappointed that we weren't brave enough to stop there (one of the options to break the journey). However, we were excited about our first stop in Mongolia, Ulaanbaatar (often shortened to UB). We disembarked the train, later joining another passing Trans-Mongolian after our stay. This stopover was also arranged through Monkey Shrine, and included a local guide to accompany us during our time in Mongolia. The three-night stay incorporated a quick tour of the city, a journey out to the open steppe to stay in a ger (a Mongolian yurt) for a couple of nights, before a final night back in the city.

A lot of our pre-reading for Ulaanbaatar didn't generally show it in a good light. We'd seen recent reports of an increase in the number of drunken attacks and petty crime against tourists. With this in mind, we were happy to have a guide waiting to meet us. We were even informed that the station was a bit of a hot spot and not to get off the train until our guide had come onboard to find us.

We had to say goodbye to most of the people we'd met on the train, as they were continuing on. The English couple also disembarked for three nights, so we thought we'd possibly bump into them again. In a way, it was a shame not to complete the journey in a single leg, but it would have been such a waste not to see these fantastic places along the way. Mendee, our guide arrived, he looked about 12 and even made me look well built, seriously how was he going to protect us? He quickly picked up

Nic's backpack and we were moving, quick sharp, into the back of a minivan. Was this a kidnapping? No, it was a whistle-stop tour of the city which included the parliament building in Sukhbaatar Square and a monument (Zaisan Memorial), high on a hill overlooking the town. The monument contained a large Soviet-themed mural, and Mendee gave us a bit of an insight into some of their history, the relationship with the Russians, and the influx of Chinese workers who were thriving (mainly because they weren't too drunk to work, unlike the local men).

The Eagle is giving me the Evils

Next, we headed out of town towards the open plains where we would find our accommodation for the next two nights. Along the way, we stopped at a roadside tourist trap. An entrepreneurial local had accumulated two camels and some birds of prey. The birds included a vulture that was as tall as me, and what looked like a large Golden Eagle. I was always a fan of these magnificent birds, as a child I used to draw pictures of them, so it was amazing to see one up close. You may raise your eyebrows, but you need to understand, I am a hypocrite. I will put my hand up as someone who is against the treatment of birds like this, but will jump at the chance to get close to them. I paid three dollars to have the Eagle stand on my arm, I was told to approach it from the side, put my arm out in front of it, but most of all don't look it in the eye.

The keeper/captor then lifted it from its post and encouraged it to step onto my arm. Crikey, it was heavy and once again I wished I'd put in that gym time before we left Melbourne. Its claws were sharp, but how many times in your life can you slip into the conversation 'oh those scars, they were just from a Golden Eagle'. Both the bird and I knew quite well that he owned me, he had that look about him. I'm sure he would have asked for my pocket money if he could speak. I bravely gave the bird's foot a submissive little stroke before handing him back. At this point, I realised the owner actually had an eye missing. Was this Karma, organising a macabre claw based accident to repay the keeper, I guess that's where the advice to not make eye contact came about. Although not a guilt-free experience it was still a memorable one.

Having a Gerrrrreat Time

The Elstei Ger Lodge was a little more organised and touristy than we were expecting. It consisted of four gers arranged in a line, with concrete paths joining them and a small building nearby where we would be served our meals. A shower and toilet block was located a bit further off in the distance. It wasn't like there was a water slide or anything, no staff walking around in big furry Genghis Kahn costumes (although Mr GK does play a big part later).

The tents were lovely inside with beautifully painted woodwork; it reminded us of a traditional narrow boat that was part Tardis. The centrepiece was a small iron stove with a chimney that would keep us warm at night. It was designed for four guests, but as it was their low season we were the only ones in ours. I sat down in the ger thinking that it wasn't quite the *Cave of the Yellow Dog* experience that we expected. Then, with perfect timing a young girl walked past the door, she must only have been around three years old and looked exactly like the star of the movie, she gave us a wave and disappeared. Quietly, Nic was hoping she'd be able to make any fermented milk offerings disappear just as magically.

We had a little explore of our new home and walked outside to see the same English couple from the train arrive in a similar minivan. Although we'd used different companies they'd been booked on a similar itinerary. We later found out that they would also be staying in Siberia at the same time too. Again, we found their enthusiasm for the adventure and location to be very different to ours, maybe they were just excited on the inside.

After a beautiful sunset, we had our first meal in a large communal ger joined by the staff, we shared some beer and vodka. Probably more than we really needed, especially as we'd later need to locate outside toilets in the minus degree wilderness. By the time we returned to our temporary home, someone had made up the fire that would keep our tent warm and water hot for those 3-in-1s. It wasn't long before we both had to make a nocturnal excursion so joined forces for protection. We made it there and back alive, well only just. I'm sure I mentioned that both Nic and I are vertically challenged. This typically protects us from low hanging obstacles. Our lives have been filled with arses who point at something clearly higher than us, and snigger 'watch your heads!'. Hopefully, just before cracking theirs on the very same thing. Heightwise, we do well in Mongolia, the people and even the horses are tiny. However, the entry into a ger is low. *DUMPH!*, the sound of my head hitting the door frame. It was the first, but not the last time I would do that. At least, in an effort to get the slightest bit of sympathy from Nic, I could blame the following morning's headache on this, and not the vodka.

Mendee was a great guide, and we talked with him a bit about the fact that his family were nomadic farmers, generally moving between two areas of the steppe depending on the season. He explained that he'd made the decision not to follow this path and go to university instead, adding that when he wasn't with us he was busy revising. He had his final exam to become a doctor in just two days. I felt for him and was sure that the last thing he needed was to try and teach two numpties like us how to shoot a bow and arrow. After hearing this news, we would often act tired and suggest the odd afternoon nap so he would get some more revision done. We did spend some time playing Shagai with him, a game which involved a bag of sheep's knuckles. Yep, you heard, not bits of plastic that looked like bones, but real knuckles, some even had bits of cartilage attached. The game was a bit like pick up sticks, you start with a pile of the knuckles heaped in the middle of the table, including a special one that was painted red. You choose a number, then throw the red knuckle into the air. As it flies up, you need to grab the same number of bones with your throwing hand before catching the falling red knuckle in the very same hand. If you succeed you keep the bones, the idea being that you possess the most bones by the time the pile is empty. There was also a horse racing-themed game that involved what side the bones landed on and was much too complicated for me to try and explain here. Great fun was had all round.

Never work with animals, even short ones

After breakfast on the second morning, Mendee asked if we wanted to travel by horseback to visit a local nomadic family. I figured that although I've never been on the back of a horse before, it would be an organised tourist event and they must cater for this fact, so agreed. Surely they must have some tame tourist-ready animals stored somewhere nearby as the only horses I'd seen so far were roaming wild.

During the morning we noticed that some of the local farmers on horseback were rounding up horses into a corral with great skill, it was cool to watch. They then proceeded to examine the corralled horses, selecting one before pulling it out and tying it up away from the others. After seven horses were chosen, Mendee came to us and asked if we were ready to go.

Surely they couldn't be for us, could they? The realisation sets in. There were no sedate tourist horses for me, our horses were running free an hour ago. I don't know about you, but this would be enough to put me in a bad mood, and that's before a fat sweaty chap climbs on top of me. We were informed that the horses were owned by the local farmer and would be fine. What could go wrong?

They needed seven horses as the English couple were going to join us, along with two staff members, and Mendee. To begin our experience, we were told to carry the saddle and put it on the horse, this would create a bond with the animal. What type of bond is that? The horse now knows exactly who's responsible for their frolicking to be interrupted. To accomplish this, we had stringent guidelines about not standing behind them, and to approach from 45 degrees. It was as though we were approaching a helicopter, not the subject of every young girl's dream birthday present. The only saving grace was that Mongolian horses are tiny, they were more Shetland that Steppe.

Just as we approached, resplendent in our chaps and carrying the saddle, it started to rain finely. That was enough for the other couple. 'It's just not going to be fun' was their reason for heading back to the ger to maybe watch some more episodes of *Only Fools and Horses* (spot the irony). This reduced the safety in numbers factor, but really, what danger could these comically looking horses get into.

With a bit of uncool assistance from behind (with multiple hands on my arse) I clamber aboard my steed. To enhance my image I was supplied with a very dodgy looking helmet to accompany my fluorescent rain mac. To help leverage our clothes bargaining in a Beijing market, Nic was wearing exactly the same dodgy rain mac and was given an equally bad helmet. We looked more special needs than special agent, but it wasn't about looking cool, it was about the experience, wasn't it? We head off, a staff member pulling our horses along with a long lead in a nice gentle meander. Looked like this was going to be easy enough after all. You could see that Mendee had been brought up on a horse as he whizzed around all of us. After about ten minutes he asked if we were okay with taking control ourselves, he was being diplomatic as I'd noticed that Nic had been riding solo for some time now.

I tried the controls to find my steed felt indifferent to them. However, he seemed happy enough just to follow the horse in front. A bit too close at times, I was praying that I wasn't going to be caught in an embarrassing tryst. Next came the call from Mendee 'let's try a trot', you notice that there was no question mark at the end of that statement. Before I could get the word 'But..' out of my mouth, the horse in front headed off with increased speed. My horse thought momentarily about waiting for an order from me, before just running off after it's mate.

People riding horses on TV look noble and heroic, Robin Hood making his way through Sherwood forest, or Mr Darcy riding across the Derbyshire moors. What you don't realise is that they are having their fillings vibrated from their mouths. Seriously, I was a short guy before I got on the damn thing and this wasn't helping as my vertebrae were slowly being compressed. I couldn't believe people would do this for fun, but then thought about the comment from the English couple which spurred me on to enjoy this, no matter what.

Of all the horses available, I had to have the one with the flatulence problem, he was a non-stop farty pants, much to everyone else's amusement. I'm pretty sure I even heard Nic's horse giggle. It was as though the gods of methane had put us together as kindred spirits. I was expecting him to have deflated to half his size by the time we arrived and was delighted to see a ger appear over a hilltop so knew I'd be able to rest soon. We hadn't been told too much about who we were going to visit, but although they were referred to as nomads, you could tell that this wasn't a temporary location. We dismounted from our horses (see, I have the lingo down, now I'm an experienced equestrian) and headed towards the ger with Mendee taking the lead.

During our short time in the country, we'd noticed a large number of big woolly dogs as pets, they were all fluff to keep them warm and looked like a cross between a Dulux dog and a St Bernard. As I approached the ger, I noticed the cutest ever example of one of these dogs, half asleep near the door. It looked like it would give the best hug therapy ever. Now, I have watched enough Discovery Channel programs to have people like Bear Grylls instil tactics about how to handle yourself around dogs, but my new-found connection with the animal world made me forget everything.

Rule No.1, don't stare directly into their eyes. This went out the window as I stared right at it, imagining us frolicking as though in a dog biscuit commercial. It turned out, this wasn't what was going through the dogs head as he suddenly sprung to his feet and started racing towards me. The change in demeanour was outstanding. I was looking to see if it was attached to a leash but was blinded by light shining off the fangs that were coming my way. What seemed like a docile beast could now suddenly give a cheetah a run for its money, and the puppy dog eyes were now red and filled with hate. This was not in the brochure.

Rule No.2, don't run. Easy enough for some smart arse to tell you on TV but not so memorable when you have Kujo running towards you. I almost remembered, but my body was already in motion. A bit like when you think of the most fantastic rebuttal to someone just as they have left the room. I managed to take about 6 steps, including a small skip while letting out a little shriek (the type an eight-year-old girl makes) before my common sense kicked in. Nic was shouting out Rule 2, but was doing it in super slow motion, which wasn't any use to me at all. I made a mental note to have a word with her about talking more quickly in times of emergency. The dog was finally brought to heal by the shouts of its female owner who'd appeared at the door of the ger while Mendee and the staff giggled at me once again.

More salt in your tea?

Tuya was obviously the matriarch of the family and was the only person there when we visited, everyone else was out working the land. The ger still had some of the lovely painted woodwork that ours did, but was much more practical with a small TV attached to car batteries and a much bigger stove area. It was bigger in size and slept the whole family. As we sat down she started to put together some biscuits and tea, could Nic's biggest fear about Mongolia be starting to eventuate? Nic hates milk, has done since a child and one of the things she was worried about was being served some sort of fermented milk and having to drink it to be polite. Thankfully it wasn't quite as bad as that, but Mendee explained that it was a very salty milky tea, Nic was brave and managed to get through it. I loved it (any chance for salt) and had a second cup, it also helped me calm down after nearly being dismantled by their pet poodle.

The homemade biscuits were lovely, a staple for them as they keep for a long time, are easy to transport, and provide energy while working. The meeting was a bit strained as I don't think Tuya had any notion that we were arriving and probably had much more important stuff to be getting on with. We asked a few questions (translated by Mendee) and then asked her if she had any questions about Australia. Her response came quickly and without contemplation, 'No!'. Mendee explained that she had met Australians before which made me think it wasn't the first unexpected visit she'd received.

As we left, I made a point of not even looking to see where the dog was and climbed aboard my diminutive whoopee cushion for the trip home. We started slow, but it wasn't long before we were trotting again, at least it would get us back quicker. After about 20 minutes we slowed to cross a river, and the three locals had a chat while looking at their watches. Mendee then turned around and said we were late for lunch and needed to speed up. Again, not a question. With my distinct lack of equestrian experience, it hadn't even occurred to me that the little thing had a faster gear. Trotting was only the equivalent to 4th, he could knock it up a cog to a gallop. If someone had told me when I woke up that morning that later on, I'd be galloping across the open steppe on a half-wild horse, I would have laughed at them. Now, not laughing. The constant vibration of the trot had now turned into moments of weightlessness as I flew through the air before crashing down as though someone had raised me five feet before dropping me on my arse.

Everything was in slow motion by now. As I flew up, my glasses would become loose and rest diagonally across my head, I couldn't let go to straighten them. As I came down, I could sense the camera that was around my neck flying up with the intent of bopping me on the nose. The thump of hitting my arse on the rock-hard saddle forced my leg through the stirrup so that it was almost at my knee, I certainly wasn't letting go of anything now. My slight allergy to horses had started to take effect and snot was beginning to fly from my nose in all directions as my eyes teared up. I'm blaming the allergy, but it might have had something to do with my man-bits being systematically bludgeoned against the saddle. This in turn, would force out another loud fart from the horse, adding a dramatic sound effect to the moment.

I guess reading this, between laughing at my inadequacy, you must be thinking that I was hating it. One thing I distinctly remember throughout the brain cell destroying ride was how fantastic this is. I was doing it; not reading about someone else doing it; not deciding to refrain because it was raining; I was there looking like an idiot who might die at any moment, but I was doing it. On our return, I was so proud of us both, even though the boys were still giggling at me. After that excitement, we were provided with one of the best tasting lunches ever. Not that I was ever likely to forget the experience, I had a nice trophy that would last at least a couple of weeks, a huge graze right across my arse.

Genghis Can't

It was such a shame to leave the camp to head back to the city, we really wished we'd been braver and stayed in the country longer. Continuing the excellent service provided during this organised segment, one of the excursions that had been arranged by Mendee was to visit the Genghis Khan Equestrian Statue. I have to admit, this didn't sound that exciting, even after being told that it included the world's biggest horse statue. Maybe we were grumpy about leaving the lovely warmth of the ger to head back to the concrete and grey Ulaanbaatar. As the minibus sped through the vast and sparse steppe, we started to wonder where this statue would be as there were no towns nearby. As the bus popped over a hill, we could see nothing but steppe and there in the middle was the imposing monument.

It really was in the middle of nowhere, we would later find out that the location was chosen because it related to a famous story where GK finds a golden whip. As we approached, we could tell that the complex was still under construction and it was going to be huge. When I say huge, I mean super expensive. If there was ever going to be a chance of making any financial return on this cultural exhibit, maybe they should have chosen another historical marker. Maybe GK's first snog or his 100th beheading could have been just on the edge of Ulaanbaatar's city centre. 'How about we build it 60 kilometres from town near no accommodation or any other infrastructure', 'Well that sounds like a great idea!'. Really?

My opinion started to change as we approached it, this had just knocked Vientiane's concrete runway from the top spot of coolest tourist attraction on the tour so far. Rising from the plains was a magnificent 40m high stainless steel statue. Its base housed a museum, and you could walk up internal stairs, popping out along the horse's mane, where you're confronted with the man himself glaring down at you with his hand resting on the end of the golden whip handle. To add to the atmosphere, we arrived in a thunderstorm and the clouds were black all around.

Unfortunately, the bad weather had also taken out the power to the site. On a positive note, this meant that we were charged half-price entry, but it did mean that we couldn't go into the museum and needed to walk around with monstrous torches to safely see our way up to the observation point. To complete the experience, as you walk into the foyer you are met with a leather boot. Not just any leather boot, one that would fit the foot of the 40m high statue. This meant that it stood over two storeys high in the buildings atrium with a staircase wrapping around it. I'd hate the job of polishing that.

We heard about their plans for further development on the site, hundreds of soldier statues and gers would be positioned around the area. It would be great to see it again once finished.

Mongolian Pickpockets

From there we left the steppe to head back into town, the trip must go on after all. Mendee dropped us off at the hotel where he would pick us up 24-hours later to put us on the train, during which time he had his doctors exam. We spent some time walking around UB. After some shopping, a huge meal, walking through a Beatles themed park, and crossing paths with the country's president at our hotel, we started to find a charm to this grey concrete city.

Mendee picked us up on time for our quick trip to the train station to continue our Trans-Mongolian adventure. He arrived with a fantastic smile on his face, confirming that he'd passed his exam. Ever security conscious, he wouldn't let us get out of the van until the train had arrived. After the previous day's trouble-free time around UB, I was beginning to think that it was overkill and merely an effort to pamper the tourists. Mendee lifted our bags onto the carriage entrance, and once in the hands of the provodnista, he waved goodbye.

We climbed onboard, along with our English travel companions and walked into our carriage to find two Mongolian men sat upright on one of the bottom seats. They were friendly and greeted us, so this looked like it was going to be an interesting and sociable leg. The compartments are well set up for travellers with plenty of luggage space under each seat or on top of a wardrobe. We started to lift up our seats to put our backpacks underneath, but the two guys began waving at us to tell us they were better being put up on top of the wardrobe. They were quite adamant, and I didn't want to strain our new relationship. After all, we were potentially spending the next couple of days with them.

As Nic and I simultaneously lifted our bags above our heads to place them out of the way, the two gents decided to leave the carriage at that very same moment. Pushing past us while we had our hands in the air looking like a rehearsal for a YMCA dance routine. What an odd lot I thought, they could have just waited a moment. Bags stowed away, we stepped out of the carriage to say hello to the English couple next door, only they weren't there, but the same two men were now sat in their cabin.

Okay, so I wasn't being the sharpest knife in the drawer and assumed they just had the wrong carriage, then I remembered that the English couple had purchased the whole thing for themselves. I went to find them and tell them about their visitors, but by the time we got back, the carriage was empty. The realisation struck once we couldn't find them anywhere in the carriage. They had just tried to pickpocket us. It was a horrible feeling, for me on a couple of levels. Firstly, the thought that people would do such a thing, I'm one of those romantics that like to believe the good in everyone, and secondly, the fact that I wasn't on to it. I pride myself in being safety conscious and can spot such risks and dodgy people a mile off. It was one of my primary duties on the trip, one that certainly couldn't be left up to Nic who would obliviously sit next to the most dodgiest axe-wielding person in the area. I had failed her, and it stung a little.

The saving grace was that we travel smart, we don't carry anything in our back pockets, and everything important is in a pocket that can be zipped away. We were not robbed because of this, but it was quite a shock that we would let anyone past our boundaries and give them a chance. Luckily, we got away with it as just a story. Can you imagine trying to get into Russia or even out of Mongolia without any visa or identification.

THE MID-BOOK PICTURE PAGE

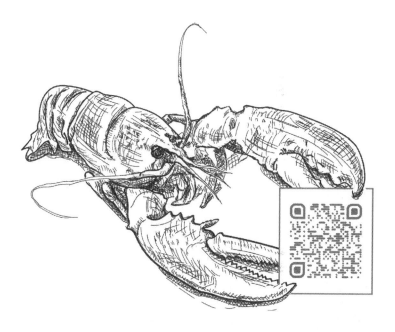

We saw our RTW adventure in high quality so
why shouldn't you. Just scan the QR code above
to view some of our pictures online.

Instagram: @worldisyourlobster

CHAPTER 8

Location: Ulaanbaatar
Days 134, Countries 11, Kilometers 23,971, Beds 69
Trains 7, Planes 11, Automobiles 28, Boats 8
Beers 41

To Russia, with love and new friends

J ust after the pickpocket excitement, our real roommates
arrived who didn't look like recidivists and both spoke
excellent English. Tyana was Russian and teaching in a UB
school, Mykola was from Ukraine and was heading home after
three months of travel. They were both super friendly, and within
minutes after we were introduced, a spontaneous picnic appeared.
A gingham cloth was placed over the table, and everyone just
started producing food from their supplies. We were a little
embarrassed by our offerings, our saving grace was some cake
type things we'd purchased in a UB department store followed
up by a packet of Mentos. Mykola was also travelling light but
Tyana opened up her large case and pulled out all sorts of produce.
Soon we were presented with a feast fit for kings, well at least for
some hungry strangers on a train.

Tyana was the entrepreneur of the bunch, and as well as the
food she also pulled out homemade crafts and jewellery from

her bag. These were available at a small price. We talked for hours about all kinds of random stuff, and as the lights went out, we broke out the alcohol. It's common knowledge that the provodnistas control alcohol intake in the carriages. On paper it's not allowed, but the practical reality is that you give the prison guards a back-hander to buy alcohol at inflated prices. We closed the door and handed around our own vodka while keeping an ear out. Every now and then the door would suddenly spring open for a surprise check, but with our plastic beakers, nothing could be proven.

Mykola – Swims like a Fish

We had lucked out with our carriage compatriots and were really enjoying this leg, even the English couple from next door would sometimes appear and have a little chat. Mykola was a young guy, approaching 30 (that is young, right?) and was super fit, he was just finishing three months of travel around the 'stans'. The girls loved him, and not just the ones in my compartment. Each morning he would wake up, climb down from the top bunk in his boxers and then start doing push-ups and pull-ups around the carriage, almost starkers. Along the corridor, female heads would randomly appear from the other compartments.

Okay, so he had a good body, that's not everything is it (yes I was feeling a little inadequate). I bet he has no personality. Wrong, he was such a nice guy, quite old for his years and would play for hours with a small Mongolian girl next door, who'd fallen in love with him. What about the coolness factor, surely I'd be up there, travelling around the world with my Hugh Grant accent and retro-styled digital camera.

Mykola even commented on how much he liked the camera, 'Ha, take that' I thought, while he pulled something silver out of his bag. It wasn't a retro-styled camera but a real retro camera, an old Zenit-B film camera from the 60's that he'd been using on his travels. He had to seek out shops that could still sell and develop the film, or have a darkroom so that he could develop them himself.

Music had to be my last foothold, I explained that I had all of my 25,000 song collection (this was before subscription music) with me as I couldn't live without them. The next item to be pulled out of his tiny bag was a reporter style voice recorder, which he'd been using to record the music from local buskers on his journey. He went on to explain that his travel would provide valuable material as he's a filmmaker. Buggerations! What the hell else does he have in that bag for Christ's sake? Actually, it was a drawing pad where he'd sketched the most beautiful portraits of people he'd met along the way. Without trying to sound like a sixteen-year-old girl, OM friggin G!

Now we really did feel like a tourist, compared to this traveller. If you were going to write a feel-good movie about a young man finding the world, then you didn't need to add a thing. I could picture the opening credits with a young Jude Law staring out through the train window, looking thoughtfully towards the Mongolian steppe. Although, the real Mykola was better looking. The English in me thought that I should hate this guy, he was perfect. The best I could muster was a bit of a man-crush. To top it all, even my backpack was jealous of his backpack. We thought we were travelling light, but his bag wasn't even a backpack, it was a soft tie string holdall, and it was all he was travelling with. After all the 'show and tell' items he'd just pulled out, there must have only been room left for a spare pair of undies and a toothbrush. Could this guy, and his bag, be any cooler? Yes actually, but more on that later.

The border crossing between Mongolia and Russia was a long drawn out affair, with an initial stop in daylight at Sukhbaatar on the Mongolian side. We weren't sure what the delay was as you don't exactly get any information on such things. This was very different from a previous trip across Australia on the famous Indian Pacific where you have a running commentary by the soothing voice of Bud Tingwell wafting through the cabin speakers. After a few hours, the four of us started to look a little worried, the Providnistas lock the toilets whenever we are at a station. It took a little pleading, but after a while we were let off the train to use the bathrooms at the station. Soon after everyone was back on board, the train moved off for a whole 10km, to Khyagt on the Russian side where we stopped again, now in the dark.

We started getting a bit stir crazy at this point, and it was now the turn of the cute Mongolian girl from next door to entertain us for a change. I think she would have been about three, and would often appear at the door so she could stare at Mykola. We found a noisy whistle that made a terrible racket, but made her laugh herself silly. This was fun at first but had to go 'missing' after a while. Then, we gave her a phone with a camera so she could take pictures of us all. We even had a trade agreement in place with her mother, who we never actually met. We would give the girl a sweet, and she would take it next door and return with a tomato in exchange, her mum had naturally packed much more sensibly than us.

It was now eight hours since we first stopped, and the waiting came to an abrupt end with the appearance of scary looking Russian police officers and sniffer dogs going through the train, checking baggage and paperwork. It was quite a nervous experience, even though one of the officers was a beautiful young blonde girl (in an 'I could kill you with a paperclip' sort of way). Once through, we could feel ourselves relax as we knew that our Russian visas worked and all the effort to get them had paid off.

Later on that night, we also had an extended stop at Ulan Ude, which unfortunately was where Tyana left us. At least we'd all bought her homemade bracelets to remember her by. This long stop was well timed as it coincided with Russia's Victory Day celebrations, and we could see the city's firework display from our cabin. A perfect opportunity to get the vodka out. Mykola, in true Eastern Block style, insisted that before each shot we would each raise a toast to something. It was after a few of these that he just matter-of-factly slipped into the conversation that he was ex-Ukrainian KGB, although couldn't talk about what it was that he did for them. First thought to pop into my head 'Seriously mate, you are killing me!'. Second thought 'Please don't kill me'. So the ever-cool Mykola just became cooler. I figured I'd best not offend him. Seven minutes later, I did just that.

He also let slip that he would be turning 30 in three days, so I quickly raised my shot glass in a toast to his birthday. His face went white, and his glass stayed firmly on the table. He believed that to celebrate beforehand was bad juju, and would cast doubt on whether he would reach the day in one piece. I apologised profusely, and we quickly found something else to toast (it could have just been a passing dog at this point of the evening). It was going to be sad to say goodbye to our comrade once we reached our next stopover in Irkutsk. I made a point of emailing him three days later, and felt relieved to find out that he had in fact, reached his birthday. No thanks to me.

Lena, our next local guide met us at Irkutsk station, and it wasn't much of a surprise to see that the English couple would join us once again. We were ushered into a posh minivan for the 70km journey to the town of Listvyanka, on the shores of Siberia's Lake Baikal. We wouldn't be staying with the others here, as we'd chosen the option of staying with a local family during our two-night stopover. Lena introduced us to Olga, the matriarch of this lakeside family, who welcomed us with a big smile and a very appreciated breakfast. Olga couldn't have looked a more stereotypical Siberian mum, which added to our experience. We were immediately intimidated by her, I guess she would be the Russian equivalent of a Yorkshireman.

After breakfast we went out for a stroll around the town and checked out the lake. Lake Baikal is the world's biggest freshwater lake by volume and contains over 20% of the world's fresh water.

It's also the world's deepest lake and considered one of the clearest. I doubt I really need to tell you that it was impressive to see. The winter ice had started to break up, and water could be seen for well over half of the surface. Some boats were even out when they clearly shouldn't have been yet. The shoreline was littered with clumps of ice, and with the beautiful clear blue skies, you could see snow covered mountain ranges across the 40 mile stretch of water. We visited a small aquarium that featured the Lake's endemic Nerpa Seal, the world's only exclusively freshwater seal. Boy were they cute, they are small but look like little water-based Michelin men who'd eaten all the pies.

We had strict guidelines about what time dinner would be served, so we made sure we returned for a hearty mix of dumplings and beetroot salad. I couldn't help but wonder if we'd been supplied this meal to enhance our Siberian experience, and imagined the family were gutted that they couldn't enjoy their regular Tuesday night, Coq Au Vin with Viennetta ice cream. We chilled in our room that evening ready for a big day ahead.

Richard's Shoes

We met Lena at the tea shop where she would introduce us to our hiking guide, Sasha. Also there was Richard, another tourist who'd be joining us for the day. It turned out Richard was actually a journalist for a well known British broadsheet and was writing a piece on the Trans-Mongolian Railway. We liked him straight away, he was charming, with a great sense of humour. After a coffee, Sasha arrived and was the epitome of a Siberian Wilderness Guide, he oozed authority and commanded respect.

We'd all signed up for a 5-hour hike in the mountains overlooking the lake, both Nic and I were a little worried about what this might entail. Despite carrying our backpacks halfway around the world, we were not the fittest, and coupled with my newly found vertigo, who knows how this adventure might go. Our footwear consisted of good quality walking sandals with toasty warm socks. Sasha examined them carefully and informed us that we 'should get by' with an unapproving expression. It was clear that he took this very seriously. Next, he checked Richard's footwear, a splendid pair of leather brogues, the type of shoe that has less grip than ice stakes. Sasha's mouth dropped, and both Nic and I had a huge internal sigh of relief. We were not going to be the weakest link, Richard's shoes were!

'First, we go to my house' was all Sasha said, and we headed off. We didn't realise at the time but Sasha ran a homestead opposite from Olga, and that was where Richard was staying. We almost had a skip in our step as we headed there. It looked a nicer house than ours, and we waited by the back door for a couple of minutes for Sasha to re-appear. What was that in his hands? Noooooooo! It was a pair of hiking boots in Richard's size. Our hearts sank. We headed off towards the mountains (note, I am refusing to call them hills). Sasha and Richard were looking as though they were ready to tackle the north face of the Eiger, and the two of us looked like we were heading to the local fete.

As we started our route through a valley between two peaks, a fire engine screamed past. We looked up and saw a substantial forest fire on one of the peaks, smoke started to pour over the town. The fire engine didn't instil confidence and looked a little Keystone Cops. Now, when I think back, I picture a fireman dangling from the back of the truck as it sped around the corner (this didn't happen). Sasha looked at the fire engine, looked at the burning trees, back at the fire engine, back at the trees, and then pronounced 'We should be okay, let's go'.

Now, let me try and recollect what direction we headed in. Oh yes, that's right, UP! Okay, I exaggerate a little, it was hard work but mostly quite pleasant. There was no real climbing, although some of the paths around the front of the mountain were very steep and slippy. Richard would never have survived in his patent leather footwear.

Sasha was one of those people that you immediately trusted your life with, he had an aura of safety. Our worries about exiting the mountain by involuntarily throwing ourselves at the scenery, or of the impending bushfire quickly dissipated. He was calm and relaxing, it didn't seem like anything could faze this guy. He looked like he should have been ex-military, something out of a Robert Ludlum book, but in fact before retiring to set up his homestead, he was a teacher. I dread to think how tough the schools must be here.

We reached the top and the view across the Lake was breathtaking, it was about as picturesque as you could ever want for. It was magical, so much so that overcome with emotion, Nic had the urge to disappear behind a tree for some light relief. As she walked back, adjusting her clothing, Sasha turned around and for the first time looked gravely serious, beckoning us closer so he could tell us some very important information.

He was very concerned about ticks, the type that give you encephalitis. A couple of people had recently become ill in the area. I turned to Nic and queried our long list of pre-trip injections, and despite the thousands of dollars, and discomfort, the only thing we weren't covered for was the thing that we were probably at most risk of. He then made us check each other for the little red ticks and told us to keep away from the shrubbery. Now Sasha, I love your work and have had total faith in your leadership, but I have to say that this information might have been handy before my beloved wife dived into a bush and started pointing her milky white arse at all and sundry.

Nic's face quickly turned a similar colour as this thought popped into her head too. Back around the tree we went again so I could examine every inch of said posterior (it's so tempting to be mischievous and emphasis the EVERY). We did actually find a couple of red tics on Nic's trousers so I knew that a much more detailed tic inspection (and a hose down) would ensue on our return home.

Sasha led us down to the shoreline and onto a small pebble beach where we set up camp at a small picnic table. Unsurprisingly we were the only ones there, but there were signs that some local youths had recently been here for a party, a cause of despair for Sasha. Within minutes he'd emptied his small backpack and laid out a great little picnic of local cheese, sausage, and even some salad (something I wasn't expecting in Siberia). We contributed with some Mentos for pudding.

A different route back took us upupup and then down-downdown, again in some pretty steep terrain. We all reached Listvyanka town and felt very accomplished. It was time to celebrate but unfortunately, Sasha had to leave us to get back to his guesthouse. The three remaining found a small market where all the stalls seemed to either sell the local salted fish speciality or beer. The local stall holders started off with their usual Russian non-smiley personas. Enthusiastic pointing and a little mime rewarded us with their wares. After a few rounds of this, they started to smile and open up a bit more (maybe it was just the beer speaking). Drinking cold beers in Siberia's Riviera, where it was cold enough to cover half of the world's biggest freshwater lake in ice, was by far the coldest memory from the whole trip. My teeth were shaking but did it stop us? Nope. In fact, if we weren't too scared of being late home for Olga's dinner, we would probably still be there.

The following morning we packed our bags ready to be picked up by Lena. As part of our usual thank you, we handed over a slightly squashed koala toy to Olga. She giggled as it was placed in her hand before ushering us into the next room which had one of those light switches on a cord from the ceiling. Clambering up the cord were another five similar koalas. Just goes to show that firstly, the world is a small place, and secondly, Australians get bloody everywhere.

The posh minibus picked us up, Richard and the English couple were already inside for our trip back to Irkutsk, where we'd spend the next couple of nights. Richard hadn't had the privilege of meeting the others yet, but quickly received a proper introduction when we mentioned that we'd be staying in Moscow for four days. 'What are you going to do for the other three days there?' was the smug retort from the couple. As soon as we arrived in town, the couple grabbed their bags from the van and left without a goodbye. That was the last time we would see them, but we hoped that they enjoyed their TV watching as they worked their way back to the UK.

Wintery weather was still hanging around, and Lena did her best to conduct a walking tour of the city before rain stopped play. It wasn't long before we pulled the plug, and crashed at her favourite cafe for coffee and cake. We spent an enjoyable couple of hours with her and Richard before saying goodbye to them both and returning to our hotel. Dinner consisted of Pringles from the local supermarket, and a beer in the hotel's English themed London pub.

Thankfully, Lena had shown us the route of a walking tour, and we hit the streets the following morning in bright blue skies, with the camera firing. Irkutsk was filled with lovely architecture, including many churches of various denominations. My favourite buildings were wooden houses with ornate shutters that over the years had sunken into the ground, so much so that the front windows were at floor level. That evening, Egor (yep real name) picked us up for our quick journey to the train station where we jumped back on the Moscow bound Rossiya service.

The World is your Siberian Lobster

Don't ask me why but we decided to watch the movie thriller *Transsiberian* a few days before we left Australia. It was quite disturbing, a bit like watching *Wolf Creek* just before travelling through the Australian outback or *Sex in the City* pretty much any time. It certainly didn't help Nic's nerves about the train journey, but there was a fundamental message she took from it.

There was absolutely no way that I was allowed off the train by myself. If I ever did disembark, it would never be without her, and even then, I would ensure we had passports, money, and sufficient papers. Fair call, I wasn't planning on doing otherwise, and sure enough for at least the first couple of days, the bravest I got was to stick my head out of the window at station stops and snap some photos. At the long border stops, we did get off (together) to stretch our legs a little, even getting told off by a police officer at one station for straying too far.

As days passed by, we started to be a little less regimented and often one person would get off to take a picture of the other still in the train. Depending on the provodnista on duty, you'd sometimes get a bit of an indication of how long you'd be at the station. Most of the Russians would stream from the train to stock up on supplies from little stalls on the platform.

As you can imagine on a journey like this, the phrase 'in the middle of nowhere' gets bandied around quite a bit, but at one particular stop, we really were in the middle of nowhere. The steward indicated with her fingers that we had 20 minutes, as she was nearly bowled over by a large Russian man keen to exit the train (yes you're quite right, he was Russian around). I was feeling in a bit of a photojournalist mood, so decided to get some photos of the passengers going about their routine. Nic was busy tidying up so I called through the cabin door that I'd be back in a mo. The station platform for this small town wasn't anywhere near long enough for the train and our carriage was right at the back. Everyone from back here had to walk over a stretch of gravel and pebbles just to get to the start of the platform. I brought up the rear, and by the time I reached the platform, the train had mostly emptied, filling the platform and kiosks. It was great people watching, and I was snapping away, always conscious of the number of people around me, mentally trying to judge what percentage of passengers they would likely leave on the platform if the driver decided it was time to go.

Then something placed on the floor in front of a kiosk caught my eye. It was a large platter of cooked lobster. We were in the middle of the Siberian plains, I was expecting a rush on bread and root vegetables, not crustaceans. I had to get a photo. Totally amused by this, I concentrated on getting some good pictures to show Nic and leant in to mess around with some arty macro shots. After what I thought was only a minute or so, I stood up feeling all smug and National Geographic, I looked around to find nothing, no one. Actually, I could see someone, it was the Japanese trainspotter from our carriage who was already back at the end of the train and climbing aboard. The steps for the carriage before ours had already been pulled up, I then saw Nic waving furiously from the window. Bollocks!

I started to run and was quickly reminded that I only had thongs on. I had to do that silly run where you clench your toes to stop your thong flying forward six feet ahead of you, lifting my feet more vertically as though wading through treacle. I could only try and make up for this with my arms. I deployed proper running arms, hand stretched out flat and raised to face height with each step in a giant pendulum motion, just like I'd seen on *Chariots of Fire*. Then, I hit the pebbles at the end of the platform which meant that on average only half of my foot would land on the thongs lovely rubbery layer, the other half on hard, sharp stones. I looked up to see my provodnista, the one that I had been generously plying with sweets for the last two days. She had an angry face and one hand on the steps. My knees seemed to get higher with each stride as though this would help my forward speed. The train's horn sounded. My knees got even higher, and it suddenly occurred to me that I had no passport or ID with me.

Could this see me spend the rest of my days in a nearby gulag, never to be seen again? The thought that at least I'd be eating lobster was only a fleeting comfort as I remembered I didn't have a ruble to my name. Surely it was physically impossible to get my knees any higher. Probably just for shits and giggles, the provodnista lifted the steps up while I was about 100m out, only to lower them again with a look that meant I'd be lucky to be allowed access to the toilets for the next 2 days. As I boarded, I was expecting a swift backhander across the head, but it never happened so I bounded into our compartment feeling very foolish and out of breath in an Indiana Jones kind of way.

Ouch! The belting came after all, but from a wife in tears who had already written me off as someone who'd fallen prey to Woody Harrelson (film reference, watch it if you haven't). It was one of those one-sided conversations where every word was punctuated with a punch. 'I', punch, 'told', punch, 'you', punch, 'never to', harder punch to account for the two words, and the start of a build up into a crescendo. I think you get the idea. I had no comeback, none. I did the only thing I know how to do at such a time. I laughed. The phrase 'blue touch paper' popped into my head as another beating ensued. I should have learnt about the laughing thing. I once did it after being told by a doctor that he thought I had Malaria, during a Kenya trip many years ago. Admittedly back then, I think it was the fact that I took a photo of Nic in hysterical tears that was the more irksome part.

However, I did have my lobster pictures as a reward, even though it took me two days to build up enough courage to show them to Nic. It certainly added yet another facet to our 'The World is your Lobster' motto.

You should never judge a Pushkin book by its cover

This three night leg on the train didn't quite have the social aspect of the other legs as our Russian bedfellows didn't really make conversation and mostly slept. I generally put this down to the language barrier although one did say a few words as he packed up to leave, which made me think he was just avoiding conversation. We had quite a turnover of people joining and leaving through the various cities we passed. It made it a little unsettling as you were constantly trying to gauge the new intakes for trustworthiness and possibilities to engage. This transition could happen at any time of the day or night, so certainly affected our sleep patterns. This highlighted the challenge of travelling with a woman who makes Jekyll look like a Jehovah witness when she is sleep deprived (not one of the three reasons I married her).

One night, things got interesting as we pulled into our next stop at around 11pm. Nic had already made her lower bunk into her bed and was tucked up under her blanket. The Russian chap on the bunk above had been pretending to be asleep for the last few hours, and the bunk above me was free. A few minutes after the train stopped, the cabin door flew open and two young Russian lads appeared with large bottles of beer in their hands. They both had a bit of a sway on, despite the fact we hadn't started moving again yet. Nic looked at them, looked at me, and pulled the blanket up higher over her face. Both guys plonked themselves down onto my seat before I had chance to turn it into my bed. Surprisingly, it didn't take them long to work out that I wasn't Russian or could speak any Russian. Enter Alexis and Paul into our adventures.

They had been away working as tradesmen and were on their way home, Paul could speak a little English and Alexis, none. Paul tried to engage Nic with a few questions, but was only mustering single word replies between fake yawning and stretching to indicate it was her sleep time. Nic wasn't in the mood for drunk young guys at this time of night and didn't look the most relaxed. I, on the other hand, still had a beer on the go, so we clinked bottles and embarked on a new friendship.

Paul asked why we were here, and when we told him that we'd always wanted to visit Moscow and to travel on this train, he looked at us as though we were a bit odd. He was from Omsk, so maybe there is a city rivalry going on here as well. He explained that Alexis was married with a young son, but he was free and single. Bit by bit, they charmed Nic out from under her blanket, and we started to tell them about our trip. We would tell Paul,

Paul would tell Alexis, and they would talk in Russian for a bit, Alexis' eyebrows would rise, so we assumed they were impressed with our endeavour. Alexis then asked Paul to inquire what our ages were and if we had any children. We explained our years and dependent situation which received a gobsmacked look from Alexis who flew into a passionate transaction with Paul. 'What did he say?' I asked intriguingly. He'd told Paul to tell us 'Have a great trip, enjoy this journey, see Russia, see Paris but then go home and have babies!'. How endearing was that from this drunk young tradie.

We talked further, and they asked if we'd heard of such Russians as Tolstoy, Dostoevsky, or Pushkin. This wasn't the direction we thought the conversation would head from these guys when they initially burst into the room. We explained that we didn't know the latter of the three and I thought they were going to pull the cord and get us thrown off the train. They were shocked. We were under strict orders to get to Moscow and find out about Pushkin, whose stories they'd grown up with as children. So put in our place, we tried to deflect the conversation and got Paul to talk about himself (in very broken English). He explained that he'd been a bit of a wild child and was thrown out of many schools, he managed to get across to us that he was not stupid but more street smart than academic. He added that he was a good actor and had performed a famous poem at school which he would often repeat years later, to impress the girls. Despite it being 2am, Alexis stood up and left for the dining carriage to buy everyone more beers.

All of a sudden, Paul checked that the third Russian was actually asleep, confirmed that the corridor was empty and closed the door, making the cabin much darker. We were a little unsure what was going to happen next when he suddenly launched into his rendition of the poem with real passion and frantic hand movements. He was obviously very proud of his ability to do this, although maybe a bit embarrassed for Alexis to see him. We didn't have a clue about the content of the poem, but the hairs were standing up on the back of our necks. He later wrote down the name of the poem in cyrillic so we could try and find it somewhere in English (*A Cloud in Trousers* by Vladimir Mayakovsky).

What we thought was going to be an uncomfortable evening with some drunk yobs, had become one of the most memorable moments of the journey. Insert here all the cliches that you can think of involving books and covers. We drank some more, even Nic joined in and had a great time. Eventually, Alexis moved to his bunk next door, and Paul finally went to bed in the bunk above me. They were only going a short distance to Omsk and would leave in the early hours of the morning, so that was the last we saw of them, but certainly not the last we've thought of them.

Apart from a few hours with two more young Russian men who just watched TV, we had the final day and night to ourselves on the train. What better way to spend it than by finishing the vodka supplies. There may have been some dancing involved, it's all a bit blurry.

Welcome to Moscow

We'd just about made it to Moscow and were at the carriage window with our eyes peeled. It was great to soak up the scenery of the city's outer suburbs, but the lasting memory from this stretch will forever be of the train surfers. No less than five trains we passed on the last hour of the journey had someone clinging to the front of it like some squidgy hood ornament. I'm not really sure what their motivation was, it wasn't like we were travelling through India and that was the only space available. You couldn't help but wonder where we were about to arrive.

The train finally pulled into Yaroslavskaya station, fulfilling an epic bucket list item. Since embarking in Hong Kong, we had travelled 11,000km across China, Mongolia, and Russia. We just can't explain how chuffed and smug we were with each other. We wanted to celebrate, explain what we'd achieved to everyone around us and receive high fives from any Americans in the area. Reality set in with sight of our taxi driver who was waiting outside our carriage, displaying a sign with our name. We climbed down and walked up to him. No high five, no fist bump or little dance, no welcome to Moscow, actually not even a hello. 'Quick, we go', and he was off.

Now just hold on Mister, we want to savour the moment and have a few more minutes of smugness on the platform, that guy over there looks American. The driver wasn't even looking back to see if we were keeping up or not. We started legging it after him, sporting both day and backpacks, jiggling down the platform. Nic was making sure I wasn't running into anything as I had my head in my bag trying to find my camera, which I pulled out just as we reached the front of the train. We stopped, joined hip-to-hip and raised the camera to get a nostril shot with the train behind, *click* - perfect first time. The only occasion that had ever happened, but still not quick enough and were rewarded with a scowling look from the driver. Welcome to Moscow bitches.

Although the hotel chosen by Monkey Shrine was a nice mid-range affair in a handy area, the staff were not very friendly. I'd say it was a cold welcome, but in a bizarre twist we'd reached Moscow mid-heatwave, and the hotel's air conditioning was broken. Despite getting them to deliver two fans to the room, we were roasting.

The hotel had a cute restaurant that served enjoyable but pricey food and was a good fall back in this scary city. For our first evening in Moscow we were both timid and tired, so just checked out the local neighbourhood, finding a great little corner shop. We stocked up on supplies (Mentos) and settled into our room for the warm night ahead.

No Bolshoi, we really did it

So for our first day in Moscow, we were eased into things with another tour organised by our great little company. We were met after breakfast by another Lena, our new local guide who would take us on a walking tour of the area. Lena was middle-aged, seemed quite sophisticated, and was very passionate about her city and its architecture. The great thing about this type of tour was that it's not centred around big-ticket tourist attractions, concentrating instead on aspects of local life that you would never pick up on your own. The smallest of statues had wonderful backstories, and Lena could speak about a 1960's concrete apartment block with such passion that you couldn't help but be brought along for the ride. Around us, other tourists were obliviously rushing past to get their pictures of Red Square. We talked in length about the type of people that would have lived in these leafy streets over the years, and what life was like in Moscow.

We were having such a great time and ploughed Lena with questions, which I think she enjoyed. She then said something that made us laugh out loud. Lena had conducted a similar tour the day before with an English couple that had also arrived by Trans-Mongolian. She was incredibly disappointed to find that they just followed her around, took a couple of pictures and hardly said a word to her. Lena looked at us strangely, and after our laughter subsided, we explained that we had a pretty good idea whom she'd just met.

After visiting a memorial to Pushkin (now that we knew who he was), we followed Lena into Moscow's equivalent of Harrods. We bought the cheapest bottle of bubbly and caviar we could find to celebrate our arrival in Moscow. We also bought Lena a posh bar of chocolate, but think she might have preferred a more monetary tip, despite the fact that she'd been rewarded with a much more engaged audience today. Just before we relaxed for a parting coffee, she took us past the Bolshoi Theatre commenting about how much she loved attending as often as possible. Months earlier, we had looked into booking tickets online, but because of a lack of knowledge, the language barrier, and being chicken, we hadn't managed it. Standing outside this iconic location, we were now regretting not trying harder. We told this story to Lena, and she took us to a box office at the side of the theatre, found someone she knew and had a bit of a chat. She returned with the news that we could get two tickets for a ballet that very night. At this point, I was so regretful of my previous ineptitude that I would have paid our next two weeks budget for tickets. We immediately said yes, without knowing the price and approached the counter. As the price was pushed towards me on a piece of paper, I couldn't help but pull that squinty face, the one that protects you from bad news or low flying objects. What was the damage going to be? Amazingly, for less than $40 each, we'd just scored fantastic dress circle seats to watch a ballet at the Bolshoi Theatre. What a day. Nic's face was full of excitement at the fulfilment of a lifelong dream, but then her face dropped - 'what am I going to wear?'

Lena received a big hug to go with her chocolate, and we parted ways. Just when we thought the day couldn't be more iconically Muscovite, we found ourselves sitting down for Borscht at a restaurant table in Red Square. Unlike our Mongolian horse adventure, I now really did feel like James Bond.

That night, we managed to scrub up well and didn't look too much like street urchins as we found our seats in the theatre. As expected, it was beautiful inside and gosh, did the audience around us look pretty. No makeup was spared, and the use of fur was so abundant I was expecting the staff to lay out bear traps in the intermission. The ballet was *The Flames of Paris*, and we actually managed to follow most of the story. This was made harder by the fact that the show would stop after the smallest of pirouettes, at which point the dancers took a bow and a round of applause and flower throwing followed. Without these interruptions, the show would have been about a third of the length. It struck me as such strange behaviour, it'd be like tipping a waiter after each mouthful; shaking a newborn's father's hand and handing him a cigar after each of the baby's limbs popped out; giving a gas attendance a big wet kiss after each litre of petrol. The evening was such an experience and still feels like some dream (set in the '80s).

Moscow No-Fly Zone

After meeting Olga and her friends, I had a very stereotypical image of Russian women in my head, based on our Siberian experience. This stereotype was blown away as soon as we hit Moscow. All of a sudden, the streets were filled with a high percentage of very wealthy cars, and the women that stepped out of them were all absolutely stunning. Even when travelling the subways, watching women go about their normal routine or on their way to work, it looked like whatever they were doing was going to involve a red carpet and an acceptance speech.

This hadn't gone unnoticed by Nic either, who quickly added Moscow to my solo no-fly list. This is the list of places that I would never be allowed to travel to without her. To be fair, this only had one other location on it, the whole country of Sweden. Just before our wedding, we'd recently visited our good friend and Welshman, Mikey, who had been based in Gothenburg for work. After our 4th bar (for research purposes only), it became clear that rather than the 10% of stunningly beautiful females that you'd statistically get in a UK club, it was sitting comfortably around the 80% mark. To add to the mix, the blokes here were not so good looking. No wonder Mikey looked the happiest we'd ever seen him. Soon after we returned to the UK, it was time for me to sort out my stag do. Before I could say a word, I was given one bit of direction. Not Sweden. I'd clearly better watch my gaze or Moscow will plummet back into the brink of Cold War.

From previous conversations with people who'd visited Moscow, it was evident that the city was polarising, but we absolutely loved it. Our second day was filled with a self-guided tour of the famous and beautiful Moscow metro system. As a target, we tried to vist each of the 'Seven Sisters', a set of beautiful gothic skyscrapers built in the '40s and '50s dotted around Moscow's surrounds. The stations were an amazing sight, and I couldn't help think that if I had to commute through their metro, I'd arrive at work a little more cheerful. In one station the ceiling was covered with ornate decorative scenes. A friendly but very drunk Russian sparked up a conversation in pretty good English and tried to explain what they depicted. He eventually sensed we knew he was just making stuff up so, instead he opened up his plastic bag and offered us some vodka. We declined. Moscow's heatwave continued and it was a fabulous day with blue skies. We toured beautiful suburbs, came across a classic car display, even walked under the Russian space shuttle (Buran) in Gorky Park. We felt totally safe in our wandering, and things only got edgy when I was told off by a very angry armed policeman for taking photos of the old KBG headquarters. This meant I had to sneak back and duck down behind a car to get the shot I wanted. It was a long slog of a day, and we covered plenty of ground on foot, as well as by rail, resulted in us sighting six of the sisters before we crashed back at the hotel.

There was one big ticket item left, and it was a doozy, the Kremlin. We'd put aside our last full day to complete it. The day was full of eclectic architecture and history, we even passed muster and were allowed to pop in to see Lenin (no thongs today). There was just something about this city. An overarching sense of romanticism, intrigue, history, and nervous anticipation, made for an exciting and memorable time.

We certainly could have stayed longer but at least having the dangling carrot of St Petersburg helped us move on. We had a prearranged ticket on the Sapsan (Russian for Peregrine Falcon) high-speed train, departing Moscow's Leningradsky Station, who's entrance was also within sight of the final of the 'Seven Sisters'. No cabin needed here as we would be in St Petersburg in a matter of hours.

Hermits of the Hermitage

No pickup was needed this time, as The Hotel Cromwell was located in a lovely little spot, only a 10 minute walk from St Petersburg train station. Our room was on the top floor, with lots of space and a small skylight above the bed. We crashed for a while researching our new home, however in a city that's so far north it didn't get dark till midnight, so time got away from us, and all of a sudden it was 8:30pm, and we hadn't eaten anything. Thankfully, part of our research included restaurants and we strolled only a few doors down to a Georgian restaurant with excellent reviews. We weren't disappointed.

Our final organised city tour from Monkey Shrine was led by Katrina, a young student. We walked quite a distance, covering some great sights that included properties once owned by Tsars, and the iconic Church of the Spilled Blood. It was at such a fast pace we would need to cover most places again by ourselves to enjoy and take photos. Although she did provide lots of great information and history about the city, it wasn't with the same passion as Lena in Moscow. This was a shame as we were also having a bout of PhnomPenhitus. We seemed to be constantly tired, and the reduced darkness wasn't helping.

The city was very different from Moscow and you could tell that it was more planned, with sensible road layouts, and standard building heights. Don't get me wrong, it was as impressive as you'd expect it to be, but I think my heart was still in the country's capital. Just like the continuing battle between Melbourne and Sydney you get a real mix of preferences from anyone who'd been to both. Similar to Ho Chi Minh and Hanoi, there definitely seemed to be a correlation between which one people preferred and which one they arrived at first.

We almost spent the following day in bed until at about 2pm, Nic discovered that the Hermitage was open till 9pm that night (every Wednesday). We used this as an excuse to surface and get going. Thank God we did, it was the perfect time to visit, no queues and free run of the place. Founded in 1764 for Catherine the Great, the Hermitage is the world's 2nd largest art museum, and mostly made up of four very impressive baroque and neoclassical buildings. We started off at the Winter Palace and covered what we could, before being ushered out at closing. A perfect example of a 'turn it around' day.

Unfortunately, half of the external building (like many others in this city) were covered in scaffolding, but one thing I liked was the fact the scaffolding was covered in sheeting that contained a life-size artists impression of what the building should look like behind. A much more civilised way of doing things.

The long shot that got us through our Russian exit

It was our last day in Russia, this made us sad, especially as we hadn't done St Petersburg justice. We rose early, had breakfast in the hotel and started to pack up before we hit the streets for one last time. While getting sorted, we came across a mostly empty bottle of vodka. We didn't want the hassle of carrying it around, or worrying about Finnish customs, so there was really only one thing for it. Mid-morning vodka shots. I was surprised that Nic agreed, in fact she jumped at the chance a little too enthusiastically (her love of booze was one of the three reasons that I married her). We exited the hotel for our last day's exploration, keeping away from the major tourist areas and wandering aimlessly through the suburbs until we started to get hungry. We found a cafe that was a real locals hangout. The manager spoke some English, which was good as the menus were only in Russian. Maybe because she could smell the vodka on our breath, we were welcomed with open arms and she explained that they had two cheap fixed-price three-course menus for the local workers. We chose one each so we'd be able to try everything. It was beautiful hearty food that you'd expect from Russia and a great last meal.

We were finally feeling that we had found the rhythm of the city, just before we left.

Our recent fatigue had passed, we were in such a great mood and having a lovely day. It could only have been the vodka. Maybe we'd been doing it wrong all this time and a morning libation should be the new norm. What harm could there be in that? After a quick stop at the hotel to pick up the bags, we jumped on the subway to Finlandskiy Station, to catch our Allegro train to Helsinki. We arrived at the station early so took the opportunity to explore nearby Lenin Square, where we were suddenly set upon by a very enthusiastic Korean woman. She initially wanted me to take her picture in front of a statue, but once she found out that we were Australian, she wanted us to be in all the pictures with her. A dozen selfies later, we politely exited stage left to get to the train, a lovely cheerful end to our Russian experience.

CHAPTER 9

Location: Helsinki
Days 153, Countries 13, Kilometers 31,562, Beds 77
Trains 11, Planes 11, Automobiles 32, Boats 8
Beers 59

Ikea-n as mustard to reach Scandinavia

The leg to Helsinki was on another superduper high-speed train, with the journey only taking a little over three hours. Leaving Russia was a significant milestone on the journey, we had now entered what we called leg 3 of the trip. We had just completed 12,000km from Hong Kong to Helsinki in 26 days, pretty impressive in anyone's book ('scuse the pun). If you don't believe me, just take a moment, put the book down and look at a map (just make sure you come back). Not bad eh?

Rather than swanning around a country for weeks at a time, our next stretch would be a cluster of city breaks, covering three countries in a week. We walked from the station on a drizzly day to find our lodging, which was our first Flipkey apartment of the trip. FlipKey is much like Airbnb where you are linked with owners of properties that let you rent either a room or the whole property. We'd chosen a property on one of Helsinki's main boulevards. It was a fantastic old building, recently converted into apartments and offices. We were met by Reijki, who was the owner's father. He was an interesting man with a quirky sense of humour and was very particular and detailed about various aspects of our stay in his daughter's flat. This accumulated in a 40 minute lecture about the use of the two bicycles, which included fitting them for our diminutive height. He wouldn't settle until he'd adjusted the seats and watched us both cycle around the building courtyard. This was despite the fact that we'd already said we probably wouldn't use them.

The apartment was charming. At around $100 it was expensive compared to our average accommodation costs but we needed to get used to the fact that costs would rise now we'd left Asia. We loved the city and enjoyed some great walks, tram rides, tasty food, and a nice day out by ferry to the UNESCO listed Fortress of Suomenlinna. Unfortunately, our budget wouldn't stretch to the Pub-Tram that circled the city centre. This was probably for the best as I'm sure it would have restricted our ability to pull off a MountyDay the following morning.

After two nights in the spacious apartment, it was already time to leave and head to the docks to catch our ferry to Stockholm. We'd arranged with Reijki to collect the keys from us as we were leaving, he then insisted on escorting us all the way to the ferry. To save money we'd decided to walk, and even though it was raining, he pushed his bike alongside us all the way. We never really did make the guy out, and unsure if he was being friendly, thought we were too incapable of making it there ourselves, or just wanted to ensure that we left his country.

Sauna ferry to Sweden

The ferry was a modern affair, sort of a cross between a Channel Ferry and a hedonistic Club-Med cruise. We discovered that due to lower alcohol prices in Sweden, the Finnish go nuts on cheap booze, and spend the cruise in one of the ships many hot tubs. We had a cheap room in the bowels of the vessel which was quite decent if you didn't mind squeezing through things or climbing up to bed. Being so far down, we were half expecting to open a little hatch and shovel in coal to progress the journey. To blend in, we decided to get stuck into the beers and even some bubbly to help us sleep, which we did quite well.

We were up early in the morning to watch as the ship traversed through beautiful Baltic Sea inlets as we approached Stockholm. It was stunning and a perfect morning with bright blue skies. After disembarking, it was a trouble-free walk, train, and walk to get to our latest home. After 158 days of travelling, it was going to be our first ever home without a private bathroom (apart from the train of course). I'd like to say we were getting brave, but it was purely down to the Benjamins, Sweden was expensive. Having said that, in true Mounty style, it was in the higher price range for a room with shared facilities and was actually part of a much posher hotel that had converted an old underground car park into a hostel. It was new, clean, very comfortable, and even had bunk beds so we could pretend we were back on the ship. With only two nights in Stockholm, we knew we were going to have to cram lots in. First things first, we stopped by the local shop to pick up some domestic Swedish beers for the stats.

We decided to take the tourist pressure off and jumped on a highly recommended free walking tour of the city. Tours like this are becoming popular in many European cities. You are charged a few dollars booking fee (if at all) and then the tour guide relies on tips, without any real hard sell. To help their chances, you'll find that the guide tries to make the experience fun, informative, and generally a little quirky. Looking at the website we saw a couple of tours that we liked, both had morning and afternoon sessions. Decision fatigued, we couldn't choose so signed up for both tours back-to-back.

Tours like these are often fast-paced to maximise what you see. Unfortunately, if you are a happy snapper like me, you don't always get the time you want to add the next few hundred photos to your collection. Quite often we would finish the tour, hand over what we felt we could afford to appease the travel Karma Gods, and then retrace the route to get the photos we wanted. After six hours of walking around Stockholm, photos would have to wait for the next day as we were knackered. Beer o'clock.

Wonderful wonderful Copenhagen

As we were getting closer to Denmark, we decided to email Cecilie and Jannik to get advice on areas to stay and what to see. I wasn't really expecting a reply. You know what it's like when you meet someone on holiday and exchange details, it's generally with the realisation that this is the last you'll see and hear from each other. I guess the Facebook era is changing things a little, so now the person you once watched a football match with in a Marbella bar will see a visual representation of how your brunch preferences change over the following 15 years. Our new found Danish friends were not Facebookers, so that wasn't an option, and I certainly hoped we would keep in touch. Meeting them had been a highlight of the trip and they had become such a big inspiration to us.

I was happy to see the reply in my inbox, but the contents were even more of a surprise. The gist of it was that we were staying with them, no questions asked, and they didn't need to send travel tips because they would be our guide to their city. I don't quite know why, but Nic and I had a bit of an emotional response to this. Partly because it was a random act of kindness, and partly because we are much more comfortable dishing them out, rather than receiving them. For me, it was mostly the fact that they wanted to go out of their way to spend more time with us, these highly intelligent worldly-wise people, with us two numpties.

Our journey between Stockholm and Copenhagen was via a very scenic train journey that included an 8 kilometre long bridge, spanning the Oresund sound between Sweden and Denmark. We hit the city and quickly changed trains to take us to our friends.

As we arrived at Klampenborg train station in the northern outskirts of Copenhagen, we were both excited and nervous. We really struggle feeling comfortable with people doing things for us or going out of their way. Both Jannik and Cecilie were there to greet us with a big smile and we immediately relaxed. Their tour guide duties kicked off straight away as they whisked us up the coast to visit the Louisiana Art Gallery. Louisiana is a famous museum of modern art, set in beautiful grounds with lovely sea views. A superb spot for lunch. Next, was a drive to Helsingør to see Kronborg Castle, made famous as Elsinore in Shakespeare's Hamlet. On the way back we stopped to pick up two of their grandchildren from school, had a quick turnaround at their beautiful home before venturing out to a nearby park. Not just any park I'll have you know, this was the Jægersborg Dyrehave, a large deer park containing a magnificent stately home. We toured the park on a large, ornate, horse-drawn carriage, a perfect way to enjoy this setting. A lovely home cooked meal with plenty of wine, ended a fantastic day. These people really know how to do a MountyDay.

The next day was spent in Copenhagen, starting off with our hosts who then headed back early, leaving the two of us to carry on exploring for a full day out. We loved this city, and our morning boat tour was a great introduction to it. More wonderful food and plenty of wine accompanied another lovely evening, full of talks about travel and some photo sharing. Once again we loved spending time with these two and wished it could be longer. Thanks guys x.

Fight or Flight

The last time we took a flight was 68 days ago, and after the cross-continental journey our overland stats were looking very good indeed. After all we'd accomplished, we really didn't expect to have a dilemma when travelling overland for the last little stretch to the UK. However, this proved to be much harder than we'd thought, after spending hours searching we still hadn't found a good solution. The time taken to do this research was also impeding our valuable time with our friends. Our best overland option meant that it was going to take around 4 days and a total of $450. This was much longer than we'd anticipated, we really needed to get to the UK to start searching for a campervan to take us on our 'Europe' leg. Just as a comparison, we checked flight prices and were immediately presented with a perfectly timed flight from Copenhagen to Liverpool for $45 each. As much as the overland travel was important, we just couldn't ignore this, and the money could then go towards the campervan purchase. We slept on it and for once, common sense prevailed. The flights were booked, we were going home.

She had a gob on her like the Mersey Tunnel

It was a bittersweet feeling as we landed at Liverpool airport, we hadn't made it all the way from Hong Kong overland, but we were excited to be arriving home. People take a year off travelling all the time, and we had only been going 6 months, but still, we felt like great adventurers and were pleased as punch with ourselves. Low cost flights to and from Liverpool are always enjoyable, the trumpet fanfare over the tannoy to announce that we had touched down safely always makes you laugh. This was tinged with a bit of concern when even the staff look surprised. It's also hilarious that in-flight announcements regarding the sale of electronic cigarettes will always get top billing over any safety procedures. Disembarking at John Lennon airport, it looked like a couple of aircraft had arrived at similar times. There was a long windy queue to get through the terminal building where we eventually reached the immigration check. For some years now we've been lucky enough to hold both English and Australian passports, so our normal M.O. when going through an airport has been to choose the shortest queue. The non-EU line was tiny, so we jumped on that and waited at the front for quite a while before the woman on the counter finally waved us forward. I was in a good mood so forgave her this indiscretion. Our other reason for getting in this line was the fact that our Australian passports were looking pretty bloody good by now, full of visas and stamps from all these exotic countries. It would be great to be able to add the stamp from my home town.

We handed over the passports expecting a welcome hug and some extended conversation about our impressive achievement. Next minute, the room went dark, everyone disappeared, we were in a small room, sat on cold steel chairs, as she positioned a bright lamp to point straight into our eyes. Okay, so that didn't quite happen, but she did start to interrogate us in her own arsey, jobsworth way. As soon as she saw that we didn't have an outward ticket, her mood just got worse and she demanded to know who we were staying with and what we did for jobs. Next, she proclaimed that I sounded English but Nic didn't, how could she prove that she was a nurse and had a position to go back to Australia for. We also had to explain that we were staying with my ageing father.

While the officer was looking down at her screen, Nic and I casually talked about what we'd done and how excited we were to get our passport stamped for Liverpool, in case this might change her mood. No response. She looked up and asked how old my father was. When I said 92, she proclaimed (pretty much to the whole room) that she could hardly phone up an old man to start asking him questions. This was the last straw as far as we were concerned. Before I said or did anything that we might regret, it was Nic who kept her cool this time, she reached into her bag and pulled out two British passports, slamming them down on the desk in front of our interrogator. Mardy bum looked at them, picked them up and handed them back to Nic without even opening them. 'Next time, get in the other queue!'. Welcome Home.

A little deflated we left the terminal, stopping by an ATM to get some UK dosh. We found the correct bus stop and waited for our ride into Liverpool's city centre. We didn't wait long at all and climbed onboard, handing over some crisp new bank notes to a balding, overweight driver. 'No change here, go away and come back with the correct money!' was our welcome. Strike two for the UK.

We needed to turn things around. Okay, so I'm not from Liverpool, I'm from Birkenhead which is across the other side of the famous River Mersey. This small stretch of water means that I am not a bona fide scouser but more commonly known as either a plastic scouser or a woolyback.

I figured we should do something special to arrive back in my home town. Those of you with a penchant for Gerry and the Pacemakers might have guessed by now, we decided to travel across on the famous *'Ferry Across the Mersey'*. It was lovely, the sun was out, lighting up the beautiful buildings along Liverpool's Pier Head, including the famous Liver Birds. Arriving home after 6 months of world travel on the historic ferry I used to ride as a kid was perfect. The day's earlier incidents were soon forgotten, and after a few swift, sharp turns with our backpacks on, any kids and infirm were soon dispersed from our prime spot at the front of the ferry.

It was because we didn't have an Alibi

Twenty-three minutes. That was the time it took my Dad to greet us at the door with tears in his eyes, make us a cup of tea, hear a bit about our great train journey, and then start slowly turning the sound back up on his favourite TV channel, Alibi. We had just conquered half the world, and before we knew it we were playing second fiddle to Angela Lansbury in *'Murder She Wrote'*. To be fair, Dad was 92 and had his routine, and it's not like we are a family of talkers. Jokers, gigglers, and drinkers maybe but you will never burst into a family meeting discussing the impact of Damian Hurst on the contemporary art scene, or what effect a robust German economy might have on the UK. Now that Nic and I were succinctly put in our place, we relaxed into the sofa with a cuppa, and it felt like we had never been away. Needless to say, Angela got her man, as did Dick Van Dyke in *Diagnosis Murder*, Yannick Bisson in *Murdoch Mysteries*, and so on. It was a fantastic afternoon of normal bliss.

Anyone for a Brazilian?

You blokes out there should be able to relate when I explain how we, as a sex, buy things. We may start out by being sensible, reading reviews and understanding what we can realistically afford. As the purchase time gets closer, we start up-selling to ourselves. No snake-oil salesmen needed, we are masters at it. 'If I get the computer with more memory, I'd be able to do so much more with it', 'If we rent the apartment with the gym, just think of the monthly fees we will save' (although we never have or are ever likely to join a gym), 'the metallic paint and leather seats will help with the resale value'. You with me?

It was time to start looking for our mobile accommodation. Influenced by the sensible around us, we initially pondered whether to buy a Toyota Hiace, like those Wicked Campers that you see driven by tourists, covered in graffiti and bedbugs. 'Well, it's not really a VW camper is it, it wouldn't be the same'. Next, we looked at hiring a VW Camper. 'How much! we wouldn't be able to have it for more than a couple of weeks'. 'Well, we could buy a banger and sell it once we finished'. 'I guess, we will have to live in it for weeks on end, so we want to be comfy, and we don't want to break down every five minutes'. End game, we are going to get a nice VW Kombi, that we may or may not sell afterwards.

Our initial plan was to have just two weeks in the UK. In this time we would have caught up with family, found, purchased, and packed up our dream VW camper. How hard could it be? Very. We searched in all the usual car sites, Gumtree, eBay, specialist magazines, and even managed to visit a VW show. As we moved around the country visiting family, we'd target searches in that particular area. Nic's Dad, Brian, and her brother, Ant, are car enthusiasts, so jumped right on board to help with our search. We started out knowing absolutely nothing about VW campers, and bit-by-bit we learnt about the difference between split and bay screens, high and low lights, Devon & Westfalia fitouts, tilting and pop up roofs. The more we discovered, the more we knew that we wanted one, but which one? There was a lot of rubbish examples out there. Admittedly our levels of hygiene and taste in accommodation had dropped considerably in the past six months, but this was going to be our home for three months.

In our learnings, we sensed the snobbery between the different versions. Split screens were more collectable and more expensive than bays, so much so that there was no way we would be getting a 'splitty'. The low-light refers to the front indicator lights that on the earlier bays were positioned just above the bumper whereas later models (high-lights) had them mid-way up above the headlights. Then there was the later Brazilian and Mexican imports, you can spot these as the roof from the windscreen rises up higher than the original.

Remember that this all started from a childhood photo of Nic's family's orange Kombi from the late '70s. In fact it was Brian that sent through a link to the first van we looked at, and guess what, it was Orange. It turned out to be a Brazilian. No, not the downstairs topiary, but rather the imported VW's that were actually still being made in Brazil. We found it stored undercover in a lumber yard run by a large Welshman. It was orange/white and had only been built in 1999 but had a private number plate that made it look like a classic from 1972. It had been regularly used for camping trips, and as such was already fitted out with cooker, fridge, leisure battery, a nice comfy bed, and wall to wall (in fact floor to ceiling carpet). The owner was a born salesman, he piled us all into the van, and threw it around some country roads. I was distracting him with conversation, while Nic and Brian were in the back rifling through all the documentation, taking secretive photographs of anything important like cold war spies. I was half expecting to turn around and find one of them dangling from the ceiling on ropes avoiding laser sensors while using a microcamera to check the authenticity of the latest MOT certificate.

At one point during our conversation, he was spruiking about the van and said 'look at this' while he madly shook the steering wheel from side to side without any effect on the direction we were going. Okay, I am not a mechanic, I generally polish a car to make it go better, but this didn't seem a valid selling point. Yet, he said it with such positivity as though he should add on a few hundred quid extra for this feature. It was a bit like someone presenting you with a necktie, rubbing it between their fingers and announcing 'look at this, it's 100% polyester, feel the quality'. Mental note made (and quickly forgotten) to chat with Brian about it later. During its life, the van had gone through a few engine changes and was even gas powered for a while, before getting its current traditional air-cooled 1600cc engine from the 1970s. This fact caused great concern, as a van built in 1999 should have a catalytic converter and be able to pass UK emission tests, but we were assured that it goes by the engine age so we should be okay.

Our next viewing was with a VW aficionado who showed us a green low-light he was storing for a friend. He was one of those guys that you automatically felt you could trust. It was a shame that this particular Kombi didn't connect with us, but we did walk away with one key bit of advice 'Whatever you do, don't get a Brazilian'. He explained that the metal was thinner and was more prone to rust and damage. Done, Brazilians were off the list (they'd actually been off Nic's list for many years).

The following day, we had another two to view, a heavily modified high-light that we really didn't trust, and a yellow

low-light that had recently been restored. The low-light was beautiful, it would need a little more work before travelling as there was no fridge or leisure battery, but it was a mighty fine example. We took it for a test drive and loved it even more. Not because it drove particularly well, but it looked and smelt like a real classic. The brakes were almost non-existent, and there was a real trick to get it into 2nd, I was already thinking about how challenging it might be to drive through the Alps. Never the less, after yesterdays advice it was top of our list from everything we'd seen so far.

Well, that was until we stopped and I jumped out with the engine running to check the exhaust. As I moved around the rear, the van suddenly disappeared behind a cloud of white smoke pouring from the back. The feedback from the now nervous looking owner was that it had just been topped up with oil and hadn't been run for a while. Any reasonable person would have exited stage left at this point, but not people who think with their hearts and not their head. We mentally added the cost of an engine replacement to the potential price. Although, this also meant that the Brazilian was back in play.

We ended up at loggerheads (no, not the place in Wales), I was favouring the cool classic low-light and thought it would be a better investment. Now, this might sound like I'm being degrading of Nic's decision-making skills, but she will agree that her choice was primarily based on the fact that the Brazilian was orange and had daisies painted on it. This is where it got hard, my passion for the unfinished classic, versus Nic's love of the ready to go orange Brazilian, versus family advice to forget it all and get a Toyota.

It took a few days to decide, in which time we were also bargaining down the two owners against each other. Without wanting to perpetuate any rumours that my wife always wins and I'm downtrodden, but after much discussion, the van we chose did indeed have daisies on it. In hindsight it was the right choice, we got a great price, and it was ready to go. It came with a cover, a drive-away awning, and even some Kombi coffee table books (including the ever essential Haines manual).

Next, one of the most critical parts of the whole campervan malarkey, choosing its name. This actually came quite easy, and we both agreed that we should name her after our late mums, so welcome to the family Maggie-Jane (almost immediately shortened to MJ).

orange is the new black

All we had to do now was buy everything we might need, pack her up, and bugger off to Europe. Rather than just buying the cheapest products available, we were strongly drawn to anything orange. This included:

- Orange plates and cups
- Orange tea towels
- Orange picnic table
- Orange picnic rug
- And many more orange things

The most extravagant of these purchases was a matching orange Nespresso coffee maker. I suppose if I were you, I'd be thinking 'What!, this doesn't fit into a backpacker trip around the world lifestyle'. Understood, but this wasn't just an impulse buy, it had been festering for some time. I have already mentioned how the Nespresso machine had helped us save for the trip by reducing our coffee shop spends. In the two years of trip planning, we would often fantasise about what life would be like on the different parts of our trip. One Saturday morning we must have been sat with a freshly brewed coffee and had been talking about the campervan leg. We'd just finished a barista course, and we were thinking that if we ran out of money, we could make coffee for the world. After remembering our poor barista efforts and sad attempt at coffee art, we decided that having a single button to press would be a better fit. Could we justify the cost? No. Would we do the same thing again? Yes, every time.

As this chapter comes to an end, it's probably a good time to introduce you to two team members that would be joining us for this leg of the trip. Firstly, our co-pilot, Hula. Hula was another of those ideas that formulated in our years of planning that we just had to make happen. She was one of those Hawaiian dashboard-dancing hula girls that bobble around as you drive. I think we must have seen one on a TV show (maybe *Breaking Bad*). As soon as we saw it, we looked at each other and the room suddenly brightening as two lightbulbs appeared simultaneously above our heads. No words were spoken, just a nod and Hula was born. Well, not just born, she was ordered in advance before we left Australia and then carefully wrapped up, travelling with us throughout Asia in our backpacks.

The final member of the crew was Betty, someone who would save our lives on numerous occasions. Betty was a Porta-Potty, and as we didn't want MJ to look like a dunny on wheels, we fashioned a wooden box with a cushion on top that covered her up, making an extra seat. I think we were ready.

CHAPTER 10

Location: Dover
Days 192, Countries 18, Kilometers 34,954, Beds 88
Trains 12, Planes 12, Automobiles 34, Boats 10
Beers 112

Bonjour, où est le camping

After calling in to see various friends and family on the journey south, we soon found ourselves parked underneath the famous White Cliffs of Dover, ready to embark on the next section of this adventure. We sat in MJ in the ferry terminal car park, feeling a little apprehensive about all the things that could go wrong once we left the comfort of the UK. I would be doing the majority of the driving which was more to do with Nic's superior navigational skills than my driving ability. It is in fact, one of the three reasons I married her. This works well, as I have complete faith in her map reading and navigational skills, and she had complete faith that she'd trained me enough to do exactly as she says.

The trip across the Channel introduced something that I hadn't really come across in the journey so far, sobriety. Previously, on a ferry crossing like this I would be on my 2nd beer by now (all for the stats of course). I momentarily contemplated whether

I was going to be less fun as a travelling partner, but hey, it's me! How could I not be fun? We exited the ferry, full of confidence, with our trusty co-pilot Hula looking after us from her centre dashboard position. We immediately went the wrong way into a busy suburb of Calais and were surrounded by unforgiving French rush-hour commuters. The situation was quickly made worse by turning into a street lined with sleeping policemen (speed bumps). MJ hit the first bump with a loud *dumpf* and we shot into the air. Hula spotted the safety of the duvet on the bed behind us and made her escape by flinging herself towards it, just missing Nic's head. This was not the start we'd hoped for.

Thankfully we'd set realistic expectations, and only planned to reach a nearby campsite, where we'd booked in for four nights. This would give us time to become acquainted with MJ, Betty and the joys of camping. It wasn't too long before Nic got us onto the right track, and we arrived at our designated spot. This arrival confirmed something we would find throughout the rest of the trip, a VW Kombi attracts smiles. Maybe sensing our inexperience, campsite management placed us behind a nice tall hedge so that we didn't need to pretend we knew what we were doing. No one could see us almost inserting the water pipe into the fuel tank, or spending 40 minutes trying to park MJ on level ground by seeing how much a can of baked beans rolled across the sideboard, or pulling the 'we are going to die' facial expression as we lit the gas stove for the first time.

Four days later we were all sorted, we knew how to connect, disconnect, empty, clean, sleep, and pack. Now it was time to grow some, and go travelling again.

Passion for France

Unlike the first six months, we weren't entirely prepared for this section of the trip and were making the route and countries up as we went. We had an idea of when we wanted to cross the Atlantic, but apart from that, the only other deadline we had, was to meet our Australian friend Susan in Berlin, four weeks from now. Because of this, we had initially thought about heading towards Brussels, and up through Germany, but then we saw how far away Berlin was and got very lazy very quickly. We compromised, deciding to head towards Italy, and then fly up to Berlin for the meeting.

It was our friends, Craig & Susan that had informed us of a fantastic organisation called France Passion. You join up by paying a nominal amount for a guide book which lists farms and vineyards throughout France where you can camp for free. Having membership meant that you can stop for free on the stipulation that it's just for one night, and that you are self-sufficient. This was one of the reasons for bringing Betty along. France Passion would be a great experience, a chance to meet real people, and embarrass ourselves at how little French we really knew. I was especially drawn to the fact that vineyards were also included in this list. We planned to mix it up between France Passion locations, and use proper campsites when we needed to recharge the leisure battery or needed a shower.

Our first France Passion site was a trout farm. We quickly realised that the biggest challenge with these sites wasn't the language barrier, or lack of facilities, it was finding the bloody thing in the first place. Each book entry came with detailed directions, but even Nic's superior map skills didn't stop us from never directly finding any France Passion site. The only indication it was a designated site, was a little five-inch rosette symbol on its entrance (and some were quite faded from the sun). So as the four of us (Nic, myself, Hula and Betty) turned off the main road, through a forest with nothing around for miles, we couldn't help but think if we would ever be seen again. More importantly, would anyone notice, and if so, how long would it take? It's not like we owed anyone any money. At least as English folk, we had that strong history of friendship and respect with the French to rely on.

Not only was this a trout farm, but it included a little shop and a lakeside bar for the fishermen to use. One of the goals for France Passion is that you would not only interact with the owners but that you might purchase some of their goods. It's not mandatory, and there was certainly no pressure, but when presented with beer and trout related products, I decided it would be bloody rude not to.

As the farm closed up, we were moved out of the main grounds. Our campsite was just outside the gates on a grass verge surrounded by fields, bordered with the most beautiful poppies. I wasn't keen on doing any 'wild' camping, and this kind of felt like it, so we were glad when we were joined by a much bigger campervan containing a Belgian family. As we supped our third beer accompanied by fresh bread and trout pate, you couldn't help but think this France Passion is a great idea.

During some beautiful days of touring through villages in the North West of France, we visited some WW1 memorials that were certainly thought-provoking, especially as one of Nic's relatives was remembered there. Almost as beautiful as the scenery was the food, we soon came to realise what our favourite saying in French was, 'Menu du jour'. We would make a beeline to any restaurant that had a sign out front. We'd quickly moved on from the 'Plate du Jour', which is basically the special of the day. The 'Menu du Jour' however, wasn't that much more expensive, and you received three courses for your troubles. They were always a great find as they were usually quite cheap, and tasted fantastic. What could be better than sitting in a beautiful cobbled courtyard with MJ parked up nearby, having a nice beer, enjoying two duck courses, followed by the best sticky date pudding in the world? It certainly wasn't helping the waistline, but as they say 'When in France, on the way to Rome...'

Red sky at night, get off my tractor!

Our campsite in Les Andelys was in a beautiful setting along the Seine River and overlooked by Chateau Gaillard, a medieval castle built in only one year for Richard the Lionheart. We spent our 2nd morning there exploring it, before returning to the campsite to say goodbye to the departing Roger & Vanessa. They had the snazzy modern campervan next to us, we'd caught up the night before, gained some handy camper advice and drank too much. After they left, it was time for a little nanna nap. About an hour later, we were woken by the rumbling of machinery moving through the campsite, I popped my head out of the window to see a tractor rolling past. Fair enough I thought, they have such a large piece of land here, it would need constant maintenance.

The tractor then pulled into the, now vacant, spot next to us. I assumed that they were taking the opportunity to do a bit of work there before the next campers turned up and quickly fell back to sleep.

We eventually came around, put the kettle on (this is code for opening the wine) and stepped outside into the beautiful evening. Not only was the tractor still in the spot, but just behind it was a small one person tent. Attached from the top of the tent to the back of the tractor was a make-do clothes line that had one T-Shirt and three pairs of women's knickers hanging from it.

The tent opened, and Ann appeared to greet us. Just when we thought we were on an adventure, we discovered that she was in the middle of driving this Zetor (a Czech built '70s classic tractor) from Holland to Portugal. It started off as a great bonding experience between her and her 18 year old daughter. The bone shaking journey in harsh elements, travelling at a maximum 25km/h (downhill), had meant her daughter had pulled the plug some time ago and jumped on the train to Paris, to fly the rest of the journey. Ann still sounded like she was enjoying the challenge but it meant the days were very tiring.

We started this conversation just as we were leaving to get some food and couldn't wait to get back and hear more about her adventure. By the time we got back, the tent was closed and the tractor's rumbling had been replaced with snoring (the tractor was quieter). Ann had crashed after her long day. The tractor left well before we emerged the following morning, keen to make some progress on the long journey ahead. We often thought about whether she'd made it safely, and what a great book that trip would make. Back to our own unadventurous adventure.

Getting an eyeful of Eiffel

Now that we were much more experienced with throwing MJ around small country lanes, and had our camping routine down pat, it was time to build up the courage to head towards Paris. This wasn't quite as scary as it could have been as we found the beautiful little town of Maison Lafitte, located about 20 minutes west of Paris. We stayed in a well-organised campsite, situated along the banks of the Seine. The town itself was a delight with a beautiful chateau and a number of other historic buildings. An express train ride from the town took us directly to the Arc de Triumph. Perfect.

It's incredible to think that this was the first visit to Paris for both of us, after living most of our lives only a two-hour flight away, we end up travelling halfway around the globe to get here. We weren't sure what to expect, but we fell in love with the city straight away. It reminded us of our first trip to New York, in that you enter a surreal world where you feel you know it so well. You've grown up, immersed in its imagery, but have not actually stepped foot here before. You feel like you have a starring role in your own movie. There were so many standouts in Paris, such as taking a nostril shot with the Mona Lisa in the Louvre, walking along the Champs-Élysée, and the Eiffel tower (which we only actually walked under).

I'm guessing you are a bit shocked to hear that we'd finally reached Paris and didn't go up the Eiffel tower. I totally understand, but it was always going to happen, we couldn't do everything. The comforting part of this, was that in most countries and cities, there would often be a big ticket item we didn't reach or couldn't afford. This meant that one day, probably many moons from now, we had the perfect excuse to do another tour.

Something that had played a part in planning our French timeline was the thought that it would be pretty cool to spend Bastille Day in Paris. Obviously, as typical English philistines, we knew little about the meaning of the day but figured that the French were sure to throw a good bash, whatever it was about. What transpired was one of the best 'Mounty Days' of the trip. The night before we hunkered down in MJ and did some research.

We started with an early morning train journey into the city before strolling off the beaten track through lovely side streets. As we approached the magnificent and familiar architecture of Notre Dam, we discovered that a choir service was just about to start. We snuck in and sat at the back for what was a fantastic experience, listening to beautiful music in this iconic setting. We then headed towards the Louvre as we'd decided that one of the bridges would be an excellent place to watch the military flypast, which follows the Champs-Élysée. It was a good choice, as we weren't caught up in the thousands of people lining the famous boulevard, and were able to make a quick exit once it was over. We picked our spot mid-bridge, chatting with a middle-aged French man who for 11am in the morning, smelt very much like a distillery. His aura was so strong, it made me a little tipsy. The weather was perfect and the flypast was great to see from this angle as they flew past us, down to the Louvre on our right.

As soon as it ended, we rushed to the nearest train station as we wanted to travel out to Versailles. As you can image, Versailles was a tourist hotspot on Bastille Day, we skipped the massive queues that were heading inside of the palace, this wasn't what we were here for. We headed straight to the gardens in search of something that had appeared in our previous night's research.

Along the banks of a canal at the bottom of Versailles' beautiful estate, a white picnic is held every Bastille Day. In a Henleyesque affair, everyone puts on their white Sunday best, and finds a spot on a lovely waterside lawn, protected by a line of tall trees. Boating, food, champagne (of course), and general frivolity follow. We were prepared, wearing smart white shirts and carrying a modest picnic, making us feel like locals for a few hours. We almost tried to interact with some nearby picnickers but were feeling a bit shy for once. After that, we ended up rushing around the interior of Versailles Palace, trying to cram in as much as we could before the end of the day. It was magnificent, but I have to say that I found the gold room in the Louvre more impressive than the halls of the palace.

Next, a quick march to the train station, and back into Paris where we enjoyed a pleasant meal opposite Bleriot's old home, which seemed fitting for an ex-aerospace engineer. We knew that Paris was going to present us with a firework display at midnight, so despite the early morning start we were determined to see it through and walked along the river to kill some time. Suddenly (not that she will want me to mention it), Nic came over with the worst bout of the shits. Thankfully, it hadn't played a part in our Versailles visit as that would have been horrible, with colossal toilet queues. However, it was now a no-holes-barred (pun intended) exercise of pacing ourselves slowly from toilet to toilet, along the bank of the Seine.

Obviously, I did look after her, but I could have been more sympathetic as I heard the loud popping of a romantic dream bubble bursting. Okay, just humour me a moment and close your eyes (read the rest of this bit first silly). Just imagine that you can click your fingers and be anywhere in the world with the person of your dreams, for a romantic tryst. Note that I'm talking romance here, so strike the furry handcuffs and waterbed scenarios from your list. How many of you chose to be in Paris, walking along the Seine, hand-in-hand? Except in our dream, I was holding Nic's hand while her other hand was on her stomach, trying to Jedi mind trick her lower intestine into going to sleep. The hand holding mine would randomly start giving me a death grip when she thought she was losing the battle. Other couples would be walking along with roses, and love in their eyes, while I was leaning up against a temporary plastic toilet because the door lock wasn't working. In some eager attempt at defence, it was just my strong disappointment for poor Nic that happened to manifest itself as me being an arse (sorry hun).

After a bit more walking and a brave attempt at some food, things seemed to be settling down on the old bum front, but we were now tired, a little grumpy and still had a couple of hours before the fireworks. We saw signs for a night-time boat trip that was only €12. We assumed it would be a horrible tacky tourist trap, but thought it would distract us and was certainly affordable on our budget. It turned out to be a great choice, we found a seat up top as it toured around with a fascinating historical commentary, passing beautiful buildings that were now lit up to show themselves off at night. We weren't sure where we were going to try and watch the fireworks from, but knew that the crowds would be deep at all the good spots such as the bridges. As the boat tour came to a close, we were expecting a mad rush to disembark, so we're getting ready to muscle our way to the front of the queue. Our plan was just to walk up to a nearby bridge, and hope for some equally small people to stand behind. However, rather than returning to its base, the boat suddenly double-moored against a similar boat and cut the engine.

Our €12 just secured us one of the best spots in town to watch the fireworks, from the River Seine itself. It was a truly memorable display with everyone on the boat singing around us, you couldn't help but feel quite patriotic with them. If this wasn't a 'turn it around' moment I don't know what is, and we were feeling quietly smug with ourselves. Actually, not so quiet, we were almost high fiving each other, while shouting out our mantra that 'you have to be in it to win it!'. That was until our thoughts quickly turned to how were we going to get home?

We knew the last train was at 12:40am, the fireworks had gone on for forever, and our now floating prison was nowhere near any of the tube stations we'd planned to use. We checked the map and decided that it might be just as quick to leg it straight to the Arc de Triumph station, rather than use a now chaotic subway system. Simultaneously, the whole of Paris seemed to have the same idea, and the race was on. In my memory, this had now evolved into a mass freerunning/parkour event with people running and jumping along rooftops, rolling over car bonnets, locals leapfrogging trash bins (see what I did there, cheeky). Everyone was encouraging others on, dogs and small children were swept up into people's arms, as we weren't going to leave a man behind. In reality, I think it was probably a bit more of a drunken, every man for himself, screw the dogs and small children scenario, but hey ho - it makes me smile when I think back.

We literally got to the station with minutes to spare and followed a throng of people all the way back to our campsite, into the open arms of MJ, Hula and Betty (who had a look of worry on her face, as she'd heard about the days earlier shenanigans). Just when we thought the day was quite special enough, we realised that the fireworks weren't over yet, and were still going off throughout the suburbs. We stood for a while in our camping spot along a different bank of the Seine, holding hands.

Wait a minute, that romantic dream moment happened after all. You know the mantra, now repeat to yourself one hundred times.

MJ, Famous in her own Underpants

To make Nic feel more confident that I had all things mechanical under control, I would occasionally spend a moment 'servicing'

MJ. This would consist of opening the engine bay, sticking my head inside, and prodding a couple of things. Knowing her love for the movie *Grease*, I would generally try to wear a tight white T-Shirt and get a little oil on it as well as my cheek. I'd then firmly close the bonnet, and walk up to her while wiping my greasy hands and informing her that we were all good. I stopped just short of performing a quick hand jive, and thankfully MJ didn't have a bonnet to jump on.

One particular day at our Maisons Lafitte campsite, this also caught the attention of a local film crew. They were filming for an advert and approached us with a pigeon English proposition. Maybe this was my big chance, *Grease 3 - The Kombi Kronicles*. To be fair it was MJ that caught their eye, and Nic was looking particularly radiant that morning. They setup a scene that panned from a Baguette perched on the bed with the back door open, to Nic writing in her journal, as I brought her a cup of coffee. Two takes and we nailed it. The team left and we have no idea what happened to the footage, it's probably out there somewhere as the intro to a *Carry on Camping* remake.

Put a Cork in it

It was a real shame to leave Paris, we really enjoyed the place, and for sure we will be back, but the tour stops for no-one. At least our next destination was something to be excited about. It involved tall glasses and bubbles, you guessed it, we were on our way to Champagne. A quick peruse of our France Passion guidebook revealed a small Champagne maker in the north of the region where we could stay. The thought of ending the day with free accommodation at a place that makes bona fide champagne quickly made us forget about the fact we were leaving this beautiful city. Although the day left a bittersweet feeling as a failure to live up to our mantra led to one of the big regrets about our trip.

Logistically, the Paris campsite was great as it meant that we didn't need to travel into the centre of Paris, but on the other hand, it also meant that we didn't drive into the centre of Paris with MJ. We just kept imagining MJ doing circuits of the Arc de Triumph, unable to exit as though we had the Griswold family in the back of the van. We even spent some time analysing traffic flow from both the bottom and the top of this monument, to get an idea of how it might be done, but we piked out. Little did we know that this failure to 'be in it' would come back to bite us later in the trip, and haunt us ever since.

It was quite a long run out to Champagne and required negotiating the busy ring-roads of Paris so we needed a super early start, and to be prepared for a long day ahead. After getting lost in the country lanes around Charles de Gaulle Airport, we quickly forgot about the Paris centre excursion. This detour introduced some choice words into our workplace, as I was frustrated at Nic for only wanting to use paper maps despite the fact that it doesn't have a handy blue dot showing where we actually were. This frostiness quickly passed, and we soon found our right path, just as a large Airbus skimmed over the top of MJ.

France Passion was true to my earlier description, as it took three slow runs through the town of Trélou Sur Marne to find the faded rosette that led us to the vineyard of Couvent-Parent. All day we'd pictured MJ parked amongst a row of vines while the vintner would sell us bottles of his ware at a few euros each, and dag nab it if it wasn't our God-given duty to support this man who has opened his home up to us. In reality, our camping plot turned out to be a small patch of front lawn on a modern house, next to a large modern shed. Not quite what we had in mind, but the thing we loved about France Passion was that you didn't know what will happen, you just need to be ready to embrace it.

The owner, Jean-Louise's English was about on par with our French, but I suppose at least there was the two of us Pommes. Nic was much stronger at translating what someone said, and I was a little better at speaking (well more willing to make a numpty of myself). He came over and said some words to Nic which she agreed to. I could make out that it was something to do with 7pm. She explained that he'd come and give us a tour of his facilities at 7pm. Then, I decided to confuse things by saying that I thought I'd heard the word dejeuner, so was concerned that he had in fact, invited us for dinner (it actually means lunch but what do I know). We are not great at accepting hospitality at the best of times, and we were getting a bit stressed. Not so much about having to be sociable while demolishing one of the world's most beautiful languages, but the fact that we didn't really have anything to contribute. If there was one place that our supply of Mentos was not going to cut the mustard, it was Champagne, France.

Our worries were unfounded though when he turned up at 7pm on the dot and did indeed show us around his winemaking shed. It was well equipped with machines that automatically rotate the bottles, slowly moving the sediment to the neck where it can be removed. He had clearly picked up a few lines of English to explain each process, which might typically work when no-one asks questions. However, we were all about the interaction and backed up by a wife that could represent her country in verbal diarrhoea Olympics (in fact that's one of the three reasons I married her). We provided Jean-Louise with what I am sure was his worst nightmare. Some mimes and machine noises later, I think we pretty much got the gist of it all, so headed to his cellar for some tasting. Expecting to just get a sip of each of his three varieties before the big sell, we were very pleasantly surprised to find that he opened a full bottle for us to get through between tastings of the other two. We cracked on with our attempts at conversation over a map of the area, he showed us where his grapes were located. I even managed to get the word 'merde!' into the conversation which I was quite proud of, whether Jean-Louise understood me or not. We bought a few of his bottles, which were certainly more than the few euros we'd earlier imagined and retreated to MJ. Another great FP experience.

The next day we knew we wanted to try and get down to the Beaujolais region, but had some important business on the way. That business was a town called Epernay, the centre of the universe for Champagne. We took some nostril shots outside our favourite brands, including our wedding bubbly, Perrier Jouet. Our Epernay experience was enhanced by an educational trip through the vast cellars of Moet et Chandon, where we were amazed to discover every bottle of Moet we see, no matter where in the world, had come through these cellars. In a day and age where everything is outsourced, it was great to see this and for once I tipped my hat to the guys and girls in Brussels with their EU laws. We stayed that night in the courtyard of another vineyard just outside of the Champagne region. Although still a France Passion site we had access to a toilet block and washing facilities, so we're really living it up.

A Nouveau experience in Wine Town

Beaujolais wasn't initially on our radar, but I noticed that we were driving south just east of what makes up the main villages for this famous wine region. It didn't take much of a discussion to decide on a side trip, before veering off onto small beautiful country lanes up into the nearby hills. We stopped at a lovely little windmill surrounded by vines and then moved up to the village of Juliénas, a town originally named after Julius Caesar, and famous for its Gamay grape and Beaujolais wine production. As we entered the town, we spotted a huge sign saying that there was a wine festival today, so of course, it would be rude not to stop.

We parked outside an old church, which was now a cellar door for the co-op of local vineyards before heading to an area where the main street was cordoned off. It was made up of stalls representing the local vineyards and intermixed with local food producers selling the most amazing treats such as bread, cheese and sausages. We hit the first stall to find out that we needed to pay for tastings. Without even prompting, Nic offered to drive for the rest of the day, this type of behaviour is definitely one of the three reasons why I married her. So, we just paid for one ticket which not only gave us access to the tasting, but I received a celebratory wineglass that came with one of the best inventions ever. It was a lanyard that went around your neck, at the end was a little nappy that your wine glass would fit snuggly into. My initial thoughts were that it was designed so you could plough into the bread and cheese unimpeded. On reflection, after watching the local villagers unable to converse without their arms and hands flying around everywhere, I think the whole event would be reduced to silence without these nappies.

Thankfully the language barrier was not a problem here, I suppose the area has a heavy footfall of tourists looking to imbibe. What helped the whole process was our meteoric rise to stardom. At the very first stall, we ended up front and centre in a little sing-song of local performers dressed in period clothing, it would be a fair bet to assume that they had already visited the stalls a few times already. One of them spoke a bit of English and asked where we were from. Without hesitation, 'We're Australian'. Oh come on, you can hardly blame us, we wanted to be directed to the good wine not the 'Wine for the English'. So, the fact that Australians are generally more liked, and that we had travelled from the other side of the world just to see them, won over their hearts. After trying out the wares on the first stall, we were manhandled over to the next, where the new proprietor would be given a full update about who we were. Word seemed to get ahead of us, and people we'd not met, knew where we were from. It was all a bit strange, as even though it was obviously a local fete, surely they must have been exposed to plenty of Australian tourists.

We spent a bit of time talking to a lovely bloke called Pascal, who ran a vineyard with his wife, and I must say his wines were fantastic, but the stand out experience was with a young guy called Arnaud. He took to us straight away, he looked like he had just left school and was looking after the stall for the grown-ups. He was very interested in our travels and MJ, which he later came and looked over. After talking about us, we turned the attention to him and found out that this young whippersnapper actually ran the vineyard that had been in his family for four generations. He saw himself as an entrepreneur and had recently travelled to New York, securing a deal with a couple of restaurants there. He took us through his wines before opening the pièce de résistance which was a wine he called 'My Fathers Secret' (Le Secret de mon Père).

Unlike Australia's trend for screw tops, this one not only had a traditional cork like all French wines, but was then secured with a coating of wax over the top of the bottle. He didn't usually open them for tasting, but I think he was very proud to show people from overseas. His skills didn't stop at the business side of things, he'd also drawn the artwork for all his bottles too. After wanting a photo with us for his website, we left the fete loaded with some great wines from our new found friends, as well as a few days supply of bread, cheese, and the most fabulous cured duck and fig sausage. I was so glad that Nic was driving the rest of the way to Mesnil St Pere, and I did my best to navigate with only one wrong turn.

As for today's detour, you know what I'm going to say don't you - 'You've got to be in it …..'

Blue Loo Juice, shaken not stirred

The thought of driving into Switzerland and arriving in Geneva seemed pretty adventurous for us. Although, MJ wasn't quite an Aston Martin, and rather than playing the nearest casino, we were busy emptying the blue juice from Betty down an appropriately authorised drain, we still felt a little James Bondesque. We knew in advance that Geneva was going to be expensive, and at €65 per night, it was by far the dearest campsite we'd stayed at, mainly because it was on the edge of Lake Geneva, and only a short local bus ride to the city centre.

We wanted to savour the feeling of achievement for getting this far with MJ, so stayed for a few days. This gave us the chance to have a mix of full-on MountyDays, exploring a city which was beautiful but not very flat, and having days on the campsite with afternoon swims in the lake. Something from my wish list, that wasn't exactly cultural, was to get a pucker Swiss Army Knife from the company's head office in the Geneva. I didn't choose the biggest one, but felt confident that I now had the tools to dismantle and rebuild MJ, as well as remove a stone from a passing horse's hoof. To top it off, they even embossed my name on it as a lasting souvenir of the trip.

We were blessed with beautiful warm weather, and on one lovely bright day I sat in the reception of the campsite using their WiFi and decided to Skype my father in the UK. Considering my call would have automatically come through on his Skype-enabled TV, interrupting his morning Alibi viewing, he was on great form. We joked about campervan life, and I filled him in with Hula's and Betty's exploits. One of the many traits that I am thankful to have been passed down from my father is the ability to smile with our eyes. Even through the dodgy WiFi connection, I could see the glint in his eye, before he started laughing so much that they were full of tears. He looked so happy, I took a crafty little screenshot of him to show Nic. We spoke for longer than usual, and his enthusiasm for our trip really put me in a great mood. I was already looking forward to filling him in with our upcoming adventures in our next chat.

It's Caper Time – knock it up a cog

As we left Geneva, heading south-east and back into France, we knew what was coming but didn't want to talk about it. Slowly, bit by bit, our anxiety was building about the thought of trying to get MJ through the Alps. So far, the oil temperature hadn't been too bad, although MJ always welcomed a little cool down stop. Now though, the air was getting thinner, and the gradients were increasing. Nic must have thought I'd developed a nervous twitch, my head moving quickly and continuously between the road and the temperature gauge. The plan was to find a campsite just before the final lead up to the Mont Blanc tunnel so that MJ only had a short run and hopefully wouldn't get too hot in the tunnel. What we didn't realise was that the last 15-20 kilometres leading to the campsite were probably the steepest we would face, and we did it during heavy traffic after a long day of motoring. The oil temperature hit the roof and we had to pull off to give MJ a rest, and calm down from its first little tantrum. This didn't help the nerves.

We made it to nearby Chamonix, filling up with petrol before finding a lovely little campsite located in a small wood at the bottom of a glacier on Mont Blanc. We had an idyllic evening, cooling some beers and gazpacho in a nearby glacial stream. This turned into a less than idyllic night when a torrential downpour proved too much for the waterproofing of MJ's roof, causing us to jump out of bed at 3am to close things up. We were also surrounded by a zombie army of slugs during the night, which gave the trips to the toilet block an interesting soundtrack. A better nights sleep would have been more ideal, before the following day's shenanigans.

We left around 7am, expecting big queues that didn't eventuate, we drove straight up to within eight car lengths of the toll. Tolls were always great fun in Europe, at least for me as they were all on the other side of the vehicle so Nic had to do everything. The entrance to the tunnel was in sight, the GoPro was turned on and suctioned to the roof, ready to record the moment for posterity. The oil temperature was already a little higher than normal as we approached the toll. The wait had given it time to cool down a bit, but I kept thinking about what a nightmare it would be to breakdown in the tunnel. I had a sudden flashback to a very dodgy Sylvester Stallone movie that featured some tunnel related disaster. There was also the fact that when researching the route we found out about the tragic and fatal 1999 fire that did occur in the tunnel, highlighting poor safety procedures and inadequate equipment that was available at the time.

Nic paid, the barrier went up, a drop of sweat fell off my brow and we were off. As I pulled away, I made a note of the mileage so that I could get an idea of when we were halfway through the 11.6km tunnel. Things would then hopefully start going downhill, so to speak. We immediately had a large truck right up our arse which really didn't help, thank you very much, but after about 4km I took my first breath, started to relax and took stock. Checking everything as though I was on my first driving lesson, I put my hand on the gear stick, Bugger.

Not only did MJ have enough to worry about today, but she'd acquired a muppet of an owner who just tried to get her all the way through the Mont Blanc tunnel in 3rd gear! I tried to be as quick and smooth as possible to change up without Nic noticing, but she doesn't miss a thing. Her tone was more 'you're a knobhead' than the normal Aussie adopted phrase of 'She'll be right'. Even when she actually did say 'She'll be right', it came across as 'She'll be right, no thanks to you, knobhead!'. Just then, I could see the light at the end of the tunnel (fnarr) and all of a sudden without any fanfare, apart from the blaring soundtrack from the *Italian Job* (the original movie of course, I can't believe you asked), we popped out like a bright orange baby into the Italian countryside.

Una veloce Italian driving lesson

Just like a newborn given a swift slap on the arse, it wasn't long before we were crying and wishing we could return to the comfortable womb of the tunnel. It appeared that we had somehow been transported into a road scene from a *Mad Max* movie. Seriously, how could seven miles make such a difference?

A few moments ago, the French style of driving would have seen an aggressive shrug of the shoulders as someone politely let you in. All of a sudden we had cars coming at us from all angles. I was scared to lift my elbow too high, because I knew if I did, an Italian car would appear from under an armpit. So far the Mountford and Mountford cockpit pairing was akin to McRae and Grist, always calm, never arguing but things soon changed.

We were only twenty minutes into the country when the relationship started to become heated, sweaty brows were suddenly in fashion and conversation was much more terse. What didn't help was the fact that the roadside had become inundated with signs, not useful signs, but ones for plumbers, pizza shops or garden centres. As we drove on, the billboards for such nonsense as dog grooming got larger and the signs for important direction changes became smaller, often hidden behind a dodgy looking realtors smiling face. Nic was busy searching for the directional signs, trying to match them to our small-print 'All of Europe' roadmap, while constantly checking her side of the Kombi for any insurgent Italian drivers.

Even Hula looked worried, her wiggle resembling a grumpy aunt shaking her head. Thankfully we'd planned not to go too far, and our first Italian campsite was only about an hour and a half into the country. We only took one wrong turn on the way which was more luck than anything. Straight away we realised how much our school French had helped us in the previous country. Now we had to employ much more arm waving, mimes, and saying things louder in English to achieve our goals. I played my 'I'm driving' card, forcing Nic to sort out the campsite with its owner. Before long we were sitting in a great spot in the beautiful Aosta Valley, with the Alps as a backdrop, and a well-deserved beer in our hand.

Our navigation capabilities were to dramatically improve that evening, as we met Adrian and Susan who had their caravan parked nearby. They were making their way home to the UK, and we joined them for a few wines. We'd been describing our turbulent Italian experience so far, and once they saw our teeny tiny map, Adrian disappeared for a moment, returning to hand over a well-loved Italian roadmap from 2007. We were now cooking on gas. No wait, that was later when we heated our pasta.

Having to be Prague-matic about our travel plans

Time was marching on, and we were getting close to our appointment in Berlin with Susan. We decided that we'd fly from Milan to Prague and then catch the bus to Berlin before flying back to Milan. This meant that we needed to leave the beautiful Aosta Valley, and head to a campsite only 14km from Milan Airport. Unfortunately, this wasn't a great spot at all, the sort of campsite where you felt like you need a shower after you've just walked out of the shower block. It was also hot, I mean really hot, and after heavy rain it was full of mosquitos. We hid in MJ and sweltered, feeling a bit low, wondering if August was the best time to be in a metal box in Italy. We were holding out for the Czech Republic to rejuvenate us (as well as being a bit cooler).

You've all heard that saying 'be careful what you wish for', well by the time we woke for the early run to the airport, the mosquito-ridden hell had suddenly turned into the Arctic. It was wet and freezing, so to reduce stress we decided that we'd throw some money at the situation and use toll roads. It certainly helped, but still had its hairy moments and we let out a sigh of relief as we abandoned MJ in the airport's long term car park.

As we boarded the aircraft, we noticed that there were at least two stag parties joining us. I looked at Nic and rolled my eyes. She very quickly reminded me that my stag weekend was actually in Prague while her's was in the less cosmopolitan UK city of Chester. Yes you're right it was a little uneven. Neither of us know quite how it happened, but it did, and for the past 10 years it's been my mission to take Nic to this romantic and beautiful city. Obviously leaving it long enough so that they have all forgotten about me there. Our hotel in Prague was a stone's throw from the Charles Bridge, in an effort to make this a special, yet brief visit.

Touring the city, I took hundreds of photos as usual. I like to think I'm a reasonably handy photographer, not so much in technical knowledge but in understanding what will look good. That was until Prague. We were walking over one of the many bridges that cross the Vltava river, this one offered lovely views of the famous Charles Bridge. About halfway across, we were stopped by a pretty girl who wanted her photo taken. I obliged, always feeling a little pressure in these situations. I took two lovely framed pictures capturing her and the bridge, before handing the camera back. She looked at the photos I'd just taken, looked up, turned to a random guy who was standing right next to me, and asked 'will you take my picture'. She didn't even wait till I'd gone. I've still yet to recover from the experience, how bad could it have been for Christ's sake?

Hopefully, this mini city break lived up to Nic's expectations, we covered lots of ground and ended up with very sore feet. Our first full day included a whopping 11 hours of touristing (that's a word), spreading our net to avoid the crowded popular areas. A highlight was to catch a funicular railway up to Petrin Hill which has an observation tower in its grounds. The tower was inspired by the Eiffel Tower and is about a fifth of the size, but unlike the Paris counterpart we actually made it up this one. Prague was an ideal place to improve our domestic beer stats, including a session in the U Pinkasu bar which has been serving beer since 1843. The weather became very hot and because of the age of our hotel there was no air-con, making it pretty uncomfortable at times. Our next location would be cooler (in more ways than one).

Not Sleepless in Berlin

Apart from when you're flying, there aren't many times when you have a little nanna nap and wake up in an entirely different country. That's what happened to Nic. As a rule, she can fall asleep within seconds, in any position, and not even an earthquake, or a Chinese man whispering could wake her up. This, in fact, was one of the three reasons I married her. When we first met, I nicknamed her 'The Hamster', because all she did was eat, run around like a nutter for a bit, and sleep.

If you drew a pie chart of her sleep against my sleep, my pie wouldn't fill a supermodel's tummy. What's that you say? 'bitter?', Okay yes a bit. I don't often use the word chagrin, but on this subject, she does rub my chagrin up the wrong way. Anyway, there she was fast asleep, while I was took up my usual role of trying to make sure we stayed alive. To be fair though, it had been a 5:30am start after a busy MountyDay, so I couldn't really blame her. We'd also had the stress of nearly missing our coach as the hotel staff on sparrows-fart duty didn't know how to check anyone out.

The coach was taking us from Prague to Berlin to meet our Aussie friend Susan. She was briefly visiting the city in a pre-arranged meet up, on her way to the UK. Berlin was always on our bucket list, this city break was something all three of us were excited about. It was only a five-hour coach trip from Prague so seemed a perfect plan, we would pop up and then fly back to MJ in Milan.

Nic wakes up, 'where are we?', 'Germany', 'What!', 'Yep', snores.

Ich bin ein Berliner

The bus dropped us off on the outskirts of town, and a train brought us right to our hotel in Alexanderplatz. We had a message waiting for us from Susan to say she'd meet us at 3pm. It was great to see her. As someone who we'd see every week back home, it had now been 6 months and really made us feel connected to Melbourne again. She is also a great person to travel with, and always up for jam-packed days. Thankfully so, as the next day turned out to be a big 14 hours away from the comfort of the hotel.

Berlin was fantastic, a bit like an edgier version of Melbourne. Just like our home town, it seemed to be one of those places that takes a day or two to grow into. It could have been the bad weather, but the locals we met, albeit all hospitality staff in shops and restaurants, came across as quite grumpy. This was chalk and cheese compared to our home town, it's twin with a sunnier disposition. We learnt a lot about the history of Berlin while we were there, which no doubt contributed to the personality of the city. Similar to Russia, once you understand and accept the fact that you may need to put in more of an effort to break down walls with the locals (I know), you can start to fall in love with the place.

Sombre Selfie

Both Susan and I are prolific photographers when we travel. If it's not in a picture, then you never saw it. With me that's mainly because I can't remember breakfast. The funniest photos were our efforts to pull off a respectful 'sombre selfie'. The three of us would get ourselves in position with a piece of the Berlin wall behind us and then 'One, Two, Three, Sombre Face!', *click*.

Unlike the regular selfie brigade, we developed a way of diminishing the significance of a historical site in a slightly more respectful way. I found the best way was to pretend I'm a little constipated. It's amusing showing people the photos when we got back home, they look and ask why we weren't enjoying Berlin.

The history we've all written essays about in school was suddenly very real and tangible here. We knew what had happened, we'd seen the films about what had happened, but being here seemed to bring that history to life, and it was often a gut wrenching feeling. We used organised tours, and free walking tours to maximise our time and soak up as much knowledge as we could. Visiting the Sachsenhause Concentration Camp and standing in the same rooms where atrocities had happened; walking through the Holocaust Memorial's powerful and disorientating art installation; seeing various remains of the wall and hearing survivors stories about life in Berlin; standing above Hitler's bunker in what's now a car park; it was all a very humbling experience.

We said our goodbyes to Susan at the end of the second day. A 3:45am start led us to the airport where we flew back to Milan. I'm not quite sure how, probably the ultra-long days spent in the last two cities, but we didn't have a plan at all from here. We landed and realised we didn't know what we were doing, so stayed in the airport to use their free WiFi and plotted over breakfast. As much as it was great to see MJ again, we decided to leave her parked at the airport for another night and find accommodation in the centre of Milan. By using that as a base, we would be able to explore the city much more easily. It wasn't the cheapest of options but the thought of driving MJ in and out of the city each day really didn't appeal.

Milan, home of the fashion thongs

We were excited about Milan, very excited. The home of Alfa Romeo, this city had always been the drawcard for us to Italy. Over the years we'd previously owned two classic Alfas. *Top Gear's* James May once said that 'everyone should own an Alfa once in their life', and when you do they are addictive. We had always dreamed of driving our old Spider to its birthplace, in what would surely have been a pilgrimage filled with mechanic bills and arguments.

Our Milan hotel, Cristoforo Columbus, was located in an ideal location. We arrived early, so dropped the bags off before embarking on a whirlwind seven hours walking tour of this great city. Before we'd even seen our hotel room, we'd managed to visit some of the city's iconic sites such as the Duomo, Galleria Vittorio Emanuele II, the Castillo, and Arc de la Paix.

Our rough plan had been to visit the Alfa Romeo museum and arrange to camp at the nearby Monza racetrack, but unfortunately this wasn't to be. With some great help from the staff at the hotel, we found out that the museum had closed, and was in the process of relocating. To top it off, the racetrack campsite was only available during race weekends too. Feeling a bit dejected, I decided to cheer myself up. It was time for some new thongs (we call them infradito in Milan don't you know). Strolling down the Corso Buenos Aires, we came across an actual Havaianas shop. Well, I just couldn't get the usual bog standard pair from here, so after about an hour of indecision, I left with a cool, wide, two-tone, extra padded affair. For the first time since my original pair was stolen in Malaysia, I had the Rolls Royce of thongs back on my feet again.

Lakeside Living

With our Alfa fun out of the window we decided that the next location should be a pretty cool one to make up for it. It was the Great Lakes of Italy. After popping back to the airport to pick up MJ, our first stop was Lake Como. This brought mental images of George Clooney dropping round for a coffee from MJ's matching orange Nespresso machine.

It was a long days journey, notwithstanding the dramas of Italian roads. As a result, we decided to camp at the first site we came across, in the town of Lecco. We grabbed one of the last spots, facing a busy dual carriageway. After a long meander through the campsite, we came across the lake. It wasn't a bad view once we found it, but we couldn't help feeling a little disappointed. It now seemed unlikely that a caffeine needy Mr Clooney would stroll up to our plot, while I cooked up a snag (sausage) on the barbie.

We decided that Lecco wasn't for us and moved onto Iseo the following morning. This place wasn't on our radar at all until we spoke to Adrian at that first campsite in Italy. Apart from a 30 minute detour to track down a supermarket, our journey went well by Italian standards. We had researched a campsite with great reviews and booked ahead to reserve a spot. The site was small but immaculate and right on the lake. Through Italy the temperature had been getting hotter, and our new supermarket purchase of a fan was put to good use, as was an afternoon swim in the beautiful lake to cool off.

This family-run campsite had such a great atmosphere it seemed to rub off on everyone, making it by far the most social of sites we stayed on. We chatted with so many nationalities, and MJ was undoubtedly an ice breaker. Although I think they were a bit worried about me after the day I nearly killed Nic. We were partaking in our regular afternoon swim in the lake when, feeling in a cheeky mood, I decided to dunk Nic. I was quite pleased with my swift nudge to the back of her knee while scooping up her legs underwater. Nic wasn't prepared for this. So much so that she didn't even close her mouth before submerging. I could easily insert a comment about her verbal diarrhoea being life-threatening, but as the perpetrator, it would be inappropriate. She surfaced and started choking. Not quietly. I like to think that in her position I'd gasp for breath in a way that wouldn't ruin anyone's serenity, or indeed bring attention. Long story short, she lived, I got hit, and everyone kept a close eye on me from that point onwards.

So, remember the drive into Paris that never was? Well on this campsite we met Steve and his family who were in a modern VW T5 camper. He was really interested in MJ, as they used to have a T2. After talking about our journey, he whipped out two of his proudest possessions; a picture of them in their T2, in front of the Eiffel tower, and a similar one in front of the Arc de Triumph. He may not have had the van anymore, but he did have the photos. My heart sank, why hadn't we been brave enough to do it. Especially after driving in Italy, it would have been a doddle. Mental note taken.

Apart from the heat, this place was magical and we extended our time at the campsite twice, making it one of our longest stays in a single spot. Our daily routine would start by preparing ourselves, and our Dutch neighbour, a coffee before we toured the historic town, travelled around the lake on beautiful old ferries, and finished with a swim in the cool water. I even managed to look handy, and put my Swiss Army Knife to good use by making a reverse polarity hookup cable. You would often come across sites where the electricity was wired incorrectly, a tester plug would show this, and you'd then use the cross over cable attached to your standard hook up. We really had gotten into the groove of campervan life.

Time to kill after oil

Our next location was another recommendation from Adrian, and we headed to Lazise on the edge of Lake Garda. Our campsite was indeed underwhelming and was a real tourist trap with a Miss Campsite pageant happening that night. However, one important consolation about the area was that it had a nearby VW garage. Just before we bought her, MJ had received a refurbished engine, and we were just over the mileage that required her to get an oil change.

The timing meant that it would need to happen in Italy, which was going to be an adventure by itself, but of course, it wasn't just any type of oil we needed. After online research and advice from Brian, we were looking for a specific non-synthetic oil used for classic racing engines. How hard could that be? We went for a tootle through the town towards the garage, after all, I think it was the Italians that put the 'toot' in tootle. It was quite a winding road out of town, and we gained height very quickly, but MJ did us proud, and with only two wrong turns we were happy as Larry to see the VW signage in the distance. We pulled up to their iron gates and jumped out, but just like an episode of the Amazing Race the entire garage was closed for lunch. You know what they say 'when 250 miles north of Rome, do as the Gardanians do' so we fired up the grill and cooked up some lovely sausage sandwiches.

I certainly hope they never get a 'Time and Motion' audit from the bigwigs at VW, it was about 3pm when someone eventually turned up. The first few employees we encountered were not interested in making eye contact, let alone investigate our oil change. Finally, they wheeled out a young female receptionist that spoke some English. As she was translating our needs to the group of mechanics behind her, you could see that they were a bit surprised by our specific oil request. However, one guy that looked like their leader gave us an approving look, providing some optimism. A quick phone call by our newfound friend discovered that they wouldn't be able to get the oil for a couple of days. Back to the campsite we returned, to wait while exploring more of the local area.

This worked out well, as what we initially thought was an unimpressive location and campsite, turned out to have a beautiful waterfront old town just a fifteen-minute walk away. Staying also meant we had a chance conversation with another Brian, an English tourist that travelled down to the area every year with his family, on a caravan holiday. He asked about our route and proposed that 'of course' we must be heading to Verona next, on our way to Venice. Embarrassingly, we declared that we didn't really know much about it and hadn't planned to go. An hour later when he had finished praising the city as one of his favourite in the world, it was firmly embedded into our plans.

With a day in hand, we took MJ for a run out to Sirmione, which has a beautiful Scaligero Castle perched on top of a long thin peninsula protruding into the bottom of Lake Garda. For once the Italian traffic and parking fell into place nicely. It was a long day but really worth it, followed by a short night, as MJ needed to be at the garage for 8:30 the next morning. The oil change went well, during which we killed time in the lovely waterfront town of Garda, having a nice brunch and browsing through its many boutique shops. We handed over our €93 to the garage and were returned MJ's keys. Not only was she replenished internally, but I had also given her the first clean and polish of the trip, so we were ready to hit the road once again. Next stop Verona (of course).

Campsite, Campsite, wherefore art thou, Campsite

Our research showed something listed as a free campsite within walking distance of Verona's historic town centre, so we headed straight there. I say straight there, but it was more like straight there, past it, hit the countryside again, turned around, navigated a one-way system for a bit, then went straight there. Also, when I say campsite, I mean car park. We'd heard horror stories of camping in car parks regarding hold-ups and robberies, so were a little apprehensive. However, there were lots of trucks, caravans, and campers around, so we decided to suck it up and head into town.

Verona was absolutely beautiful, and if by chance we'd bumped into Brian wandering its streets, we certainly would have bought him a beer or two. I can't believe this place wasn't on our radar and we nearly missed it. With beautiful blue skies, we wandered the streets, laughed at all the tourists getting selfies in front of Romeo and Juliet's balcony. We then got a selfie in front of Romeo and Juliet's balcony (you would too, don't lie) before crossing the river for a hot climb to Castel San Pietro, rewarding us with spectacular views across the city.

The Combination to my Heart

To gouge the tourists as best they could the locals had constructed a false metal fence nearby the famous balcony where love struck visitors are encouraged to hang a padlock with their names on it. We'd seen something similar in many other cities, but they are normally attached to a bridge before throwing the key in the water to represent the everlasting bond they have. The fence here was a good idea, as this practice has caused issues in cities, where they have to regularly cut off the keys to protect the bridge.

That would be a horrible job, it must feel like killing an angel every time you snip each one off, sending discombobulating relationship-ending waves across the Universe. The thing that always makes me laugh though, is that without fail you will always see at least one combination lock. Just in case. Now, I'm sorry but unless you are both diagnosed with early onset dementia, this isn't a thing. It's a statement that our love is forever but if we get bored then at least we have a 'get out of jail' free option.

One of the big-ticket items, literally, is the magnificent Verona Arena, a first-century coliseum. Unfortunately, we were unable to get inside for a tour as they were setting up for an opera that evening, this was quite a disappointment so there was only one thing for it. Rather than trying to beat them we decided to try and join them. We had no idea what the chances were of getting tickets for an opera in one of the most spectacular locations in the world with only a few hours to spare. Well, a wise man once said to me 'you've got to be in it to win it!'. The 'it' for this scenario was the ticket office, and we won. The ticket price was pretty cheap which meant the seats might not be great but we didn't care, we got to go in.

The day got hotter and hotter, so we retreated back to MJ for a nanna nap. Going to sleep in a metal box on a 40-degree day while it's sitting in the middle of a car park with no shade, windows or doors closed (in case we were robbed), was not the greatest of ideas. We wanted to look good for the evening's excitement so pulled out the smartest of the travel clothes we had. The fact that we had been sweating profusely for the last few hours was offset by the fact that we looked more svelte in our attire after losing a few kilos. Anyway, a couple of dozen wet wipes later, and even our mums wouldn't know us.

The hot day made for a fantastic evening, and we arrived at the Arena just at the start of a most spectacular sunset. The seats were cheap because they were up in the gods, all but a few rows from the top which couldn't have been more perfect. It's not like we were there for the opera and it meant we could survey the whole coliseum and watch sunset come and go across the city's skyline. Not only that, it turned out to be a commemorative 100-year performance of Aida in this arena. Even the Mayor of Verona appeared and made a speech where he presented the lead male actor with the sword that was used in the original performance.

Well, that was our goal to see inside the Arena ticked, but there was still the opera ahead of us. Although a fan of the arts, the thought of four hours of indecipherable opera while sitting on stone steps, wasn't high on our agenda. We planned to watch a little before exiting stage left. However, between a bottle of Jean-Louise's champagne in plastic cups, an incredible performance, in world-class setting; four hours later we left the arena at 1am for a lovely, still warm, wander back to the car park. It seemed quite a juxtaposition that we quickly went from feeling like a movie star to then sleep in a car park.

Unfortunately, lots of the other vehicles had left, leaving only a handful remaining in the whole car park. With our safety by numbers plan out of the locked window, it meant very little sleep for the trip's safety officer. Not so much of an issue for the navigator, who somehow managed to pillage a foghorn from somewhere and hide it under the duvet, where it would be used to replay Aida all night. The next day would have been very tiring if it wasn't for the excitement of being in Venice by nightfall.

Not even one Cornetto

On the excellent advice of Brian No.2, we knew about a convenient campsite with easy access to Venice, so headed off early (I was awake anyway). Between our hangovers and the dodgy Italian road signs, we performed a 30 minute detour before pointing the right way. The scenery everywhere had been beautiful so far, but all of a sudden the roads were also a bit quieter, and we were able to relax a little more and take it in. The roads towards Fusina took us along rivers, and past lovely historic houses. Even the one wrong turn we made was a pleasure, as we got to explore another beautiful area. The campsite was easy to find, as it was huge with lots of facilities. Our Kombi was a big hit with the staff and we immediately scored a 15% discount on the ground fees which, at their prices, was appreciated. It catered for all types of campers from tents to cabins, and had quite a busy trade of coach trips full of young budget travellers, earning the place a bit of a party reputation.

We moved around a bit to find the right spot, choosing a waterfront pitch looking out across the Venice lagoon. It seemed ideal, but we found out later that this prime spot was empty because of the 36.2 million flies that lived within the 3x2m plot. We were not going to be beaten, no matter how bad it was. It was bad. By the end of the stay, our lungs contained a 50/50 mix of damaging fly spray, and the actual pests themselves. However, as we sat in MJ's front seats (smelling of fly spray), we could look straight across the lagoon and see the skyline of Venice beckoning us.

The journey to get there couldn't have been easier. We walked out of the campsite, turned left for 200 metres and boarded a ferry that ran every hour, straight into the centre of town. The previous day's activity meant we slept well in our hot tin can, but our excitement made sure that we were on the very first ferry of the day. This decision definitely turned out to be one of our better ones, as we soon found out how busy Venice got from mid-morning. We arrived and it was relatively quiet, with a slight mist in the air. Just as we approached our first iconic bridge, we saw a proper Venetian gondola with waiting gondolier, sat on an empty canal. We looked at it then looked at each other, after all it was one of the top things you have to tick off while you're here. We decided to defer it as we still had so much to see, and hadn't yet researched what we should expect to pay.

This decision would turn out to be one of the bigger mistakes of the trip. The first two hours of our morning in Venice was relaxed and relatively quiet, but slowly more and more and more people arrived. A more touristy place, I don't think I had ever seen. By 2pm the concept of taking a romantic journey through quiet canals in a beautiful gondola was decimated with views of major canal traffic jams full of camera-snapping tourists. It was so crazy that you could hardly spot water between the black wood of the gondolas. A scene punctuated with sounds of *O'sole o mia* coming from every 5th or so vessel. The moment and the romance were gone. We never did take that ride.

Apart from the 'poor man's gondola' which takes a larger number of people just a short journey across the Grand Canal for a small fee, and a larger ferry ride to the Lido for the day, we covered most of Venice by foot. Each morning, we would get the early ferry across and hit the laneways. If you visited the big ticket items such as St Mark's Square, Campanile, and Basilica early, you could then find quiet areas off the beaten track later in the day. This way even in Venice, it could still seem like you had this beautiful city to yourself and feel like a local. There is nothing more surreal than wandering alongside a quiet canal as a UPS gondola passes, stacked with boxes, making its rounds. If you end up in the wrong place at the wrong time, the city can be no fun at all. However, if you time things just right, it's as beautiful and magical as you've ever dreamt.

CHAPTER 11

Location: Venice
Days 232, Countries 21, Kilometers 39,472, Beds 92
Trains 12, Planes 14, Automobiles 35, Boats 11
Beers 152

News from Home

While walking along a small side canal that had the most beautiful reflections of the sunlight in the water, light dancing around the surrounding buildings and beautiful wooden boats, I received a text message to call my brother urgently in the UK. He'd recently driven across the UK to pick up my father and take him back to stay with them for a short break in Newcastle. I still hadn't seen Dad again since that fun chat in Geneva, it had been long overdue and was on my mind. I phoned the UK to learn that while visiting, Dad had become ill and was taken into hospital with suspected pancreatitis. After speaking to my family, it seemed that he was stable and they would keep in touch. Although obviously worried, we'd been through this before with a similar life-threatening episode a few years earlier. Last time, I'd travelled straight back from Australia to spend time with him, and miraculously at the age of 89, he pulled through with a great recovery. Before that, he did the same with bowel cancer. I know it's not realistic, but in my mind he was now indestructible, there was nothing that could stop him, even at 92. So, being the eternal optimist, I was expecting him to have a rough spell before getting better, and would soon be telling bad jokes in his dodgy Irish accent (he wasn't Irish, he just put it on to improve what would typically be a bad dad joke).

After the call, we walked on a bit further, but I couldn't relax, so we returned to the campsite to wait for some news. The next 24 hours contained numerous calls to and from the UK. His condition kept changing, one minute he was stable and doing well, then things would deteriorate, then seem a bit better again - and so on. There was only one thing to do, and luckily there was an early morning flight from Venice direct to Newcastle.

The car park is not full!

The next morning, we headed off early to the airport with little planning under our belts. Normally, we would have researched and memorised the airport layout and car park plans, knowing with military precision where we would park, and what we would pay. This time we turned up blind and headed to what was billed as the cheapest long stay car park. We were immediately halted by a large sign saying that it was full. It wasn't by any means. Next, we transited around the airport's one-way system to the next cheapest car park, it was also pretending to be full unless you had pre-booked. Each move meant the car park pricing was going up, as was our frustration. As we completed our 2nd loop of the airport, we joked that rather than be named Airport Marco Polo it should now be called the George Armstrong Custer International Airport. If we stuck a feather in Hula's headpiece, she would have really looked the part.

Finally, we ended up back at that very first car park, staring at empty spaces just metres away on the other side of the closed barrier. Enough was enough, we parked MJ across the entrance and pressed the help buzzer on the intercom.

'Hello.'

'Hi, we are at car park 4, and it won't let us in.'

'It is full.' - line goes dead.

I press again.

'Hello.'

'We are still at car park 4, it's not full, I can see plenty of spaces.'

'They are for pre-booked customers.' - line goes dead.

I press again.

'Me again, I can't believe that many are for pre-booked customers and the website won't let me do it this late.'

'Try one of the other car parks'.

Now I could handle things two ways, one would be to explain the fact that I am in the middle of an emotional situation, and have reached the end of my mental tether, plead to their better nature, maybe get a bit tearful. Or there's the other way. I press again.

'We have, they also don't let us in, even though they are also not full. We fly in an hour and we are not moving from this spot until you open the barrier and we park in the bloody empty spot that I'm staring at right in front of me!'

The line goes dead, a loud buzz precedes the barrier lifting, and we were in, just in time to make the flight.

Arriving Home

This 3-hour flight felt longer than a 24-hour flight from Melbourne, however, there was a slight distraction when we landed. After our welcome to Liverpool, I really wasn't in the mood for a similar experience, and thankfully we didn't get it.

While waiting in the queue (the UK one this time), border security staff were walking along the line to check that everyone had their documents ready, but were also welcoming people and asking about their holidays. This is what we wanted in Liverpool, but the process was like chalk and cheese with these Geordies.

It was great to see my brother Mick waiting for us. Not because it was one of the very few times in our life that someone was waiting for us at an airport, but it meant that we were one step closer to get to Dad. Mick drove us directly from the airport to the hospital where I finally saw Dad for the first time since Geneva. I could hardly recognise that it was the same person. His face was pale and gaunt, but as he looked up at me, you could still see that flicker of a smile in his eyes. I had been warned that he was a bit confused and was not always making sense. He beckoned me a bit closer and welcomed me with a joke 'I still see you've got that woolly hat on', referring to my now lengthy head of hair.

We left him to get some rest, with the promise that we would see him that evening. Mick drove us to his home to see the rest of the family, and I can't portray how comforting it was to see everyone, including my sisters, Eileen and Tracy. We were all handling the situation in our own way, some cleaning, some trying to keep spirits up, and some locked away in their own thoughts.

It was only about an hour later when the call came to advise us to return to the hospital as soon as possible. In my memory, this started a slow-motion scene as you saw the worry on people's faces as we grabbed coats, called for others and tried to assess who would be more suitable to drive. After all, this wasn't the call we were expecting. Any other news we'd had from Dad's previous hospital visits had all been positive; he was on the mend, or had a much better night, or we could pick him up later. For most of us, we were in denial that there was any other type of call to expect.

We didn't get to the hospital in time.

Nic and I felt blessed we had taken that flight and were able to have that last joke with Dad, and felt for others who hadn't had a chance to get to the hospital in time. At least for now, the tour would stop. Due to our lack of work commitments, we were in the best position to sort out arrangements and estate matters. It would be a couple of months before we started travelling again.

As for this book, well, I don't want to belittle the impact that this had on us or the fantastic support and help I had from my wonderful wife over that time, by skipping over it. After all, the journey that we are going on in this book is not just a physical journey, it's about the personal journey too, and it doesn't get more impactive than this. I could spend half of this book talking about my late parents, how they influenced their kids and how much we miss them. However, I might just take the liberty to cover off some of the ways that my Dad has influenced my life to help create this trip, and why it wouldn't have happened without him.

Thank you Dad

You blessed me with the skill of finding joy in even the smallest things. You instilled in me the notion that you get more from life by not putting yourself first. You provided the true north to my moral compass. You gave me the strength and understanding to know when to stand up and be counted. You presented me with a toolbox to manage life's tricky challenges. You were my friend as well as my father. You enriched my life by bringing me up with a love of music. Yours and mum's love for each other showed me that life can be like the movies. You gave me your face, and the cheeky glint in the eyes, although, you did also give me your nose hairs. You gave me the inability to keep a straight face when I really need to. You showed me that there is nothing stronger in this world than the bond and connection with the person you love. You gave me a glimpse of other worlds and created a traveller. You showed me that the world really is your lobster.

William George (Bill) Mountford 1921-2013

The quick way home

Although the trip's pause button was pressed, there was still something to remember. Three members of our travel party (MJ, Hula and Betty) were still trapped overseas in an airport car park. In a twist of fate, a family holiday had been booked many months before to the Norfolk Broads (one of Dad's favourite spots). It was an annual event that family would attend and we would join if we were in the right hemisphere. It had been booked for the week after the funeral, and the family made the decision straight away that they still wanted to go. Our mission was to fly back to Venice, retrieve the remaining team members and try to get back to be with family as quickly as possible. It had taken six weeks to get MJ down to Venice with an ever watchful eye on the oil temperature. We had no idea how much we could stretch her, and how long it was going to take, but at least the mission gave us some focus and distraction.

Our best option for a flight was one from Manchester, six days after the funeral. The journey was uneventful, and MJ was there waiting for us in the spot that caused so much controversy two weeks earlier. She must have been pleased to see us as she started first time, and we left the car park at around 11am with no real plan or idea as to where we would get to that night.

Bone Idle MJ

We had to take our hats off to MJ, over the next three days we pushed her to the limits, and she took it in her stride. Our route used quicker toll roads where possible, and we used all of MJ's gears going back through the Mont Blanc tunnel. One day, we even managed to cover 620km and by the end of the third day we were in Dunkirk. Despite trying our best, we were unable to get onto a ferry and had to stay just outside of town for a frustrating full day. We didn't use MJ during that day, so the next time she was run was the very early morning ride down the road to catch the ferry. As usual, she started straight away, and we were off.

It must have just dawned on her that her time on this trip was drawing to a close and she still hadn't seen Rome, Southern France, or Spain as we'd promised her. She got grumpy, and as we pulled up to the back of the queue for the ferry, she cut out. It was a bit strange, but I put it down to the cold morning, and the short run to get there. She started first time 'phew!' then stalled 'bollocks!'. After a few attempts, it became obvious that although otherwise fine, she just wouldn't idle. This realisation coincided with a burly French docker waving our orange tin can forward towards a steep metal gangway into the belly of this larger tin can, making MJ look like the small relative in a babushka doll.

I had no real idea what could be causing it, and at least she was Brazilian, so there was no smart arse comments to be had about being defeated at Dunkirk by a German. There was no way we could miss this ferry, so we proceeded. Despite two tall sleeping policemen we made it onboard, and into our parking spot without the need to idle. MJ cut out at this point like a teenager that had just been told to do the dishes. Time to head upstairs, have a cuppa and put our head in the sand about what might happen once we got to the other side. Moments later, hands tightly wrapped around a warm cup of tea, my thoughts tended towards the great Australian phrase of 'She'll be right'. I'm not sure about Nic's thoughts, but suspect it was along the lines of 'I do the cooking and navigating, this is your problem buster'.

On the one hand, I wanted the crossing to go quickly so that we could get back to the family and make sure they were all okay. On the other, I wanted enough time for the ambient temperature to rise in case that would help (I'm no mechanic, don't judge me). It was a very short crossing, so back to the van we went, fingers crossed. Nope, still the same. What do we do now? What we did was the least sensible of all options on the table, and that was to try and drive four and a half hours to Norfolk. Remember, this wasn't just an issue when we stopped, but whenever I took my foot off the accelerator, say when braking, or changing gear.

Luckily, we were able to follow a stream of cars leaving Dover that hit every green light. This was going to be okay, wasn't it? How much braking could possibly be needed in the next 200 miles through London's famously empty M25 ring road? If we thought driving through Italy added a little excitement, then we were truly mistaken. Roundabouts were interesting, Nic would keep an eye on traffic heading towards us from the right, and we would time it to not stop, but to shoot out and swerve around the roundabout, resembling a drifting scene from a *'Fast and the Furious'* movie. Betty needed to be wedged into place with the steering lock, everyone else including Hula wanted to use Betty. All we needed was a lack of traffic on the M25.

At about the same time we'd escaped Dover, around 100 miles north of us, a car was just about to catch fire in the Dartford tunnel causing miles and miles of traffic queues. The next few hours were really not much fun and tested the patience of everyone inside the van and those in the cars behind us. It also caused a few worried looks from those in front. Eventually, we were on the 'A' roads towards Norwich, which had far less traffic, and our average speed was faster. By now, our roundabout methodology was to pretend we were French, I would just drive out, and Nic would shrug to the oncoming drivers.

It was a very long hard day, but we eventually made it and introduced the ill-behaved MJ to some of the family for the first time. All my siblings were there, as were Sam and Scott, my brother-in-law Mark, and sister-in-law Val. A nice cuppa, and to be back with everyone made it all better.

A Cheap and Honest Mechanic

The time spent with the family at one of Dad's favourite holiday spots was both thought-provoking and relaxing. However, our time there was passing quickly, and we didn't want to have the same adventurous driving experience for the five-hour stretch back to Birkenhead. We needed to get MJ fixed. A bit of internet searching came up with a VW garage about 5 miles away, so we dropped her off with the friendly local mechanic to be picked up the next day.

Now I don't know about you, but I'm always very dubious about mechanics, and this one had a captive audience. He knew we were holidaymakers and needed to get home. Bundled with the mythical black art of carburettors, it meant we were ripe for exploitation. Nervously we returned, wallet in hand as he took us into his office and closed the door. How bad was it that he needed to close the door? Was the apprentice now on the other side of said closed door with a defibrillator under his arm? He looked up from his chair and announced in a cheerful voice that it was only a loose wire on the solenoid so just give him a tenner.

A tenner! Ten Great British pounds. About a tenth of what I was realistically expecting. Who was this unknown phenomenon of an honest car mechanic? To show our appreciation, Nic legged it back to MJ and pulled out a 6 pack of beers which was handed over with a crisp TWENTY pound note. His good karma needed repaying after all.

Apart from the trepidation about returning to the family home in Birkenhead, knowing a certain well-worn armchair would be empty, the journey itself was a nice run in a much more jolly MJ. Our new opinion that maybe the UK hadn't become the ripoff nation we'd thought was soon blighted when the M6 Motorway toll insisted we pay the cost of a truck. Why, because we didn't have a bonnet of course.

Moving On

As time went by, more and more jobs were completed in the family home, and we knew we should turn our thoughts onto climbing aboard this rollercoaster journey around the world again. Only, we felt numb about the idea of it. It was a mix of guilt for having these recent wonderful experiences, and a strong feeling that it didn't seem appropriate to carry on. The later was appeased by the knowledge that if Dad were to suddenly appear, he would have a stern look on his face before calling us 'bloody idiots' for even thinking it (before making us a nice cup of tea).

As I was mentally preparing myself to move on, I realised that a big part of my motivation for the trip was to share it with Dad, letting him know where we were and what we'd achieved. I guess with a view to make him proud and show how happy our lives had turned out, thanks to his and Mum's support and influence. It was enough for me to doubt why we'd continue. We'd also lost our safety net, the thought that whenever it all got a bit too much, we would pull the plug, get on a flight, and turn up to Dad's sofa for a cup of tea and some crime-solving TV. This wasn't just a backup plan for the tour, but had been for life in general for many years. Could we continue on an emotional tightrope with no safety net?

I really could never explain how wonderful Nic was during this time, and she never once complained about the fact that nearly two months of her 'once in a lifetime' experience had now been spent on a council estate in the North West of England. I could however, sense that she was getting a bit stir-crazy as we waited for letters to arrive from pension companies or banks, so we needed to do something. There was one place nearby that we had been to before, somewhere we loved and felt at home in, making it ideal for a small city break, Amsterdam.

Dambusters, dipping a toe in the water

We had to make it easy, which was an excuse for blowing the budget. We needed this trip to be enjoyable enough to convince us that we could still do this, and in fact still wanted to. We found a charming boutique hotel, in a lovely quiet area on the east edge of the Jordaan district. A spot that we knew and loved. We booked nice easy flights that unfortunately left from our now least favourite UK airport. This time, we would be prepared with plenty of change for the bus.

Amsterdam was wet, cold, and beautiful. The benefit of going somewhere we knew well, was that there was no pressure to hit the sights or take copious amounts of photographs. We chilled and wandered the streets as though we were locals. Well I say that, but we just couldn't pull it off, there is something undefinably cool about the Dutch. As a nationality I love them, they are not as photogenic as a monk of course, but they are always a pleasure to come across when you are travelling. This was doubly confirmed after our time with Michel and Agmar through South East Asia, and the numerous Dutch campers that would appear, wanting to talk about MJ in Europe. Everything about the Dutch in Amsterdam just oozes coolness; they dress cool; they cycle in a cool way on their cool retro bikes; they laugh in the face of privacy, allowing everyone to see how cool the inside of their homes are.

It was a bit of a solemn and soul searching time, but it did us both wonders to get away from a house full of memories at every turn. I returned still not knowing how I might be able to engage with the rest of the journey. I had no interest in photography or carrying on with the writing. We just knew that we needed to try.

The next few weeks were spent finishing what we could for Dad's paperwork, and preparing for the next stage of the tour. MJ was mothballed at a farm near Brian. A local farmer had realised that he could make more money from his land by storing caravans and campervans in a secure area. Although, it was a bit disturbing as it sounded like something you tell a child when the dog dies 'Yes Nic, we have sent MJ away to spend her days on a lovely farm, she is much better off there with others of her kind'. I'm picturing sheep sharing a lovely blue cocktail from Betty, while Hula bounces past in the background on the back of a leary goat. The loss of MJ was another psychological blow, especially for Nic as being tucked under her bright orange (of course) duvet was one of the few places in the whole world she felt most at home.

Our first stop was to spend a lovely couple of days with Brian as we started to make our way down to the South Coast and kickstart the next stage of our trip.

CHAPTER 12

Location: Birkenhead
Days 318, Countries 23, Kilometers 42,878, Beds 96
Trains 12, Planes 16, Automobiles 35, Boats 11
Beers 195

On the road again

To recap. So far on this journey we'd been presented with the whole gamut of emotions from supreme joy to devastating tragedy. At this point, we had travelled over 42,000km, through 24 countries, 68% of which had been without flying. We really aren't the sort of people that do this, and it was a huge personal achievement to get to this point. It certainly helped to instil a little confidence to continue.

With regard to my physical appearance, not only did I still have my 'travel hair' (uncut for 11 months), I decided to support Movember. For those who haven't heard about it, it's a worldwide fundraising event originating in Australia and raises money for men's health, especially prostate cancer. The long and the short of it, is that you receive sponsorship for nurturing a moustache or other random facial hair for the month of November. Over the years, I've had a tumultuous history with beards, and we're still not on speaking terms so I decided to just go for a full-blown

Burt Reynolds style mo. I now looked like the offspring of a Sasquatch and an Ewok.

The big smoke

Although both from the North, Nic and I first met each other in London, twenty years previously, and had both lived there for some time. It seemed fitting that we should stay in the city as part of our world tour and take the opportunity to catch up with old friends and stalk old haunts. Boy, did all those memories make us feel old (our livers are only just talking to us again). Our Airbnb was in the very swanky Bayswater area, in a property called 'The Short Let', the clue was in the name. It was a beautiful four storey Edwardian townhouse that had been subdivided into many small apartments. Ours had to be the smallest, it felt like we were in the galley of a longboat. The location however, was perfect for our adventure, as we buzzed around the city and its suburbs, visiting friends and family, even catching a West End show.

One of the highlights was the opening night of an art exhibition for the fantastic artist Scott Paterson at a SoHo gallery. He is a multi-genre genius, despite the fact that he's also a family member (the better half to our niece Sam). It meant we had the chance to catch up and say farewell to some of the family who had travelled to the show. There was also free booze, which is always welcome when on a budget. Our last day in London fell on Remembrance Day, our trend of being in the right place at the right time continued. It was a lovely day, and quite emotional to be at the Cenotaph and thinking about Dad.

Our journey to Southampton was via a National Express Coach, which was excellent value but did mean we had to wait around Victoria Coach station for a couple of hours. From a long list of places to visit in London, this one was down near the bottom. It lived up to expectations.

Our hearts will go on

Yet again, it was one of those incongruous and surreal moments of our year, similar to the argument over a dollar with a tuk-tuk driver as we exited Raffles. This time we were carrying our backpacks, daypacks, and pulling along our new addition of a suitcase for a mile across Southampton because we didn't want to pay for a taxi. Our destination was in view for most of the trek, the world's only remaining ocean liner, Cunard's flagship, the Queen Mary 2. It would set sail that evening on a direct non-stop route to New York, meaning we could cross the whole Atlantic without flying.

On the one hand, we were musing that this wasn't exactly conquering the world as a backpacker, and on the other, our scruffy appearance made us feel like we were disrespecting the legend that is Cunard. The more dominant thought, however, was 'fuck yeah, look at what we are doing!'.

Anyway, let's go back a paragraph. 'What's this about a suit-case?!' I hear you shouting after all my preaching about baggage. Well, let me explain. So far, the trip had not required much cause for dolling ourselves up. Although climbing up a temple in Burma in black tie would have made me look like James Bond, I think it was best to have stuck with the Keen sandals and trusty zip-off travel pants. We'd been on a couple of cruises before, so knew the dress code required, and they weren't Cunard. We were a bit worried about how we'd manage with our thongs and Sea Shepherd T-shirts. Trying to jazz ourselves up with a distracting hair fascinator wasn't going to cut the mustard.

Cast your minds back, remember all those lists after lists we went through back in Melbourne, well one of those was just dedicated to the next seven days of the trip. It was one of the few things we knew we were going to do, and it was a big ticket item that needed some preparation. Luckily, not long before we left, our good friends Nic & Matt travelled from Melbourne to the UK and kindly took back a suitcase packed with clothes for this very leg. It also had a few warm clothes, ready for our travels through Canada. The key items were my dinner jacket (the one I got married in), and some elegant dresses for Nic. We topped this up with some last minute shopping in London's Oxford Street Primark (aka Primani), a low price clothes shop. I was now armed with a couple of shirts, and a cheap tweed suit for this part of the adventure. We even had accessories ready for the fabled masked ball. Once again, thank God (Gusset) for the Magic Shirt.

Our suitcase was an old dilapidated one with a broken wheel, so it knew it didn't have long for this world. When we reached New York, we would parcel up the valuable items, posting them back via the slowest, cheapest method possible. The rest would go to charity, and the suitcase thrown away, leaving us with just our trusty Osprey backpacks again.

As the limousines were passing us, we trundled past the harbour security guards and up to Cunard's welcome marque. We arrived and plonked our backpacks (by now decorated with the odd trinket or cuddly toy) up against our one wheeled suitcase to stop it falling over, next to someone's lovely Louis Vuitton leather baggage. It was safe to say we didn't blend in. With the last two months of comfort-food binging, I'd put on a few pounds. Between this, the mo, and my long hair, I looked like an honest to goodness 70's Porn star as I approached the check-in desk. If Ron Jeremy and Danny DeVito ever had a lovechild that sweated a lot, that would be me.

Living in Australia had provided us a level of comfort in who we were, as there isn't really any class system. A place where you can walk into any high class restaurant wearing whatever you want. However, we weren't in Melbourne now Toto, and if there is anywhere in the world where you expect to see a well oiled class system in action, it's when you're climbing aboard the friggin Queen Mary 2. Fair dinkum to Cunard (see how Australian I am), they were perfect hosts and made us feel completely at home. The boarding process took a bit of time and provided the best people watching you could imagine. Despite my worries about being judged, I have to say there was a bunch of 'book cover' judging going on from the Mounty household as we boarded this floating behemoth of luxury.

I know, you're worried about the budget aren't you? The Queen Mary 2 sounds like it should be super expensive, but in fact, this transatlantic crossing was cheaper than most cruises. Mainly because there were no other ports of call. Coupled with the fact that we found a handy website offering discounts on cruises as they get closer to the departure date, it meant that we would eventually hit a price point that we could justify. As this crossing is scheduled monthly, we were able to see how cheap the deals tracked from previous months, gauging when to buy. It wasn't the $15 per night we were paying in Cambodia, but it could have been a lot worse. So, with the thought of approaching the famous Manhattan skyline by sea in our minds, we upgraded to a balcony room. Don't look at me like that!

Pulling away from Southampton on this grand ocean liner was quite an emotional moment. This was helped by the complimentary champagne that we rushed down before a quick change for dinner. Despite banging on throughout this book about how the people we meet are some of the most memorable parts of the trip, we guiltily decided to choose a dinner table for just the two of us, rather than join a group. I guess this was a symptom of the recent emotional upheaval. This didn't quite work to plan when we realised that our table for two was placed only a few inches away from the next table for two. However, what a result that was, within a few minutes we were chatting away with Barrie and Kaye, who became great travel buddies during the crossing.

The seating arrangements for breakfast and lunch were a different matter altogether, we were directed to an arbitrary table containing complete randoms. It was great meeting such a breadth of people, and each sitting always started with the same routine. I would sit down looking like a mini-me Burt Reynolds, everyone would stare. I quickly move my hand in a circular motion in front of my face while declaring 'Hi, my name is Lee, and I don't normally look like this', at which point Nic would whip out a passport photo showing her real husband. If anything, it was a great conversation starter and a summary of our world trip would often ensue.

The journey so far had been such an achievement for us, it made us passionate in our portrayal of it, and I think that made others excited for us. It was funny seeing the reactions from different nations. The Americans we met, loved it and couldn't ask enough questions, one bunch almost adopted us. Some of the English, on the other hand, were sometimes resilient in their efforts not to be out-done. They would ask where we'd been, and for each location, they would have a comeback, 'been there', 'Oh yes, went skiing there', 'our Kevin lived there for a while'. They never asked what we thought of a place, surely it must have been the same as how their dentist's cousin had found it.

Cunard-ly see a thing

The whole transatlantic nature of the journey made us feel like we were on an old-time adventure. Despite the budget bashing, it seemed the perfect addition to our tour. The epicness of the voyage hit home in the early hours of our sixth morning onboard. Our alarm woke us at 5:30am, we rugged up, went outside, and headed towards the bow (the front, to you landlubbers). The reason being that, at that very point of the journey, we would pass the closest distance (about 40km) to where the Titanic had famously sank on a similar journey some 101 years previously. So far, the weather had been very consistent with clear skies and a brisk wind, so we were quite taken aback to push open the heavy door and find that we were in a white-out, surrounded by fog. It was incredible to see (or not as the case may be) and made even more eerily when, at the closest position, the Queen Mary 2 turned on all its external lights in tribute. The lights made the fog seem whiter and thicker, as though we were wrapped in cotton wool. The moment was both magical and poignant. It was a shame that we only saw a few other people who'd made the effort.

Quickstep to Quebec

The plan was that during our 7 days crossing the Atlantic, we would have nothing much to do accept research our itinerary for Canada. We'd previously decided that we would cross the continent through this country rather than the U.S.A. Even though we'd been on cruises before, we hadn't done a crossing like this, so pictured deckchairs and research books, not quizzes and Martinis, or planetarium talks and Martinis, or historical talks about New York architecture and Martinis (getting the picture?). Canada was the furthest thing from our Martini soaked minds. The afternoon quizzes were held in one of the many bars and were quite popular. We would often meet new people, and join their team to make up numbers. It was always a bit disappointing to see how hard they tried not to make eye contact as we wandered into the bar the following day.

Oh yes, back to Canada. We had a rough plan in our minds that included Montreal, Ottawa, Toronto, Jasper, and Vancouver but we still knew so little about the country and its locations. This wasn't the time for a text-heavy Lonely Planet book, we needed books with pictures. In a fleeting half hour between a Martini and a masked ball, I pulled out the *DK Eyewitness Guide to Canada* to have a flick through. Okay, I may have exaggerated for comedic value, and I don't want to offend any Canadians out there by how little interest it looked like we had in our preparation. This totally wasn't so, Canada has always been towards the top of our destination list as soon as we came up with the idea for the trip, but we fell into the trap of thinking we had all the time in the world to research while we travelled, as we were not working (or were we?).

The book slammed shut, and as I fumbled about making my bow tie look semi-presentable, I announced to Nic that the route seemed okay, but we needed to add a quick trip to Quebec too. Not knowing much about it, she was quick to query the cost, time implications, and the fact it was in the wrong direction. I gave her my 'Trust Me' look. In my mind, her internal monologue goes something like 'Ah that's the trust me look, I know not to question that as he is never wrong when he brings out that look, I can't wait'. One night, after some red wine, and some loose lips, I discovered that it's more along the lines of 'What the hell is he getting us into now, I'd better hide some of the money'. Anyway, let's get on with the journey so we can find out how I faired later.

Gangplanks of New York

I'd be lying if I said that we weren't excited about the thought of sailing into New York past the Statue of Liberty. It wouldn't be our first sight of this majestic world-renowned monument, but what a perfect way to arrive. We were due to arrive at around 6am in the cold and dark, and weren't sure whether our balcony was going to be on the best side or not, so we rugged up and made our way out on deck at around 5am to get a spot. After a few location changes, we settled in and eventually could see its green outline in the distance.

There was quite a turnout on deck, and everyone was trying to find shelter from a bitter wind. I positioned myself nicely behind Nic and waited. The cold weather meant it wasn't as romantic as we'd imagined, but still a great experience watching this colossal liner only just squeeze underneath the Verrazano Narrows Bridge as we approached Manhattan. We hadn't done any research into where the ship would dock and were surprised to find that we eventually came to a halt in Brooklyn. A nicer surprise followed once we returned to the cabin to find our view was facing directly towards Ellis Island and the big girl herself. We still had a few hours before breakfast and disembarkation to marvel at the sight.

For any Americans out there that might think the immigration entry into their homeland is nice and convivial, I'm afraid

I have to disappoint. The words unfriendly and intimidating spring to mind when I think back to my previous experiences. This one was no exception, as we felt like guilty culprits for no reason whatsoever. We didn't have a terrorist hiding in our broken wheeled suitcase, or a kilo of heroin sewn into my dinner jacket. However, there was one thing that we were losing a bit of sleep about, the fact that we didn't have any onward travel booked. We knew that some countries don't like this fact (remember Liverpool).

It was a great leveller to see all the passengers from back-packers to the ultra-rich having to snake their way through the same queue together, heading towards the angry looking officials ahead. Unlike us, the wealthy contingents looked resplendent, but also nervous in case customs discovered the lama hidden in their Luis Vuitton case, or the Star of India inserted inside a perky chihuahua. Some just uncomfortable hanging around riff-raff such as us. This prompted us to have fun, latching onto them for a conversation whether they wanted to or not, our bogan scale off the chart as we tried our best to insert a fart gag or two for the captive audience.

Our customs officer looked like this was just a side job to support his NFL/MMA career, which really didn't help the situation. I figured, the worst that could happen would be our refused entry and Cunard would be obliged to put us up for another seven days on the return leg. The slow movement of the queue added to the nervous suspense, and we had worked ourselves up into a right mess by the time we reached the counter. It felt like Vietnam all over again. A drop of sweat dripped down my brow in super slow motion, running along my nose and falling from the tip. Just as it hit the stainless steel counter, making an unrealistic boom, the officer's rubber stamp pounded my passport to welcome us to this wondrous land. Crisis averted.

You talkin' to me about a Taxi Driver?

Unexpectedly, we now found ourselves on a wharf in Brooklyn with no seemingly good public transport option, and our awkward extra suitcase. We decided to get in the queue for a taxi. The long line gave me plenty of time to work out what future country we might need to drop from the list to pay for this taxi ride. Once our turn came, we gave the driver the details to our pre-booked hotel in Tribeca. It felt like the travel gods were looking down on us today, or maybe some good Karma had been paid back, as we hit every single green light on our way to the Cosmopolitan Hotel. Once there we both took a loud gulp as the driver turned around and announced that the fare would be a whopping US$15. Now that's a nice welcome to New York.

We sat in the small lobby of the hotel waiting for the very friendly staff to help us lock away our bags until the room was ready, when a loud English accent suddenly appeared. It was attached to a tall, portly man in his late '50s, accompanied by a small frail-looking wife by his side. Her nose seemed to be constantly stuck up in the air, maybe from some horrible gardening accident. By his accent, he was unmistakably a Yorkshireman, and seemed to fit the 'I say what I like, and I like what I bloody well say' stereotype.

We proceeded to eavesdrop for amusement and kill time. It soon became evident that they were leaving New York and coincidently about to embark on the QM2 for its return voyage to Southampton. He rudely asked the concierge about the cost of getting a taxi to the dock, the reply was that he could take his chances with a cab that should cost around US$50 or the hotel can arrange an executive car for US$100. At this point, I just had to pipe in with some assistance, whether I liked the guy or not. I explained that we'd just come from the QM2 and the taxi had only cost US$15, to which the concierge looked surprised. The English couple also looked surprised, but that was more in disbelief that we could have been Cunard passengers. They decided to ignore our advice, and pay for the executive car. I sat back down feeling frustrated, but I guess it couldn't have happened to a nicer guy.

The hotel room was small but was a cool boutique affair with a mezzanine bed area at the top of a narrow ladder. Once upstairs, even us two short arses couldn't stand up, but after a busy day hitting the pavements of New York, standing was overrated. We felt very trendy to be in the middle of Tribeca which was compounded by our visit to The Laughing Man coffee shop owned by Hugh Jackman. It was great to be back in NYC, one of our favourite places in the world. We'd visited previously to celebrate my 40th, so had ticked off a lot of the big-ticket items then, leaving us to mooch around like a local this time. Dinner that night consisted of a hot dog from a street cart, I was already starting to talk like Robert De Niro.

Wanting to maximise our time in this fabulous city, we hit the streets early the next morning, and headed to the massive Federal Post Office on Church Street. We had sorted our cruise costumes into piles, either for charity or sending home. The suitcase disintegrated before our eyes as we pulled out the last item, in what looked like a homage to Jake and Elwood's Bluesmobile. We called into a local grocer at the Amish market to pick up some empty boxes and bought packing tape along the way. Once we reached the Post Office, finding the most cost-effective way to post it back to Melbourne was a challenge, but the staff were great and soon sorted us out.

Drive by Selfie

$200 later we walked out of this impressive art deco building, feeling both skint and relieved. Relieved to be left with only our backpacks, our whole world in two bags, just as God had intended. It was one of those moments that required a nostril shot. I manhandled the camera from underneath the hundreds of layers I was wearing to keep warm, pulling Nic close (Well as close as we could, dressed as Michelin Men). I hadn't really paid attention to the car in front of us that had its engine running, until the electric window opened and a head popped out. An Andy Garcia lookalike appeared through the window and offered to take our picture for us, at which point I automatically handed him my camera with a smile. Correct, I just gave it to the guy who looked like he was a 'made man', in a running car with tinted windows. How could I have let my guard down so badly? I was already picturing the car speeding around a corner knocking over empty cardboard boxes, while I was spreadeagled across the bonnet trying to recover my camera, safe in the knowledge that if I flew off, my many layers would protect me.

I was busy trying to decide whether the theme music would be by Harold Faltermeyer or Hans Zimmer, when he raised the camera, took the picture, and handed it back before driving off. I wasn't quite sure how to feel, silly to be so gullible, or jaded for being so untrustworthy. The ensuing bagel would undoubtedly be food for thought (Yes, of course it would have been Harold Faltermeyer). The excitement had been forgotten about by the time we'd walked all the way to midtown, up 5th, through SoHo, then Broadway, passing icons such as the Flatiron building, Time Square, lunch in Macy's, and the ice-skaters at the Rockefeller Centre. We caught the subway home to get ready for dinner. Nic asked where I'd like to eat, given that New York was our lobster (for a price). I opened the curtains and pointed directly across the road, 'There!'. Partly because I was knackered, and partly because my research had shown that Mudville No9 had some of the best reviews in Tribeca.

It was famous for Buffalo Wings which was one of Dad's favourites. Boy oh boy, were they good. This restaurant is now the standard by which we hold all Buffalo Wing comparisons to. In fact, they offered a two-hour, eat as much as you want, wings and beer session, but it has a minimum number of people, so we can't go back to New York until we find four friends to join us (anyone?). After second servings of both beer and wings, we strolled back across the road to our teeny tiny room, crashing out before another big day ahead.

The Lady and the Tramps

The day started with a chilled subway ride down to the South Ferry terminal, arriving in time for our date with the Statue of Liberty. The trip which includes a climb inside this magnificent monument gets booked up way in advance, so we'd arranged it during our weeks in Birkenhead. Just as the subway approached our final destination, I looked down at the tour tickets in my hand, feeling very relaxed and on time. That was until I saw the statement 'Photo ID is required', unfortunately, it didn't carry on to say 'is required to be securely left in a hotel safe halfway across town'. My relaxed demeanour quickly turned into nausea. Only one thing for it, I left Nic and ran across the platform onto the northbound train and raced back to the hotel. I made all the transfers in good time, sliding through closing doors like a young Tom Cruise. I was out of breath and pouring with sweat by the time I found Nic in Battery Park, just as the queue started to board the Miss New York, Ellis Island bound. She was getting worried and had a coffee waiting to greet me. This thoughtfulness is one of the three reasons I married her.

Although we'd seen Lady Liberty to point at before, she was spectacular up close, and once you're in a small staircase, spiralling up to her crown, you realise she's actually smaller than you think. The views and overall experience was outstanding, our trip finishing off with a reflective walk through the large halls of the Ellis Island Immigration Museum. That was enough excitement for one day, so we slowly wandered home from Battery Park, through Wall Street, past City Hall, picking up Sushi from the nearby Amish Market on the way. The following day, we had a whole other city to get to and still hadn't worked out how we were going to get there.

CHAPTER 12

Tea Parties at Never Never Land

The stories we'd heard about travelling on Greyhound Buses had really put us off using them, but there was a feeling deep down that it was something we needed to experience for ourselves. This was coupled with a sense that lately, we weren't following the defining principles of our backpacker year. After much discussion, we hardened the fuck up and booked our US$30 tickets to Boston. Early the next morning we checked out of our chic hotel, feeling light on our toes with just our Ospreys to contend with. A subway ride took us to the Port Authority Terminal, which was probably no worse than getting a bus from Victoria Station in London. That's all I'll say.

Our bus was actually subcontracted to the Peter Pan bus company who's off-duty coaches showed the destination of Never Never Land in bright lights above the driver. I dread to think how many drug or alcohol affected people try to get on board these (I was even tempted while stone cold sober). The bus was in great condition, it was half empty and also had WiFi. We felt very safe and had a lovely journey. We probably hadn't taken into account that our standards might differ from others after the bus journeys through South East Asia. Boston welcomed us with cold and rain, but nevertheless, we decided to walk the mile to our hotel. Again being nervous about America, we'd booked a decent hotel in the centre of town. As we dumped our wet bags at the Omni Parker Hotel reception desk, we sparked up a conversation with the very friendly staff. A brief summary of our world tour later, and coupled with the fact that Nic had joined their membership scheme on the bus journey here, we were upgraded to a top floor room with hot drinks delivered to our door each morning.

We crashed onto the softest pillows ever made, and just as we couldn't feel more blessed, there was a knock at the door. I was expecting them to have realised their mistake with the room, but when I opened the door we were greeted with two free Boston cream pies (a dessert invented in this very hotel in the late 19th century, don't ya know). Not to be confused with the Boston Bun which is one of the many things that Australia and New Zealand argue about owning (this includes the racehorse Phar Lap, and the actor Sam Neil). If the two countries ever went to war, you could imagine one battalion's coat of arms actually depicting Sam Neil riding Phar Lap, deep in battle with another whose flag has Russell Crowe eating a Pavlova. Both sides living off Weet-Bix as though it's gone out of fashion.

I digress. Our free desserts were also accompanied by a complimentary book on the hotel's history, we were going to like this place.

Where only one person knows your name

The day ended with a real real treat for me. You may josh at my philistine ways, but a trip to Boston would not be complete without a visit to the *Cheers* bar. Luckily, this city had two of them. The first was located within the Faneuil Market Hall and was configured with the same layout as the one from the TV show. *Cheers* was a sitcom that ran for 275 episodes, starting in the early '80s. It had always been a favourite of mine, even though I had to watch it on a small tv upstairs as Dad didn't get American humour. Even 10 years later, we couldn't get him to watch an episode of *Friends* without him making tutting sounds throughout.

I walked into the bar dreaming that everyone would look up and shout 'Mounty!', as I came out with a witty remark about beer nuts. Only in my head did it happen, but it happened. A beer, great food, lovely company with Mrs M, and spending too much money in the souvenir shop, ended a great day. Although, I was a bit worried about the fact that I now had a *Cheers* pint glass to securely get around the rest of the world, in my soft, full, backpack.

Starting a jam-packed day with a hangover wasn't ideal, but hey-ho. We walked the three mile freedom trail (renamed by us to the freezing trail), back to the beautiful marketplace, and then across the bridge into the northern suburbs to tour the USS Constitution, before climbing the 294 steps to the top of the Bunker Hill Monument. Sustenance was of course provided by the city's 2nd *Cheers* bar, which is actually called the Bull and Finch pub. This was the location for the exterior shots of the pub, with a green canvas walkway and the stairs that descended in front of the main window. My Cheersometer was overflowing. I'm sure Nic enjoyed it too, but she was already thinking ahead to our evening trip to Walgreens, her new favourite store. It was close to the hotel and had everything we could possibly need, and that particular night, we needed DIY frozen yoghurts.

Harvard, but not as you know it

With all the film and TV shows set there, we've all seen Harvard, haven't we? Actually no, we haven't. The efficient and cheap subway (or "T") took us to Cambridge, and we jumped on a free walking tour of the Harvard campus. The first thing we learnt is that the university never gives permission to film there, so all those film and TV locations were shot somewhere else. The tour was informative and covered some lovely campus buildings. We'd surprised ourselves just by venturing out these last two days, as the temperature didn't get above freezing, even before factoring wind chill. But, we felt very much at home in Boston and thought that we could easily live there if it didn't get so cold. The weather and the city's lovely decorations certainly made us feel Christmassy, our summer Decembers in Australia make that a rare occurrence these days. In turn, it made us miss family and friends, so it was a good job that we were going to catch up with some of my family the very next day.

I actually had a bunch of cousins that live in the Southington area of Connecticut, whom I'd not seen for many years. Although we'd grown up on the same estate, they were all a bit older and emigrated to the US while I was still quite young. In an oversight by us, we didn't think in advance that we'd be so close and hadn't been in touch. In the same way that we struggle accepting help, we also don't get why anyone would want to see us, so feel uncomfortable forcing ourselves on people. It was bothering me that we were so close, but luckily my cousin Gary had been keeping an eye on our Facebook posts, knew we were in the neighbourhood, so reached out. A quick conversation, and a review of bus timetables later, we'd arranged to call in on the way back to New York.

This time our bus wasn't quite as nice, and there was a long queue to get on which meant we couldn't sit together. I ended up at the back with the cool kids. When I say cool, I mean 'please don't hurt me' kids. Thankfully, it was only a quick journey, and Gary was there to pick us up from the station with a friendly smile. We had a wonderful evening catching up with my cousins Gary, Lyn and Suzanne and their families in such a lovely home full of Christmas decorations. It was as though we'd last spoken only yesterday, and to spend time in a welcoming family home was just what we needed. A perfect day.

New York New York, so good we went there twice

After being treated to an American sized breakfast at a local diner, we were dropped off at the bus station for our return to New York. We needed to retrace our steps a bit for the journey into Canada on the Amtrak train from New York to Montreal in two days time. This bus was even busier, and we were lucky to make it onboard, many didn't. The journey was mostly in the rain at breakneck speed which was a little unsettling at times. So much so that it was actually a relief to be back at New York's Port Authority bus terminal. It was short-lived, and within minutes we were whipping across town on the 7 subway line to Grand Central Terminal. We knew our hotel was just around the corner, so grabbed a beautiful bagel from Zaro's bakery at the station, reliving one of our first ever meals in NYC, four years earlier.

The nearby Fitzpatrick Hotel didn't give us the best of welcomes, and there was certainly no upgrade to be had here. We didn't get a chance to explore the room, as we dropped the bags off before heading straight out, walking west to Times Square. A conversation with the family in Connecticut about seeing a show on Broadway had prompted us to do something about it. We knew where to get cheap deals from, so headed straight there to try and purchase tickets to see *Wicked* that night at the Gershwin Theatre. They had two tickets left, great. At opposite ends of a row, not so great. It wasn't ideal, but it meant that we could see the show and when you think about it, you don't speak to each other during the show anyway. And if you do, expect a heavy sigh and flared nostrils from the short English guy in front (Oh, that's me). The show was terrific, and we were pumped on the way home, it had felt like a real MountyDay. The next one certainly was.

Feeling Thankful

The date was November the 28th, Thanksgiving in New York City, and we were pretty excited to be once again in the right place at the right time. Our day started early so we could make it to the Rockefeller Centre for our 7am session on the ice rink. We booked in advance for an hour slot, and they provided the skates and a nice hot chocolate to keep us warm. It seemed such an iconic thing to do, we had to lock it in, but there was only one problem. I can't skate. It didn't take long for Nic to pick things up and she looked elegant, gliding past the large gilded Prometheus statue. In fact, her skating skills were one of the three reasons I married her. I on the other hand, held on to the edge. Even that wasn't easy for me. From the top half I looked like I wasn't moving, but if you looked downwards past the white knuckles holding onto the barrier you could see my feet in furious involuntary motion. To the untrained eye, it looked like I was auditioning for *Riverdance on Ice*, when really I was just trying to stay alive. I felt terrible that I couldn't be out there sharing the experience with Nic, and she was great at coming to see me for the odd photo opportunity. I pushed the envelope of my fear and skill by working my way around the fence, hand over hand, feet going ten to the dozen in all directions. This came to an impasse when I reached a gap in the fence, it was only a metre across but might as well have been a shark-infested ocean. Time for a well deserved hot chocolate.

With beautiful clear skies, it was a truly cold day and the warm drink didn't do much to raise our core temperature. Nevertheless, we had our next deadline to meet. Of course, Thanksgiving in NYC makes you think of one thing, the Macy's Parade, and we were determined to see at least some of it. We figured it would be popular, with crowds camping out to get good spots, so we set our expectations low. If we just got to see one balloon floating past in the distance, we'd be happy. We wandered past the Rockefeller Centre and along West 49th Street expecting to meet crowds almost immediately, but before we knew it, we were at the junction with 6th Avenue and at the very front of a barrier on the midpoint of the parade's route. Admittedly, it was still an hour to the parade, but we couldn't believe our luck. We killed time by chatting with others around us and kept warm with a couple of large coffees.

The parade was as magical as you'd expect, it was surreal watching a building size Snoopy float past, followed by Sonic the Hedgehog and Superman. After two hours of parade, the excitement culminated with the sight of Santa on his sledge. Not only did we see him but he saw us, he looked right at us and gave us a wave. Magical. If only he'd brought us a flask of tea or a portable heater as a present. After three hours of standing in sub-zero temperatures we were suffering, so headed straight back to the hotel.

We climbed fully clothed, still with coats on, into bed. I put the heating on, turned it up, and waited. Nothing. I turned it up to the max. Nothing. Nic was starting to turn blue, so I called reception. After some 'discussion' with the staff, who were obviously grumpy about working on the holiday, we arranged to move rooms. After ten minutes there was a knock at the door. Expecting a porter, we were greeted with more of a security guard whose job was to ensure that we vacated the old room before showing us to the next. No help with bags, no smile, just the occasional raised eyebrow. The heater in the much smaller second room made up for the lack of congeniality, as we hibernated for the next few hours.

A local cafe provided an orphan's Thanksgiving meal, and after our pumpkin pie, we headed for a stroll down 5th Av for Nic's obligatory play on the giant piano, the one from the movie *Big* in FAO Schwarz. It's a bit embarrassing watching your fully grown wife barge small kids out of the way while trying to complete her rendition of chopsticks, her boobs alone nearly knocked one poor girl to the floor (you bet your ass, that's one of the three reasons I married her). The walk home seemed magical, it really was like walking through a Hallmark Channel 'Christmas in New York' movie. There was still a real chill in the air, and plumes of smoke poured from the city's underground steam system. A lovely last evening in one of our favourite cities in the world.

CHAPTER 13

Location: New York
Days 342, Countries 25, Kilometers 50,008, Beds 104
Trains 13, Planes 16, Automobiles 36, Boats 12
Beers 223

The Mounties Streak into Canada

Our journey into Canada was provided by the iconic Amtrak service, leaving from Penn Central station. I was very excited about this and couldn't help but think of the classic Gene Wilder comedy *Silver Streak*. I wondered if we'd get through the journey without a body flying past the window, eventuating in a cat and mouse espionage caper. By comparison, it was quite uneventful and relaxing, apart from a brief heart-stopping and flatulence inducing moment, just before we boarded the train when we realised that we had no idea whether or not we needed a visa to get into Canada. This was so unlike us, how on earth could we get to a border crossing without knowing this information? Thankfully we didn't need a visa, but it provided a reminder that we shouldn't let our guard down. The journey was picturesque and comfortable, buoyed by the fact that I was riding on an Amtrak.

Keeping it Montreal

After years of talking about it, we'd finally made it to Canada. Our research struggled to find any really cheap accommodation and like America, we were not as brave with our choices compared to South East Asia. We eventually found a hostel about a twenty-minute walk from Montreal's old town.

Although only a hostel, I gave them my usual upgrade banter. It was a special trip, a lifetime dream to visit your country, this establishment is our lucky first stop, yadyadyada. Surprisingly it actually worked, but the result backfired somewhat as we were shown into a room whose entrance was off the main busy foyer. Right away you could see that it was probably the largest room in the building. However, the first point of interest was the mirrored ceiling; second, was the jacuzzi in the middle of the room with no privacy; third, was the faulty window blinds that meant there was no separation at all from your jacuzzi activities and the small smokers area on the other side of the glass. If the bedside lamp had been sporting a red lampshade, I would have sworn we'd just been transported back to Amsterdam. We declined the offer and instead took a smaller, equally dodgy room upstairs. This one however just had the standard stained ceiling, no water amusements, and absolutely no chance of introducing Lee Junior to any unsuspecting Canadians.

It certainly wasn't the ideal locale for our introduction to Canada, and the bitter cold was deflating our first impressions further. In hindsight, this would be no comparison to the feeling we had arriving in Hawaii in about 23 pages time. Only one thing to do, have a 'turn it around day', and the best place to do that was the beautiful old quarter, along the banks of the St Lawrence River.

Not lovers of the cold, we were having a bit of a tug of war battle with it. The cold would slowly sap our energy (and joy from our souls), and then we would be revitalised by Montreal's beautiful architecture and lovely surroundings. And repeat.

The day ended on a high with the fantastic light show at the Notre-Dame Basilica. It was unforgettable, and gave us more than enough *oomph* for the cold, slippery walk home. We were beginning to doubt our 'not follow the sun' route around the globe, we'd always expected that our first time in Montreal to be in the summer, coinciding with the Formula 1, or maybe the world famous comedy festival.

A day out crossing the fast-flowing St Lawrence River, over St Helen's Island and onto Ile Notre-Dame (the island home of the F1 circuit) was a must. It was pretty surreal to be able to walk the length of the track in deep snow, taking a nostril shot against the Wall of Champions (known for being the demise of many a great driver's race), and building a highly accurate 1/20 scale F1 car from snow in the empty pit lane. It's now impossible for us to watch the start of a Canadian F1 race, seeing the cars head into the first hairpin, without thinking of the snow angels we made on that very same spot. We both twinge a little from the safety of our sofa as the cars run over us. Thankfully, the island's casino provided free coffee to keep us warm before a walk through Olympic Park.

It was quite romantic walking through the snow-covered grounds, hand in hand. I can say with some assurance that Nic loved me a little more this day. For the only reason that the moustache had been finally shaved off (after raising $300 for a great cause). Moving forward, I think Nic will just donate that amount each year to prevent me from doing it again. During the train journey home, we stopped off at the Canadian rail (VIA) office to ask a few questions about our planned cross-country rail journey. We met the friendliest lady at the counter who loved Australians. She gave us great advice, and made sure we were booked into one of the train's best cabins. For her troubles, she received our 2nd to last Koala.

Jumping to the top of the Quebec

Montreal eventually grew on us, but considering it was a city we once thought about moving to, it wasn't as welcoming as we'd hoped. Let's see what Quebec holds for us, after all, my 'Trust me' look was on the line. Just between you and me, I tilted the scale in my favour with a secretive hotel booking.

We disembarked after a comparatively short train journey, and our first impressions were good, helped by the fact that we'd arrived at the historic Gare du Palais train station, with its beautiful sloping copper roof. We walked outside to get our bearings, and our second impression was just how bitterly cold it was. I mean really cold. As we looked across to the city centre, we could see the building that inspired the construction of the train station and is synonymous with Quebec. Chateau Frontenac dominates the skyline and has to be Quebec's most iconic building, perched on top of a hill overlooking the St Lawrence River. The building adorns the majority of postcards that you find here. Nic was impressed with the view, which turned to excitement when I pointed to the chateau and told her that's where we are staying. I quickly helped to pick her up off the floor. Literally, I did, she'd just gone arse over tit on the ice.

In yet another extreme budget juxtaposition, we decided to save money and walk the 1.5km uphill route to our 5-star hotel, carrying our bags on treacherously icy paths. $7 well saved if you ask me. I hoped the room had a spa bath. We checked in, and despite the fact I'd found a ridiculously cheap deal, our 5th-floor room was quite spacious, facing an internal courtyard. The excellent rate might have been connected to the fact the hotel was part way through a refurbishment. There was some scaffolding to the rear of the hotel that didn't really affect us at all. We were going to sleep well that night.

I wrote that too soon. The courtyard was also where the deliveries for both the hotel and I think the construction work, started at 4:30am. The sound of trolleys being brought to and from trucks across the cobbled yard sounded like machine gun fire to a tired, grumpy tourist. I called the reception to complain, they said they couldn't do anything at the time but to come and visit the day staff later that morning.

We appeared later at the desk, bleary-eyed, and a little deflated that our fairytale location could have anything negative about it at all. We explained our situation, and of course, included the details of our journey (as well as the other room upgrade tips and tricks we had up our sleeve). The lovely woman at the desk was very apologetic and informed us that it was difficult to do anything due to the renovation work, but she had one room that we could move to. However, she said there is just one problem with this room. 'Here we go' I thought, it's going to be in the cellar, or the last tenant died and they haven't changed the bedding yet. To our surprise, she was concerned about the fact that there was a jacuzzi in the main living space and it wasn't separated in its own bathroom. What is it with Canadians and jacuzzi voyeurism? We explained that she was sweet to be concerned, but after 20 years together we'd recently grown out of that shy stage in our relationship and took the room. She made a point of saying that it should be far enough away for the deliveries.

It's probably a good time to try and explain what the hotel looks like (maybe just google it, I'm not a great writer). It resembles a fairytale princess castle with the main structure forming a semicircle around the offending courtyard. Halfway around the semicircle, a tall part of the building shoots into the skyline, the beautiful green copper roofing is broken up with the cute dormer windows of a few small attic rooms. One of those attic rooms wasn't just any attic room, it was OUR attic room, with a jacuzzi that you could sit in and look out across the city's skyline. The upgrade resulted in numerous high fives, a couple of victory dances and of course the line 'I told you to trust me'.

From Montreal's dodgy upgrade, Quebec had gotten off to a flying start with what ended up being the 2nd best upgrade of the trip. I jest you not, but you will have to keep reading to find out what topped this. Quebec was beautiful, it was full of snow, making the hotel look even more like a fairytale scene. The people were so friendly, and the town was so cute it looked like a Christmas card. Once again we got to practice our terrible school French, as we strolled around a lovely Christmas fair, hugging a cup of Gluhwein to keep us warm.

Back Ottawa

After Nic had fallen into a deep mulled wine sleep on our last night in Quebec, I stayed up to sort out the next Canadian cab off the rank, Ottawa. I locked in a hotel with the usual tips and tricks (including a quick prayer to the travel gods) and also worked out a public transport plan to get there from the train station. We woke to a beautiful morning in Quebec, although still very very cold. It provided a perfect opportunity to get some final photos of the beautiful train station before we settled in for our journey to Canada's capital city.

It was dark when we arrived, and the wind, sleet, and snow was very unwelcoming, and to be honest a little rude. Nic didn't quite realise how much planning I'd put in that previous night, so was a bit taken aback when I rushed her off the train, grabbed her hand, and shouted 'This way!'. I dragged her, at pace, through a subway, over some stairs, across multiple platforms, over a road bridge, and down to a bus stop, just as the 95 bus pulled up to its stop. She sat down with a slump in the bus seat, looked at me and asked 'what just happened? Do you know what you are doing?'. I have to say, I was a little dejected at her lack of confidence in my direction, and despite my assurances, she still spent the next 10 minutes of the bus ride confirming that I wasn't bonkers. Getting off the bus, I resumed my march with Nic in tow, still not feeling the support for my organisational or directional skills. A direct walk, straight to the hotel's door without even needing to refer to the map, preceded us both bursting through the doors and out of the horrible weather. We were soaked, had bright red noses, and enough bags strapped to us to resemble those blown up sumo wrestler outfits.

Before we could even take off our bags, the night staff suddenly presented us with a glass of champagne each. With our hands busy concentrating on the alcohol, we were stuck in Sumo costume until we reached the room. We squeezed into the lift sideways, popping out at the correct floor, eventually waddling into our room, which had been upgraded to a junior suite with a bath the size of a small town. Thank you travel gods. Nic, doubt me, really?

Our time in Ottawa was a pleasant surprise. Like Australia's capital Canberra, it instilled thoughts of offices and bureaucrats, however, the city was full of nice coffee shops, beautiful walks, markets, and historic buildings. During our mooching around the area, we sourced some nice cheese and wine as sustenance for a marathon 5-hour soak in our huge bathtub that evening. The day ended with a trip to Parliament Hill to view the Christmas projections on the magnificent gothic revival Parliament buildings. Quite a fun packed day for our only full day in the capital, this place is certainly worth a visit if you're in the area.

You never saw Murdoch wearing a woolly hat

After a very early morning start, we were back at the train station, this time with thick snow falling as we climbed aboard our train to Toronto. Just like all our VIA rail experiences so far, it was very efficient and friendly. By the time we arrived at Toronto's Union Station, the sky was clear for the walk to our hotel. After our stay in Quebec, we were very much endeared to the Fairmont chain of hotels. The company had purchased a number of the great railroad related buildings from the 1920s, similar in style to the Chateau Frontenac. The equivalent in Toronto was the Royal York Hotel. It looked beautiful and grand, but unfortunately not possible on our budget, pushing us to a cheap hotel about five blocks east of the city centre. One of the handy things about Toronto, especially in winter, is that it has a network of underground walkways joining office blocks and shopping malls, allowing you to traverse across town without having to venture outside. We made the most of this on our journey from the station, but still had about three exposed blocks to our lodgings. Just the perfect amount of time to make your cheeks start to ache.

Toronto felt like a cross between Melbourne in winter, and London in winter (I hope you are getting the fact that it was cold). We had two missions to complete in this city and were determined not to let the weather stop us. The first mission was a tribute to Dad. Remember his love for the TV show *Murdoch Mysteries*, the program will forever remind us of him, especially his frustrations, as an eternal romantic, that the two main characters never hooked up despite their love for each other, for series after series. The show is produced in Canada and set in Toronto during the early 20th Century. More specifically, it's set in Police Station House No 4, and guess what, it exists. It's obviously now a modern functioning police station, but is still partly housed in one of Toronto's older historical brick buildings. In its foyer, there is a little police museum with a special display that highlights the links with the TV series. It was one of the trips highly surreal experiences as we stood in the foyer getting all emotional at the display when just to our right was a long plexiglass window with police officers staring out at us while helping people report stolen wallets or cats up trees.

Chocolate, on bacon, on a stick!

Where else would we head for sustenance on our exploration of Toronto, but the enticingly named distillery district. This is a lovely area of town with cobblestoned streets meandering through converted 19th Century industrial architecture. A bit of a trendy spot so we obviously felt quite at home in our many layers of clothes, restricting movement with just our red noses peeking out for identification purposes. The red noses were quite on topic, as the area also hosts a large Christmas Market which was buzzing with stalls selling food and gifts. It was in this industrial area that I found the greatest invention ever built.

We've already established that anything edible is greatly improved just by presenting it on a stick, well what about doing it with my two favourite food groups, bacon and chocolate. My heart skipped a beat of joy, when I saw the Pig Candy stall. It probably fluttered a bit after trying out this delicacy, in what clinicians call a Sinus WTF rhythm. Only the Canadians would and could pull this off, and I take my hat off to them (well two hats and a hood).

With mission one complete, the next was going to be taxing on the budget. During the many months of planning back in Melbourne, we had numerous discussions about how much money we would need. After speaking with others who'd travelled around the world on a budget, we wanted to ensure that whenever we reached a bucket list location, we had enough money to enjoy it appropriately. We would give each other examples of situations that might arise. A re-occurring scenario was that if we ever made it to Niagara Falls or the Grand Canyon, we should be able to take a helicopter trip over it. Now as we find ourselves within 130km of Niagara, we had to put our dwindling money where our mouth was. We chose an organised tour that would visit the falls before heading to the local Reif Estate vineyard to experience the region's famous Ice Wine.

The minibus first stopped at a small airport where we could opt-in to the helicopter trip. Hells yeah we did! The fact that it was the same cost as living for a full week in Cambodia was firmly out of our minds. We had a wonderful time in this truly great way to experience this iconic location, added to by the smugness of feeling that we'd completed one of the major scenarios we'd originally set out to do. This warm fuzzy feeling soon became a cold fuzzy feeling by the time we were on the ground and standing at the edge of the Falls. Even the Ice Wine failed to warm the cockles. The sight was as magnificent as you would imagine, it had a beautiful frosty frame as all the surrounds were covered with snow and ice. Very Christmassy indeed. It was cold enough that the spray from the Falls had turned into ice by the time it landed on us. This certainly added to the atmosphere, but detracted a little from the romanticism that you usually attribute to the location. We managed just a quick peck on the lips in fear that otherwise, we'd become quickly inseparable, having to be whisked to a local Emergency Department for surgical extraction. I scoured the fine print of our travel insurance before we left, and was pretty sure that bizarre kissing related injuries were not covered.

After four days of dashing around and exploring Toronto, it was time to move on and we said goodbye to our budget lodgings. We were excited about the next chapter of our adventure, a journey on the iconic 'Canadian' train, travelling right across the country. As I walked out of the hotel, I obviously hadn't woken up yet. My sight seemed to be quite blurry, all I could see was white. I rubbed my eyes, white. I looked down, white. I looked up, white. I looked at Nic, NOT white (apart from the knees down). Things were starting to fall into place, well actually many things had been falling all night and there was a thick 'white-out' of snow which was still coming down hard. Initially, this was great fun, but if you were to plot the fun on a graph against the number of blocks we'd walked from the hotel, you would notice a sharp decline in sales. At least we had the excitement of the train journey to keep us going, and we eventually made it to Toronto's underground city, just before an ear dropped off. From there, we were safe all the way to the station.

We shivered our way up to the check-in counter to be informed that the train was going to be delayed. Apparently, there was thick snow on the tracks, something we now refer to as 'Storm NoShitSherlock'. They informed us to sit tight, have some free coffee and wait for updates. We waited. We waited some more. We went to a nearby cinema to watch a movie, came back, had a coffee, and waited. Eventually, someone brave enough to face the passengers appeared in the middle of the waiting area to say that the train would not be able to leave until the morning, so they were going to put us up in a hotel for the night. Great (sarcastic).

We weren't sure how they went about allocating accommodation, and were hoping that we didn't have to walk back a similar distance to somewhere. Maybe it was because we'd booked a private sleeper cabin, but when it came to us, we found out that we were staying at the hotel just across the road. None other than the Royal York Hotel. Great (not so sarcastic).

Crossing the road, I had a warm glow that, once again, someone up there was looking out for us. As I flew through the air, in super slow-motion, after slipping on ice, arms flailing, facing up towards the sky, the warm glow was punctuated with a 'don't get cocky about it' statement. *Dumpf!*

This stopover meant we would have less time at our next stop, Jasper, but we weren't thinking about that right now. The hotel was as lovely as we expected, with a grand lobby, an old station clock in the middle of the foyer, and a magnificent Christmas tree. We didn't get too much time to enjoy it though as by now it was quite late, and we needed to be back at the station by 6am the following morning. We just had time to contact the Jasper hotel to reduce our stay, which they were very Canadian and understanding about.

The Champagne (not so) Express

Morning came, bringing clear blue skies to the still white Toronto landscape. The train was ready to leave and was just as we had imagined it. It sat somewhere between the posh Chinese sleeper train from Hong Kong and the Trans-Mongolian. Originally designed to be more utilitarian than luxurious, it now had a very cool hipster vibe, like an Airstream caravan on rails.

Our cabin was tiny, with a single small armchair packed in, designed to get in the way whenever you wanted to do just about anything, unless only one of you wanted to unsociably sit and look out the window. Once unpacked, we went for an explore, finding ourselves in the communal carriage at the end of the train. The last compartment was nearly all windows, having a bulbous end to clearly see the track behind us. The seats were set around the edge facing inwards, making it more of a social gathering place. The next section along was on two levels, the bottom level was the bar, above it was a cabin with rows of seats to relax and make the most of a large glass domed roof. This section was higher than the other carriages, enabling you to see the whole length of the train ahead, watching it snake along the tracks.

What we didn't realise was that the railroad company (VIA) would employ people (or give them a free ride across the country) to entertain us. This became apparent when the noise of a ukulele wafted through to us in the upstairs viewing area. The staff started to usher passengers to the last carriage to meet each other, and the ukulele playing Shelley who would be with us for our journey.

Again, I'm going to blame the fact that I'm a northern Englishman, but sitting around in a small confined space with someone making direct eye contact and singing to you is a little confronting. This was compounded by the fact that some of the passengers had no qualms about singing along. We sat with our complimentary glass of champagne praying to any God who would listen that there wouldn't be an 'over to you Lee' moment, where everyone would look to me to continue the next verse of a moving folk song I'd never heard before. In times like this, alcohol is your friend, and luckily it was on hand. I'm not sure how often the Canadian gets delayed, but the staff did a great job of making us know that they felt bad about it. Their years of experience and training had taught them that the best way to bring everyone around was with free champagne and finger food. Both just kept coming and coming. A couple of hours later I was trying to catch Shelley's eye to get me to sing the chorus of her latest tune.

The bubbles also meant that everyone's guard was down and people quickly got chatting with each other. We had a great mix of people, although mainly English and Canadians, some travelling as tourists and others just wanting to get somewhere. This made mealtimes in the dining car easier, as there was already a good chance that you might know someone on your table. We shared a few meals with Shelley and by now I was totally hooked on ukulele music. It seemed to be a very fitting soundtrack for this cross country journey. She was a singer/songwriter and teacher who'd completed a similar engagement before, helping with the costs of travelling across the country to see family.

The journey was just magical, the snow covered winter wonderland reeked of Christmas with hours and hours of beautiful white forests and frozen lakes.

We often got to study the scenery in a bit more detail as it became apparent that passenger trains like ours played second fiddle (or uke) to freight trains. We would often spend hours in a siding waiting for a goods train, some over a mile long, to pass. At one long siding stop, we were even able to get out and have a play in the snow. This delayed the schedule even more, so only one thing for it - champagne and finger food.

Don't poke the Bear

The comradery between our fellow captives was very reminiscent of the boat trip through Laos. It was going to be a shame to say goodbye to everyone when we reached Jasper. We all swapped details and had one last singalong (no I didn't) with Shelley before spending the last few hours glued to the viewing car windows as we approached Jasper. This was real Rocky Mountain country, and the views were supposed to be fantastic. I'm sure they were, but said views were behind the latest snow storm and fog, so it could have been anything really. We were teased with a tiny glimpse of an outcrop or mountain top before we came to a halt in the blizzard that was Jasper. It was sad to climb down from the Canadian, as not only were we saying goodbye to the team, we also knew that we couldn't afford a sleeping cabin for the next two-day leg. We only had seats booked. 'No champagne and finger food for you!'.

We'd arranged a pick up to the hotel and couldn't really see much through the van's window on the transfer. Now, is probably a good time to let you know that this was another Fairmont hotel. I'm conscious you might be doubting that this really was a backpacker trip around the world and I'm not, in fact, Donald Trump Jnr. Let me just take a quick moment to justify this. You will have all seen those iconic pictures of the Canadian Rockies, the ones with a lovely lake, surrounded by snow-topped mountains and tall trees (usually Lake Louise or somewhere in Banff). Well, this hotel had that view, or it should, somewhere beyond the whiteout. It wasn't just a frivolous expense, it was one of those 'helicopter over Niagara' moments, admittedly we were clocking up a few of them.

We arrived and walked into a foyer that looked like the set from the movie *Holiday Inn*, I kept expecting to see Bing Crosby sat in front one of the many fireplaces in a rocking chair. The interactions with the hotel to arrange our delayed arrival had given me opportunity to make a personal connection, explaining how excited we were to be there and to pass on the general gist of the trip. Between this and our sincere disappointment of having time cut short with them they, you guessed it, upgraded us to a lakeside lodge.

A little dance ensued.

Although the train was great, the thought of a 5-star bed was better. We decided to crash out for the evening, putting a pin in the day and see what weather we had waiting for us the following morning. The sleep was fantastic and lengthy. We woke, put the coffee machine on, slipped into our Fairmont, thick, warm, dressing gowns and opened the curtains. I shit you not, we were looking straight at two elk, and behind them, I really shit you not, was the view from those magazine photos I promised you.

More dancing ensued.

I can't explain how beautiful this place was, which when you think of it, is a bit of an epic fail for someone writing a travel book, but hey ho. You've come this far already, you might as well stick with it. After a hearty breakfast in the hotel, we rugged up for a walk around the lake. The snow was still in abundance, and it wasn't long before we could see our breath and not feel our ears. We were a little on edge after reading a note in the hotel room, telling us to report any aggressive bear or elk behaviour to reception. This sounded a lot more civilised than crapping yourself while trying to remember whether you should run or stay completely still. I was still traumatised by the big cuddly dog in Mongolia, so who knows what I might do if faced with a grumpy Bambi on steroids, let alone a Grizzly.

I think we only saw two other small groups on our four-hour walk of this magical place and were kept on guard after noticing various scratching marks on tree trunks. The whole area was so photogenic, I couldn't work out what to take a picture of first and hope Nic wasn't an abandoned camera widow. By the time we reached the cabin, we were officially colder than our Thanksgiving Day in New York. At this point, the thought of jumping into an outside swimming pool isn't typically high on the list. But that's what we did. We were assured that the lodge's pool was kept lovely and warm, and you even entered it from within the hotel in the warmth, before making your way through a plastic flappy door, into the extremes. At which point my glasses misted up and blocked my vision, but my other senses were obviously heightened as I could clearly make out Nic's giggling.

It was marvellous, looking at that view, almost naked, in temperatures of minus F.F.S. A perfect day was rounded off with a hearty meal in the *Holiday Inn* lookalike. I was still on the lookout for Bing, and after a few reds, I'm pretty sure I did spot him. We woke with a slight hangover, feeling grumpy about the thought of two days sitting in train seats, with no finger food or even a private toilet. It must be time for a bit of luck and a cunning plan.

The abundant champagne on the previous journey would have completely compensated us for our Toronto delay, but it turned out that VIA had a policy where if you're delayed over 10 hours you get half the journey's value awarded in VIA reward points. This, coupled with the accumulation of our previous points, meant that we had enough for an upgrade on the next leg.

We were, however, not confident of the availability at such late notice as we presented ourselves to Jasper's VIA counter with nervous smiles. Bingo! The last, smallest cabin was available. We were back in the good life. We even came across a few fellow travellers from pre-Jasper, which made it even better. Although comfy and well looked after, the camaraderie with the new passengers wasn't the same. They hadn't been through what we'd been through, hadn't downed the significant levels of alcohol or vol-au-vents that we had, they just wouldn't understand what we'd been through. Next stop, Vancouver.

Meeting Melbourne's Nemesis

As I mentioned at the start of the book, our wanderlust saw little action after our first big relocation to Melbourne. Voted the world's most liveable city repeatedly since arriving, it was hard to leave. Vancouver, however, would be the city that could occasionally drop Melbourne to the number two slot. We arrived with an exciting thought that this might be a nice place to settle down for a bit, but also feeling a bit defensive for Melbourne.

We stayed in a nice mid-range hotel near Stanley Park which had an art gallery built into the ground floor. Our usual trickery had rewarded us with not only an upgrade, but the lovely gift of a book about Vancouver. We loved Vancouver straight away and hit the pavement to explore as the snow was clearing (still enough to make the odd snowman, and when I say odd, I'm referring to our bad snowman making skills).

We clocked up the miles, checking out the parks, the waterfront, the seaplane port, the bars and microbreweries. It felt like a cross between Sydney and Melbourne, and I think if we'd been there in the warmth of summer we would have been looking for jobs by now. Between the fact that we'd been constantly cold for a few weeks, and the realisation that this wasn't anywhere near the worst of Canadian weather, it was clear that we are just a bit too precious for this country. We decided, our backup option was to cherry pick the best bits of the city and send encoded emails back to the Mayor of Melbourne, in a covert mission to further edge out our rival.

Top of this list was the cutest little bathtub shaped boats that ploughed the waters of False Creek on the south side of the downtown peninsula. Including, transporting passengers to and from the Granville Island Market (a very cool spot full of great music, crafts, and foodie stalls). We always did find it irksome that Melbourne has done little to make use of any maritime history or better still, its waterways. Our ferries are not cute, not even nice. I felt sure with our covert information received, we would return to Melbourne after the tour to find bathtub ferries aplenty, and another nail in Vancouver's coffin for the 1st place prize.

One Year Update

It was in this wonderful city that we hit a tour milestone. It was 22nd December, and one year since we left Melbourne on our trip. I can't believe how quickly it's gone. We've had some real highs and one real low, but we have made it so far, and we were feeling very chuffed with ourselves.

On the statistics front, it was also time to celebrate one significant milestone. By arriving in Vancouver, we had clocked up a total of 56,172km since we left home, 42,162km of these were without flying. That's 75% of our journey so far without flight, but more importantly, that distance is more than the circumference of the Earth. Remember back at Melbourne airport, we'd started the trip really thinking that we weren't cut out for this, and were expecting to end up on Dad's sofa within weeks, but here we were, seasoned travellers.

It was the perfect time for fist bumps, high fives, and whatever else Canadians do, as we knew we'd soon be flying across the Pacific and our overland stats would suffer. We'd tried to secure onward travel on freight ships but nothing seemed to fit our timelines. We had certainly changed as travellers, as people, and as partners. I like to think it was for the better in each case. We felt proud and happy, but it still just felt like we were starting something rather than coming to the end of it. It really did feel like the world was our lobster.

'Twas the night before Christmas

During our time on the train, Shelley our ukulele playing companion had convinced us that the city of Victoria (the capital of British Columbia) would be much more Christmassy than Vancouver. Out of the various forms of transport available (including a seaplane), we took the cheapest option of a bus/ferry service. Despite the cost, it was one of the prettiest journeys of the trip. We'd made the saving here so that we could spend it on the hotel. I think you might have an idea who owned it.

The Fairmont Empress Hotel, located on Victoria's waterfront is a beautiful imposing neogothic chateauesque building, much like a smaller version of Chateau Frontenac. Luckily, we had now accumulated some discount due to our hotel membership and previous Fairmont stays. No upgrade this time, and our room was okay, but in these temperatures, it didn't take long to realise that we had another room without heating.

Engineers came to try and fix it, without luck. We were shown to another room which was bigger but not as homely. All we could hear in the nearby vicinity were the screams of a large family with what sounded like maybe 50 kids bouncing off the walls like they had all eaten something blue. Back to the original room it was, with the addition of two electric heaters, and extra blankets. This was the foundation of what became a very Christmassy experience, as one of the heaters was an old school model with the orange bars across so, if you squinted a little, it could be a fireplace. Even better, one of the TV channels was just showing footage of a roaring fire. The scene was set, we just needed a bit of Christmas decoration.

We wandered into town to try and put together a Christmas Eve buffet for the room that evening, and eventually found a large supermarket. We thought we might find some tinsel or a poinsettia but right there at the front of the supermarket was a florist who was about to close for Christmas. Staring right at us, from a bargain basement table was a miniature fake Christmas tree with stand, baubles, tinsel, and even a set of lights. It was all made up and good to go. In another surreal conversation about what to spend money on, we must have spent about 30 minutes discussing the whopping $25 expense, before carrying it back to our $280 a night hotel, via the liquor store. It was a perfect Christmas tree for our cosy room.

By the time we finished, there couldn't have been a more Christmassy hotel room in all the land. The sideboard was emptied to cater for the tree, a C$10 present from each other, some nuts, and a satsuma each. We then nipped out to find a local pub for a drink but at 8:30, the city had shut. Tails between our legs we returned to our own little buffet, and a Christmas movie. I came from a family where Christmas celebrations were huge, and for sure, it was my fathers favourite time of the year. I don't think there was a gyrating Santa, or singing snowman ornament that he didn't have. Our room was perfect, homely, comforting, with a dollop of sadness.

We slept well and awoke early on Christmas Day. While opening our C$10 presents, we heard rustling outside our door as a group of staff sang carols through the hallway. Thinking it was the morning paper, I checked to find that the hotel had put a stocking on everyone's door with little treats inside. It really did seem that someone was looking after us this Christmas.

The most expensive meal ever

So the phrase 'Our most expensive meal ever' is certainly not something I would have expected us to come across when we started our trip with a budget of $50 a day through South East Asia. However, that is what happened on Christmas Day in Victoria. We decided that, understandably, we needed a bit of looking after this Christmas so signed up for the Christmas meal in the hotel's exclusive restaurant. We still had some credit on Nic's salary packaging Visa card so it wouldn't hurt our cash flow right away.

Our first obstacle the previous day, was getting a reservation without causing an international incident. We approached the front desk just as the receptionist walked away, but another member of staff stepped in as she saw us approach (at least I think she worked there). We requested a reservation, the response came quickly 'Now, you do know how much this is don't you?'. Which wasn't patronising in any way. Rather than being rude, the English in me could only manage a shrug of the shoulders, and slight raising of the hands with the phrase 'Of course'.

Simultaneously, I was getting a flashback to a trip to London as a teenager. While walking into the front door of Harrods, my brother Mick was refused entry for wearing a singlet. Val, my sister-in-law, took great offence to this, turned to the doorman and shouted 'Well you can fuck right off, we are all leaving!'. Correct, we were all Northerners. Now, by this point, three of us had already made it inside the store successfully. A lengthy pregnant pause ensued as the successful stared at the unsuccessful through the revolving glass door. One side of the door full of treasures, and the enticing smell of the Harrods Food Hall, the other side a flurry of arm waving, rudely pointed fingers, and swear words. Dejected, heads down we exited the store. I remember my brother just had this look of acceptance as though it happens a lot.

Anyway, back to the cleaner or whoever she was. She showed us a computer screen so we could choose our table. Being who we are, we'd memorised the restaurant layout, and selected the table we had already set our minds on. All sorted, I tried to make a quick exit, while we were still ahead. We weren't fast enough. While slowly looking us up and down, she added 'You do realise that people will be all dressed up, nice and smart?'. Hmm, now what would Val do? It took every ounce of restraint, but I didn't. This meal was now too important to us. And after all, she was right. We had ditched our QM2 clothes and were back with just what we had in our backpacks. This was a turd that we needed to try and polish. Time to go shopping.

Back to Christmas Day. We managed to cobble something together (of course I had the Magic Shirt), and headed down to dinner. Our private waiter showed us to our beautifully arranged table, and we were handed the details of the set Christmas menu and wine list. People certainly did look smart, in fact, they all looked like dignitaries. How do you do that? Are you born that way, or is it just smoke and mirrors with good posture and a fancy haircut? Are people chosen to be dignitaries, because they look like this? You don't see slumpy shoulders in a Ferrero Rocher advert, and I'm pretty sure that I haven't been served a burger by anyone looking like the ambassador of Liechtenstein. We stood out, purely because we don't look like dignitaries, too small for starters. I think they have one of those height limit things, like at an amusement park.

We started off feeling a little unrelaxed. Only one thing for it, booze. I opened the wine menu and filtered out the affordable offerings to choose from. What was left was a short list. Our waiter appeared and asked for our choice. I mentioned it was great to see they had a lovely wine from one of our favourite vineyards back home, and well, that was that. We had a lengthy conversation about the area and our local wines, and I think all three of us suddenly became much more relaxed. We also took a moment to remember that we have a good life in Melbourne, and have been lucky enough to eat in some of its finest restaurants.

The meal was magical, it was a really special evening, and although to this day, still has the moniker of the most expensive meal ever, it is one we will remember forever (something we probably can't say about the 2nd or 3rd most expensive).

More FooBar than Foo Fighters

Despite our plan to not miss big ticket items because of money, we decided that we couldn't afford one of the many Orca spotting trips from Victoria or the seaplane journey to our next destination, Seattle. Instead, we booked a reasonably priced fast ferry shuttle to cross back into the US. While boarding, we were warned that the trip could be a bit lumpy, and if there was any chance of feeling green, then they had some sea sickness tablets to hand out. I'm generally okay but do have random bouts of queasiness, so grabbed two at the counter, taking them quickly without consulting my medical officer.

Nic was shocked to find out what I'd done and quickly explained why. These tablets were antihistamine based and similar to something I'd used before to help me sleep. 'You mean the tablets that even though it says take one to two, I can only take a quarter as they knock me out so much?'. 'Yep'. 'Shite'. The good news for me was that, as much as I tried, I couldn't get anxious about it, in fact, I was feeling quite chilled and dreamy. The same could not be said about my travel buddy.

I had an incredibly relaxed journey into Seattle port, before seeming to drift through American customs inches from the ground (thankfully it was late, and they weren't paying too much attention to pupil dilation). By all accounts, it was a long cold walk to the hotel North of town. Not for me. I vaguely remember thinking I was in a Buck Rodgers movie as a monorail shot overhead making me look up to see a towering, needlelike, white space station raised up into the sky. Seriously these drugs were good. I woke the next morning all sleepy-eyed and groggy, turned around to find Nic starting at me with bloodshot eyes, hair like the Wicked Witch of the West, and a sore finger from poking me at regular intervals throughout the night, making sure I was still alive.

I sensed a little tension that day, as we went out to tour this city of grunge (music that is, it's not a grungy city in any way). We only had two full days in town, so they had to be MountyDays. And they were, starting with something for Nic to help me get in her good books again. It was a boat trip on Union Lake to see the boathouse from *Sleepless in Seattle*, although I was more interested with Bill Gates' boathouse, the only one with a helicopter pad on top. From there, we didn't have time to waste in queues, so bought a VIP ticket for the Space Needle (I had a real déjà vu feeling about this place, and it made me think of Buck Rogers for some reason). Handy tip: we arrived for sunset to get both day and night views.

Pike's Place Market has a great vibe and sells, hands down, the world's best clam chowder. Although, there was a side street out back that drew our attention. It was crammed with people taking a walking tour. They were looking at what seemed to be an art installation down one of the laneways. It was only when we got closer, we realised it was basically a wall covered with chewing gum. Now I'm sure if this was my city, it wouldn't be something I'd want to advertise. Paris has its 'love bridges', covered in padlocks adorned with romantic messages, and Seattle has a wall with people's gob and leftover food all over it. It has to be said, it was indeed colourful.

A Later Latte

Seattle is of course famous for being the headquarters of the Starbucks Corporation, whose green emblem is seen in over 30,000 cafes around the globe. Our feelings towards Starbucks has changed during our travels. Back home in Melbourne, it's just not done. We have some of the world's best baristas and a seriously dense population of hipsters, creating amazing coffee shops. Many Starbuck establishments have actually closed down in the city. However, when you are travelling and in an unfamiliar Asian city in need of a caffeine fix, it's a comforting site to behold. It was often expensive for our budget but just like walking into a Costco or Ikea anywhere in the world, the familiarity was sometimes worth it for our mental health.

Pike Place also happens to host the location of the first ever Starbucks coffee shop, which is still in operation. We looked quite smug with ourselves, holding our buckets of coffee, ticking off a quirky tourist attraction. That was, until we later realised that the market area had two Starbucks cafes. The real first one was about 300 metres from our smug little faces. It felt like an *Amazing Race* fail.

Another great tip for this city is a visit to the top of Smith Tower. A historic building built in a beautiful neoclassical architecture style which has an observation level on the 27th floor. A cheap ticket affords (see what I did there) great views of the city and the benefit of this, over the Space Needle, is that the views from here actually include the iconic Space Needle. Much in the same way that the view from the Rockefeller Centre is almost better than the Empire State Building.

Despite a busy last day, we managed to research the location of our bus stop for the early morning run to the airport. Although our next location was still in the US, we were Pacific bound, heading to one of our all-time bucket list destinations. Hawaii.

CHAPTER 14

Location: Waikiki
Days 373, Countries 26, Kilometers 60,748, Beds 116
Trains 19, Planes 17, Automobiles 40, Boats 14
Beers 258

Blue Hawaii

So we were finally making it to Hawaii, a big ticket destination filled with images of lush mountains, and beautiful
women greeting you with a Lei (flower garland) and a
cocktail when you walk off the plane. Maybe our time with Hula
had created an even greater connection with the islands. We've
travelled enough to know having any kind of dream sequence
in your head about a location before you get there will nearly
always end in tears. With Hawaii, however, we couldn't avoid
it. The end credits for the Elvis classic *Blue Hawaii* scrolled up
the laptop screen as we started to descend into Daniel K. Inouye
International Airport.

Our plan was to stay in Waikiki for a couple of nights, to
enjoy New Year's Eve on the beach, then fly to Kona on the big
island, before heading to Maui. Needless to say, the budget was
well and truly decimated for this whole leg of the trip. Obviously,
with it being New Year there was a shortage of hotels and they

were at a premium, but we found and booked a spot before we arrived. It looked great on the website and was only two streets back from the beach.

We disembarked the plane, full of beans, and walked through the crowds of people being presented with a Lei. We remembered that while booking our flights we'd ummed and ahhed about paying the extra $20 for the experience, and because of the whopping cost of this leg, we declined. Something that we fully regretted at this point. No worries, let's just get out there and visit this beautiful island, the one where everyone drives around in classic cars, knows everybody, and waves as they pass by on the way to the local pineapple plantation to stock up on fruit. You just thought, 'Naive, numb asses', didn't you? You may be right. Our next bad decision of the day was to refuse to pay for a US$30 taxi, or nice airport shuttle, in favour of the US$2 public bus that would eventually drop us right outside the hotel.

The bus stop was almost underground in the armpit of the airport so no palm trees in sight, just concrete. *Dumph!* The sound of us both slamming back down to earth. I won't go into who's *dumph* made the loudest sound, it's not the time and place, and wouldn't be gentlemanly.

Rather than being full of like-minded travellers who wanted to see the real Hawaii, our US$2 bus was full of real Hawaiians that couldn't afford the expensive alternative. The bus took around twice as long, traversing through industrial areas and some less affluent housing estates. Our hearts sank further and further as we drove past probably the largest homeless tent city that we'd ever seen. Just as we pulled up to a set of traffic lights, Nic looks out of the window to see an old woman urinating into a McDonalds cup. There was such a mix of feelings; sadness for the people we'd seen; a reminder that we were about to be thrown back into the real world in a matter of weeks; fed up that our Hawaiian dream sequence had been ripped apart, and then guilt that we were thinking of ourselves rather than the people around us.

We needed something to break the silence.

The doors opened at the next stop and a huge (I mean huge) islander, full of tattoos and bleached blonde hair climbed onboard with the aid of a crutch and sat down next to me. He was a jolly character, talking to anyone around, including himself. Sensing an air of despair about the vehicle, he decided to start singing. Fair dues, he had quite a good voice as he dedicated a song about angels to his mum (and any other mums that weren't with us anymore). As his arms raised into the air, to indicate that everyone should join in, everyone else's head lowered to stare at their feet or phone. I never sing, despite twenty years of Nic trying to make me, I was damn sure that this Hawaiian Hulk Hogan was not going to fair any better.

Next, it was time for his joke repertoire, including the one about why don't blind people skydive? Because it scares the dogs. Again, the sound of shuffling (isn't that a Simon & Garfunkel song?) from the rest of the bus. Except me. I laughed. 'Now that's what I'm talkin bout!' he shouts before performing his half of a fist bump. Picturing a Hawaiian version of *Of Mice and Men* where he was Lennie, and I was a cute little bunny rabbit, I decided not to leave the man hanging, we were now besties. By the time he reached his stop, he'd asked if I wanted any amphetamines, cocaine, or ketamine as he was also a bit of a pharmacist on the side. I put the fact that he thought I might want to partake, down to my long hair and crumpled clothes, and tried to pull off a cool 'no, not today thanks' response.

Welcome to Hawaii. Well, at least we had the nice hotel, didn't we? We entered our small, dated room and pulled back the curtains to see a multi-story car park meters away from the window. We had three options in front of us:

(a) To have a little cry

(b) Hit the beach and have a Mai Tai

(c) All of the above.

We chose (c).

Walking along the beach, in front of the hotels that we couldn't afford, we still felt a little down and dejected. As the sun started to set, the sky turned a beautiful colour, providing a wonderful silhouette of Waikiki's iconic Diamond Head. It was the perfect Hawaiian vista as a large catamaran departed for its evening cruise, the icing on the cake. Suddenly, we see something in the water. Surely it couldn't be, could it? A beautifully chunky green turtle had come to cheer us up and remind us that in the scheme of things, we were still doing quite well. We then realise that he'd brought five of his mates to meet us too. This nice 'turn it around' moment was improved further with a 'must have' Mai Tai at the famous Dukes beachfront restaurant. It now felt like we'd arrived in Hawaii.

The Cross-Continental Nostril Shot

Our second day in Waikiki fell on New Year's Eve, and it was another up and down day in the neighbourhood. It was a beautiful start as we walked south along the beach, past Diamond Head and back, before crashing in the hotel. We had a bit of fun along the way with Mick and Val back in the UK. They told us about a public webcam along the beachfront they'd been checking out in case we wandered by. We arranged a time, stood in front of it, texted, waved, and other silly stuff. This accumulated with a Nostril Shot with Me, Nic, and the webcam which obviously meant Mick and Val were in there too (along with a few hundred other people). A new record for my Nostril Shot skills.

Before long, the room's multi-storey car park views got the better of us and we came down with a case of the fuckums. We hadn't arranged to do anything particular to celebrate New Year as we were conscious about our disappearing budget. We finally decided that we'd eat in a Hawaiian themed restaurant, next to the hotel. Unfortunately, the theme didn't go much further than its name (Da Big Kahuna) and the staff costumes, in what was a real tourist trap. Out of everything on our deluxe share platter,

I think the only thing that wasn't deep fried was the plate itself. We walked out, feeling even more grumpy and with a reduced life expectancy to boot. I was close to heading back upstairs to the room, but Nic insisted we head to the beach to see the fireworks. I agreed but peppered the walk there with positive remarks, 'it's going to be heaving, we won't get anywhere near the front', 'it's already looking a bit lairy around here, will it be safe later?', 'Was that rain? Did you feel that? I'm sure it's spitting!'.

We walked through the crowd, straight onto a small raised area of beach, just as the fireworks started. During the long display you could see the silhouettes of surfers riding waves to shore, making the experience even more magical. I shut up and put my arm around my wife, pulling her close. Wow, what a year that was. For many many reasons, it will standout amongst all of them, and what a perfect way to end it.

Book 'em Nicko

Unlike Nic, I am just old enough to remember the original *Hawaii 5-0* TV series, and we'd been watching the modern remake before and during travelling. The show made Hawaii look beautiful, apart from the constant crime of course, something we just put down to artistic license. Although now, not so sure. We were not organised enough, or cashed up enough, to do some of the prominent tourist attractions like the HMS Arizona. Instead, we decided to have a day on our favourite US$2 bus and head off in search of some of the famous sites from the TV show, which included some of the city's historic buildings.

Now that we knew what to expect from the bus, it was much more of a normal MountyDay as we ticked off various landmarks, such as Iolani Palace, and the statue of King Kamehameha. We were surprised at how few tourists were around, everyone seemed to concentrate around the shopping centres and bars near the beach. Much like New York, it was great to visit sites for the first time that felt so familiar due to their TV and media exposure.

Also thanks to NYC and our new found love of all things Buffalo Wings, we ended up in a Hooters Bar for lunch. I guess you have to take the rough with the voluptuous.

Farting at the splashy kids

Now that the budget had long been blown for Hawaii, you know the rule. If it's blown, then it's blown, so just go for it. We decided to do something that we'd heard about a few years earlier, and has been on our bucket list ever since. Kona on the big island (the actual island of Hawaii) is famous for its year-round Manta Ray population. Some of which, come to shore at night to feed. Organised trips allow you to dive or snorkel, letting you get up close to these magnificent beasts. This was something that just had to be done. We have a long-standing love of these creatures, especially, after spending a week assisting Project Manta scientists on Lady Elliot Island some years ago.

The budget breaking didn't quite end there. There is a certain Kona cove that's particularly popular for this Manta activity. This cove has a hotel on the cliffside that enables you to see the Mantas from the shore by illuminating the water to attract its food, microplankton. An ocean room at the Kona Sheraton was a far cry from our mice infested beach hut in Cambodia, but it was a year of different experiences after all.

A small propeller aircraft transported us from Honolulu to the Big Island for a very reasonable price. Once there, we picked up the dodgiest of hire cars from the airport. We had realised that when you book a hire car through a US website, it doesn't include any insurance, so you end up paying much more than you expect on pickup. However, if you book through a UK or Australian website, the insurance is often included in the price. If you then book using the right type of credit card, the ridiculously large excess amount is taken care of. This means that when you reach the hire car counter, you can't be sold anything, you have an answer for all their doomsday scenarios. As an unfortunate side effect, we found that we would often be assigned the fugliest car they had. It took a good 30 minutes, recording all the bumps and scratches before we left the car park and headed to our posh hotel.

Unfortunately, we didn't pay quite enough for the room, and my upgrade skills failed me, so we were not able to see Mantas directly from the room, but we could hardly complain about the view. Our next dilemma was whether to snorkel or dive. We hadn't been underwater for over a year but wanted to make sure we had the best experience, so had a chat with the tour company owner. He advised that generally, people get the closest experience from just snorkelling, so we signed up. The trip consisted of packing a catamaran full of people, heading just a couple of hundred meters into the cove before throwing everyone off to dangle on a floating rope ladder.

Onboard, the staff gave everyone clear instructions about not splashing or paddling, just to float relax and watch. The staff would then pull the ladder to the best spots. The fact that the English are bastions of polite queuing meant that Nic and I ended up being two of the last to get in, next to a family with two younger boys. Once in the water we all waited. After a while we notice a dive boat appear, eight divers then jump off and descend underneath. Having heard stories of the possibility of 12-20 Mantas appearing, we stayed excited. We know from diving that everything can change in a heartbeat.

Forty, cold minutes later, we notice the diver's lights moving around excitedly, and we see the silhouette of at least one Manta. It was great to know that they were out there, but it wasn't really close enough to tick it off as a Kona experience. I'm pretty sure the main reason that nothing came close was because of the two little shites that were holding onto the rope near us. They had become bored by now and were splashing around and leaning on one side of the ladder which meant that everyone holding onto that side got a dunking.

Again as an Englishman, the biggest weapon in my arsenal is my furrowed eyebrows and disapproving stare. After a third dunking which left me with a snorkel full of water, I drew on all my inner grumpiness and pulled off the best eyebrow/stare combination that I could muster. Then it struck me, I was wearing a mask, they couldn't see any of it. It was my kryptonite, I figure at the most, it would have looked like I'd just squeezed out a little fart and it was working its way up the back of my wetsuit. After about two of these, the mother finally gave the kids a serve, probably because she thought the rocking might have been causing my flatulence. Finally, we could concentrate on the Mantas.

It must have been a rostered day off for the Mantas, as there was only one on duty, and she much preferred flirting with the divers, with their fun lights and bubbles. Why hadn't we dived instead? Then, just like a young child that's made to go and kiss the smelly uncle goodbye at the end of a family party, she swam underneath us. Her eyebrows (cephalic lobes) in a kind of 'whatevs' look, she performed a barrel roll to present her belly to us, before heading back to the divers. That was that. It was enough to tick it off the list, but probably not enough to travel the world, convincing others to add it to theirs.

Dodgy car trip to the end of the world

Next day, we spent a day out in our crappy hire car on a 140km coastal drive to the Hawaii Volcanoes National Park. Although beautiful scenery, our first refreshment stop was a little sombre. It was Kealakekua Bay, where Captain James Cook was killed (and maybe made a broth out of). More coastal road and whale watching ensued before we reached the volcanic park. We'd seen great pictures of the Kilauea volcano spouting lava from its main crater, as well as massive lava flows pouring into the sea, creating a plume of steam.

We arrived full of excitement to find the volcano just performing some mild burping. If we climbed onto a fence, standing on tiptoes, we could see the odd little lava spec fly through the air. Not quite what was in the brochure, but it's not every day that you find yourself sat on the edge of an active volcano. It was still pretty cool enough to cause plenty of pinching ourselves.

From there, we went to the end of the road. Literally. A previous lava flow had covered a road leading down to the coast making it a tourist attraction and a visible insight into the damage that an eruption can cause. The journey home from here was timed nicely with a torrential weather front. The drive would have felt dicey in a decent vehicle, but in our hire car, we were once again finding religion and having flashbacks to our South East Asia experiences. In a scene reminiscent of *Jurassic Park*, the wipers couldn't keep up, as locals sped past using their muscle memory of every bump on the road to keep them alive. It was a horrible 3-hour drive, but later back in the apartment sipping on a Kona beer after surviving the journey and visiting a volcano that had mild indigestion, we felt alive.

Maui Wowi

So, remember when we first arrived in Hawaii it didn't meet our dreamy expectations of the islands, well this was about to be rectified with a trip across to Maui. We'd booked inter-island flights and arrived at Kona airport on a beautiful sunny day. The 'airline' was based out of a hanger that didn't seem much bigger than a double garage. We checked in, ready to board our small Cessna Caravan. There aren't many check-ins where you get weighed as well as your luggage. Our unhealthy diet, post South East Asia, was front and centre of conversation that morning.

We waited, watching islanders come and go from their flights, all looking like the cast of a *Magnum PI* episode. An announcement called us to board, and our pilot arrived with his Khaki shorts and bright white sleeved pilot shirt, topped off with confidence inspiring epaulettes. The problem was that he only looked about twenty, certainly not old enough to be flying a passenger plane. I'm no spring chicken, and a good proportion of the people that I now meet are younger than me. However, I'm fairly confident that I could have been this guy's father (if it wasn't for his ruggedly good looks).

While I was living in fear that he might think he was back playing shoot-em-ups on his PS3 during the flight, at least Nic had some eye candy to distract her. Then the co-pilot arrived, a stunningly beautiful young blonde. Nic and I elbowed anyone in our way, ensuring that we secured the two front seats behind these spunks. They strapped themselves into their seats and slotted an iPad into the plane's dashboard. Maybe this was a multiplayer game.

We took off, staying at a low altitude to give the most amazing views of both crystal blue sea and luscious green mountains. Nic kept one eye on the scenery and one on her pilot, I did the same with the co-pilot. It really was something out of a movie, as we flew through beautiful valleys on our descent into Maui. We both hoped that the rest of our stay on Maui lived up to this introduction, and it truly did.

The best upgrade of the trip

I honestly don't know what happened to our budget for this leg, we seemed to have no intention whatsoever of keeping it under control, or try to travel within our means. Maybe it was the fact that they were important places to us, or we were a bit further out of our comfort zone in the US and wanted to play safe. Maui was no exception, in fact, it led the way. We'd booked into the most expensive hotel of the trip, the Makena Beach Hotel and Spa, located on the island's south west coast. It was whale watching season, and we wanted to make sure we had a prime spot for it. We'd heard that the hotel had great views and a lovely, almost private beach. Of course, we forked out for an ocean view room.

Our hire car was even worse than the one on the big island. We arrived at this posh hotel in a clapped out disgrace of a car to be quizzed about valet parking. On finding out that we could just park in the car park behind for free, we went for that option (see, saving US$20 a day thank you very much). We checked in and headed to our room through the hotel's lovely atrium with lush trees, and extensive Koi pond.

Our room was lovely, and as billed there was the ocean. It was a bit off at an angle, but there it was. I laid down on the bed taking in the serenity, but instead could clearly hear banging and drilling from outside. From the balcony we could see that we were directly over a building site, this certainly wasn't in the very expensive brochure. This hit hard on two fronts, firstly we felt guilty enough about spending so much money on the room, it would really seem a waste if things weren't perfect; secondly, we'd spent many years in Melbourne living opposite one building site or another, so were highly sensitive to construction noise. I headed off back to the reception.

This was going to be another of those moments where one slight twist of fate would make the world of difference. I was standing in a queue listening to an American woman checking in and demanding an upgrade. No justification given, other than she thought she deserved it. It was lovely to hear the receptionist explaining that it's their policy not to provide free upgrades, much to this annoying woman's disgust. Because this conversation had been dragging on for a while, another staff member appeared from the back room to help me out. It was Paul, the hotel's assistant manager to whom I explained my predicament and pre-existing allergy to construction noise. I remained very polite, rambling about how beautiful the hotel was and how the stay was the fulfilment of a bucket list item. This got us to talking about Melbourne and, of course, about our trip. I sensed none of the disdain I was expecting towards the scruffy looking backpacker standing in front of him.

He reached under the desk and programmed two door cards, explaining that I should check out these two rooms and select the one I liked the best. Paul informed me that one room was the furthest away from the noise but had restrictive views, the other was only halfway along the hotel, but he thought I'd prefer it. I initially went to the furthest room and walked in. It was much bigger and at a similar angle to the sea than our current room. I then moved to the next location. I walked in, then walked out immediately, closed the door and tried the key again as surely there was a mistake. The door opened again and led me into a suite with three balconies, all with perfect ocean views. The suite had a living area, a separate dining area, and two bathrooms. It was huge, bigger than our apartment in Melbourne.

You know those muscle spasms you sometimes get in your feet or neck, well I had one in my face as a silly grin appeared that I had no control over. I had to show Nic, so rushed back to our original room, the atrium filled with the song of my thongs, flipping and flopping along the internal marble walkways. Every muscle in my face was fighting the silly grin as I walked in and explained that they had offered another room. I said that it was kinda okay and we could move if she really wanted.

I led her to the new room, carrying all the bags and opened the door for her to enter. Five minutes of discussing whether it was a mistake followed. Both, leaving the room and checking the swipe yet again. My face spasm suddenly became contagious as we both stood there looking at the ocean, then each other, then the suite, then the ocean. Needless to say, we decided to keep the room. We legged it down to reception before they changed their mind, armed with a toy koala to say thank you. Paul had disappeared behind the scenes again, so I explained the situation to the 'we don't do upgrades' receptionist. Just like us, she double checked at least five times before making a phone call, probably to Paul, to confirm. She even waved over a colleague, her eyebrow nearly hit the hotel's high ceiling. I passed on the koala which looked pretty unsubstantial now, bordering on embarrassing. It was our very last one, and although well travelled and worldly wise, had taken a bashing over the previous year. We made a quick exit (flip flop, flip flop) back to our new home.

This upgrade probably affected the extent to which we saw Maui, as we just didn't want to leave the hotel. Each evening, while enjoying a Kona beer, a magnificent sunset would provide the background to numerous whales breaching and slapping tails as they passed. Only if the cast of *Magnum* and *Hawaii-Five 0* joined us on one of our three balconies, could the scene have been more Hawaiian.

Close Encounters of the Turtle Kind

Maui delivered so many lasting memories: driving the Hana Highway, a spectacular coastal route that's only 85km long but takes around three hours due to its 620 curves; the abundance of whales; and our first Hawaiian shaved ice. But, one of the stand out experiences happened just off the hotel's doorstep. The resort had a beautiful little beach that wasn't officially a private one, but few people knew about it, so it felt like one. We were disappointed that we hadn't been diving in Hawaii so decided to try some snorkelling on a small reef just off the beach. Although a bit fresh getting in, as soon as you submersed your head, you could see how crystal clear the water was. What transpired was probably one of our best snorkels ever, even beating many scuba dives.

We started by swimming over some lovely reefs and bommies (outcrops of coral or rocks) that were full of life. As we cruised by a small solitary coral bommie, we spotted a cute little green turtle alongside it. You already know how much we love a bit of turtle time, especially Nic. We were in about 10-12 metres of water, and I tried a few dives to get some Go-Pro footage. I'm not a water baby, nor a great swimmer, or comfortable without scuba gear for that matter, so was quite pleased with my achievements. The turtle, let's call him Thomas, looked me up and down during my momentary visits, not surprisingly, he wasn't threatened in any way whatsoever. However, Thomas must have sensed that there was someone up on the surface that would really like to meet him. He slowly rose and headed directly to Nic. After surfacing for air only a few feet from her, he had a lovely nosey around for a full investigation of my wife. Although I was a few metres away, I could see Nic's eyes were like footballs as she stared at Thomas, who in turn was staring at her. I gave Thomas a thumbs up, indicating that I'd taken some great footage, and he slowly headed back to the protection of a large fan coral. We've probably used the phrase 'magical' too often but it certainly summed up that last 15 minutes.

Evening Ladies

It was hard not to feel cool in Hawaii, the sun was shining, the sky was blue, and we were surrounded by surfer dude and dudettes. As the year was marching on, my hair had grown into flowing locks. Surely it couldn't have been timed better for someone who's never had long hair, to find themselves in a laid back surf Mecca with hair that looked like it just walked off the set of *Big Wednesday*. All I needed was some cool surf clothes to complete the look, time for some shopping. I was feeling a little less out of place than normal as I swaggered into the surf store with Nic, a staff member even shouted out to greet us. 'Evening Ladies!'. A quick double-take by the clerk preceded a sincere apology. I figured I must have been blocked a bit by Nic. It was a simple mistake but my confidence dipped slightly.

Three days later, I walked into a local ABC store to receive my fourth call-out as a 'Lady'. Clear line of sight, a slight beard, no fascinators, and trying out my deep Barry White voice, didn't help. Admittedly the UK and North America had kindly presented me with a pert set of man-boobs, and after a relaxed few days I might have had slightly less hairy legs than Nic at this point. But still, what was next? Wolf whistles from local construction workers? I walked out of the store in a strop, googling locations of local female-only saunas to try my luck. Why? Because I'm worth it.

Tokyo Drifters

Despite a relaxing time in Hawaii, we were still feeling a little fatigued from the journey, and dare I say it, ready to get home. Remembering the immediate relief and relaxation as we left Vietnam for Hong Kong, we were feeling a little anxious about how much we were going to enjoy our next location, Japan. Would it just be too much for us, to be thrust back into a more challenging environment with such a high density of people and intense sensory overload? Well, I guess we would find out soon enough.

The United Airlines flight went smoothly enough, Nic was preoccupied as she'd heard about a perfect Melbourne based job, so was busy putting together an updated resume. I settled back with a Bloody Mary and a dodgy Ben Affleck movie, trying not to think about the upcoming onslaught. Surprisingly, the disembarkation and train journey from the airport was easy to traverse, and we had a relaxing 50 minute journey from Narita to Shinjuku, the world's busiest train station. Just working out the best way to exit this station could be a reality survival TV show hosted by Bear Grylls. I guess it's times like this we realised how much we'd learnt over the past year. We took it calmly, used the resources at hand, and exited the station in the right direction with only one wrong turn.

Strangely, we found that we were surrounded by so many people, just like the other cities in Asia, but we weren't being pushed, prodded, or shouted at. No taxi drivers tried to kidnap us, it felt as though the crowds were parting before us, as we made our way through the bright lights of this lively area to our short stay apartment. Maybe, we were just delusional after too much airline booze, I'm sure things would be back to normal the following day.

It turns out that Tokyo is a city of organised chaos, it really is impressive and refreshing. Polite orderly queues form at each side of a train door, allowing people to get out first, no-one jumps queue or pushes (unless you need a bit of help squeezing into a jam-packed train). If you produce a map, then someone will present themselves to help, whether or not they speak any English, or indeed know their way around. Far from being the busy, tiring, and stressful experience we were expecting, it was actually a lovely relaxing country to be in. I can only describe it as one of those TV or Film scenes where a person is moving in slow motion as everyone around them is frantic, speeded up, and blurred as they rush around.

We loved Tokyo. Like Melbourne, there isn't that central location to head to, or a clear set of Top 5 attractions to go and point at. This was great, as it meant we could just mooch around different suburbs and soak in as much as we could in the little time we had there. We had plenty of opportunities to try different types of food. Although, it often relied on us dragging a member of staff outside and pointing to a picture of food they had in their window.

The stand out food experience was Tokyo's waterfront market and the food stalls therein. We weren't too adventurous, as being supporters of causes such as Sea Shepherd, we hated the thought of inadvertently eating something we'd rather not. To play safe, we headed to a sushi restaurant, highly recommended by TripAdvisor. I say headed, but that sounds like we took a direct route, when in actual fact we surrounded the place twice, taking 20 minutes to hone it down to the correct one. It was worth it, a genuinely authentic locals place with the boisterous greeting of 'Irasshaimase!' by all staff members as you walk in. For us, this was both welcoming and intimidating. Thankfully, there were also lots of pictures to point at.

I'm dreaming of a white Kyoto

Without doing enough research before visiting Japan, we knew of one obvious place to visit as well as Tokyo, and that was Kyoto. It also gave us the opportunity to travel on one of the famous

Shinkansen bullet trains that travel up to 320km/h. Our first challenge was working out the best value tickets, and where to get them from. Like everything else here, it was easier than we expected. The train left from Chiyoda station, a beautiful building with a mix of old and new architecture, the old section had a very westernised brick exterior and was rumoured to be inspired by Amsterdam's famous Centraal Station.

We boarded the train and found our allocated seats. As the trains run every 10 minutes and are rarely more than a minute late, we definitely felt the pressure to get on and sorted efficiently. British Rail's overweight, unshaven ticket collector, with one side of his shirt untucked, was replaced by a pretty stewardess that would quietly enter each carriage and bow to everyone. Can you imagine fat Dave running the 10:30 from Crewe to Liverpool, battling a hangover, performing a bow without throwing up. I love this country.

Kyoto station is a vast, impressive, modern construction. If it was located in a more boring part of the world, it would be on your tourist itinerary. It has a hotel and lots of great restaurants, including our regularly visited cheap sushi train. Despite its low cost, the staff didn't hold back on their 'Irasshaimase! gusto. However, there were more beautiful wonders we wanted to discover outside of the confines of the station.

Our hostel was just a 15 minute walk from the station and only a couple of blocks from two of the city's more prominent temples. It was a great location and reminded us of the Hop Inn in Hong Kong, with a cool travellers vibe going on. We woke up the next morning and saw that it had been snowing, we weren't expecting this and it was a complete surprise to see the white roads. The young guy on reception confirmed that it was an unexpected snowfall, before ordering us to head directly to the Golden Pavilion. I think if he had a broom, he would have swept us out of the door. The Buddhist temple Kinkaku-Ji was already on our list as it was one of the more picturesque of Kyoto's temples. We'd researched a local bus, and boarded with the map preloaded into the iPhone so we could jump off when the blue dot reached a near enough spot to walk from.

It seemed that after sweeping us out the door, our receptionist quickly jumped onto the phone and internet to give the rest of Kyoto their marching orders too. You could sense that something a bit special was going on. We paid our entry and followed a path around the grounds until, there it was. It was absolutely beautiful. The snow either hadn't stuck to the famous golden roof, or had been cleared off, leaving a lovely contrast between the snow, the now bright blue sky, and the shiny golden roof. The still lake in front, providing a mirror image for perfect photos.

As you can imagine by now, this wasn't my first bite at the apple when trying to photograph a major attraction while surrounded by a few hundred people. I prepared myself by handing any superfluous clothing and baggage to Nic, making myself more slipstreamed to get through the crowds. My camera settings were already selected, my elbows were out and pointy, and my accent became Italian in case anyone pulled me up on their use. I took one step back, head down, and surged forward to a predetermined spot for the best photographic results. In what must have looked like a staged World Wrestling Federation routine, the crowd parted before me, almost letting me hit the fence and bounce back further than my start position. I couldn't believe it, everyone was politely giving each other space and time to take the photos they needed. Seriously, what was the challenge in that? Although, I greatly appreciated it by the time I'd taken my twentieth photo of the temple including three nostril shots. I fell in love with this country even more. It was a lovely experience apart from some annoying pushing-in from an Italian (or was he really?).

Geisha Paparazzi

We knew nothing about Geishas before arriving in Japan, even to the point that we didn't watch the movie about her memoirs until after we'd arrived in the country. We thought we knew what they looked like with traditional garb, pretty makeup, and a white face. We were stoked to see girls looking just like this at one of our first temples in Kyoto. I managed to get a sneaky pic of them while they were busy getting a selfie of themselves. That in itself should have fired alarm bells, but we didn't think anything of the fact they were ladened with trimmings such as Digital SLRs and phones. We ticked it off our list of must-see sites in Japan and carried on. Fail.

A last minute decision to complete a walking tour of the Gion district, famous for the Geisha scene, quickly educated us to the fact that they were not Geishas at all, just people who enjoyed dressing up. The tour was incredibly interesting, and not only journeyed through some pretty side streets, it gave us a much better insight into the real life of a Geisha. The tour had a funny juxtaposition of wanting to educate the tourists and ideally enable them to see a Geisha, while wanting to protect their modest lifestyle and much needed privacy. This made the guide seem both excited and nervous. It was a case of 'there's one', 'don't look', 'don't look', 'now quickly look'.

We only had the smallest of sightings during the tour, so decided we'd have better luck without the other noisy rabble. As soon as it ended, we doubled back to retrace our route. It felt like we were paparazzi and were trespassing into things that should just be left alone. Did that stop us? No. Actually, it was only the fact that we were hungry and a long way from our hostel that stopped us. Then, just as we were heading to a bus stop, we saw a real life Geisha crossing a busy road with her wooden souled shoes, much more basic traditional makeup, and a plain brown kimono. It was now dark and raining, but I managed to get a discrete photo from a distance. It was an 'in it to win it' moment, but with a small serve of guilty tourist on the side.

Keeping the Golden Pavilion company, Kyoto was packed with many other significant experiences such as walking through the relaxing and almost meditative Arashiyama Bamboo Grove, and the Fushimi Inari Shrine. Fushimi Inari will be familiar to some from a classic scene from the movie *Memoirs of a Geisha* and is famous for its thousands of bright orange torii gates. This Shinto shrine complex is set in a beautiful forest hilltop location, and after the full 3-hour walking loop, we definitely deserved the cold Asahi at the end.

In the end, we became Pod People

Our hostel in Kyoto was our last home for the whole trip, a very sad thought indeed. As you may have picked up during the book, our various homes over the past year have included all kinds of styles, comfort, and price. However, there was still one aspect we'd managed to avoid for the whole thirteen months, and that was to stay in a dorm. I suppose if we are being pedantic, the Trans-Mongolian was a little four-bed mobile dorm, but we didn't think of it that way. So that we could say we did it, we decided to split our stay in the last hostel between the two types of accommodation they had.

The first three nights were in a private, double ensuite room. It was a mixed experience, the room was small, the bed hard, but in the corner of the room was a high tech bathroom. The toilet would do everything but poo for you. You would exit the room the cleanest you'd ever felt in your life with a posterior at the perfect temperature. Even the shower had LED lights and a radio system to keep you entertained. It was a miracle that we actually left the room to see any of Kyoto.

The next room we chose, our very last for the whole trip, was a capsule dorm. You know, one of those coffin type contraptions where you each have your own self contained little world. Its base was a hard mattress, it had shelves and small individual TVs. It could have been on the set of the next *Alien* movie, I didn't want to fall asleep in case I woke up a thousand years later in another galaxy. My pod was above Nic's and there were only about eight pods in the dorm, so we didn't have to mingle too much with the great unwashed. It seemed a perfect quirky ending to a great adventure.

This model of capsule had its entry through the longer side (the length of the bed), but we didn't realise in advance that the pod door wasn't solid, instead kind of a window blind material or that stuff you place at the bottom of a drawer to stop things slipping. This was fine unless you wanted any protection from light or noise. After spending some time squished together in one capsule, reviewing the day's photos, I moved upstairs and settled in for the night.

We probably should have realised that everyone else in the dorm would be half our age and their usual time to 'head up the wooden hills' would be far different from ours. They didn't even start returning to the dorm until after midnight, and despite the number of capsules, I'm sure about twenty people eventually rocked up, noisily depositing their bags and chatting away. Maybe one was a clown capsule that allowed for an endless number of people to appear from it, I think I did hear the honk of a horn at one point. The noise was endless, I feared for one poor German backpacker's life as it sounded like he was being fatally attacked by a noisy plastic bag for at least half an hour. Don't worry, he survived. I know this because the ordeal made him hungry, and I could count the individual Pringles he was chomping on (not exactly the sheep I'm used to counting). It struck me that this capsule door material not only didn't cancel any noise, it seemed to amplify it. How else would it be possible to hear, One Down-Three Across (as we liked to call her), turning the pages of her book? I was being kept awake by somebody reading!

So for the last night of our whole trip, we were not only separated from each other, but had one of the worst night sleeps of the 124 different beds we'd slept in. At least we had the saving grace of waking everyone up, as we left for the airport at 5am.

Take that, you smelly herberts! Now get yourself a haircut, and get a job (something I was now mentally preparing myself for).

Homeward Bound

The flights home were long and drawn out, partly because they were cheap, and partly because we were in no rush to end our adventure. It consisted of an AirAsia flight from Osaka to Adelaide with a long wait in Kuala Lumpur, and then into Melbourne with Virgin Australia. We were exhausted, apprehensive, sad, and very proud of what we'd achieved. It was only fitting to end the trip as we'd started 378 days earlier, by raising a glass of bubbly. So we did it everywhere we could, Osaka, KL, and Adelaide.

On arrival in Melbourne, in another of the few times in our lives we were actually greeted at the airport. This was lovely and emotional, although, the fact that our last leg was a domestic flight robbed us of being able to burst through the sliding doors into international arrivals like the intrepid explorers we were. Instead, we were stuck in queues of pale businessmen and women, with their pull along cabin bags, muttering about sales forecasts and agenda items. Susan picked us up and took us home, her and Craig's home would also be our home for a couple of weeks while we found an apartment and resumed our normal lives. By nightfall, we'd all caught up. Of course, all the big stories had already been told by virtue of social media, so it didn't take long. Before we knew it, it felt like we'd never left.

Surely we hadn't just done what we did, had we?

What do we do now?

EPILOGUE

Location: Melbourne
Days 397, Countries 27, Kilometers 77,427, Beds 124
Trains 22, Planes 24, Automobiles 41, Boats 14
Beers 276

Heading back to work wasn't the hard part. Nic had a job waiting for her and I'd managed to get myself hooked up within a few weeks of returning. Believe it or not, after 13 months it was actually lovely to return, be productive, be sociable, and be constant. We were empowered with an extra air of confidence that came with the experiences and achievements we'd accomplished. Unaccustomed as we were, we even felt just a little bit cool for the first time in our lives. Looking back at what we'd done, and the many big-ticket items we crammed into the journey, it never ceases to surprise us. From the Great Wall of China, to the top of the Statue of Liberty, to the Bolshoi Ballet, to sitting on the edge of an active volcano, the list goes on. The fact that we actually did it, have the memories and pictures to prove it, is still sometimes not enough to convince us that it really happened.

What did we learn along the way? Well, the prominent thing is that we can achieve much more than we thought we could.

All the comments from those self-help books (from the library) about creating a mental image and working towards making it real, do actually work.

It validated our belief that life is better if you make it an adventure. However, that adventure doesn't have to be a round-the-world trip. Our life is made up of continual micro-adventures together. Even a visit to the local DIY store can be an adventure. It puts more fun into your life and makes you look at things differently. This means that it doesn't necessarily have to cost anything to have an adventure or to push the envelope of your comfort zone a little. The rewards from doing this are immense. It builds confidence, it's an apple a day for your mental health, and a laxative for your laziness.

Although not strangers to loss, we were again presented with its challenges and used it to make us stronger, not only individually, but as a couple.

Having the ability to travel does change how you look at the world, life, and other people. However, you realise that you can travel, without actually travelling. Try it in your own home town. Even after being back in Melbourne for some time, I'll often walk around and pretend that I'm still travelling through the city. Try it, you will look at what's on your doorstep in a whole different light.

I could easily bang out a couple of pages of cliches that are accurate and relevant. That's why they are cliches, right? Three of the most cringeworthy examples that stick out like a lazy writer's sore thumb are:

- It's not about getting there, it's the journey.
- It's the people you meet that make it special.
- Wrong turns could lead to great things.

Sure, we did hit big-ticket, shiny destinations, but if you think about it, there is very little time spent in this book talking about them. This isn't just because I'm inept as a writer and unable to portray them with any degree of justice. It's mainly because most of the memories happened in-between them, and with the fantastic people we met along the way.

Personally, the past 13 months wouldn't have been the same if I hadn't had the most amazing partner in crime. As you may have realised by now, there are endless reasons why I married Nic. I couldn't have imagined being at any one of those locations without her (apart from maybe Moscow of course). The trip has made me thankful for many things, but mostly that I have a perfect travel buddy and life partner. Without her, none of this would have happened.

It was inevitable that the honeymoon period back in the real world wouldn't last. It didn't. Surprisingly, it wasn't the jobs and the bills that bothered us. It was a constant pull to travel, the urge to just jump on a plane, bus or train, and piss off to somewhere unknown. We were literally homesick to not be at home. When we weren't reminiscing about this trip, we were talking about when we could do the next. It was so strange to feel like a transient in your own home town, living with one foot out of the door.

We were walking on eggshells, like a ticking time bomb. Generally, one of us would feel worse than the other at a particular moment in time. However, there was an underlying risk that if we both came home after a bad day at work, to be faced with an inane 1st world problem like no milk in the fridge, we'd be in an Uber to the airport within minutes.

Months and years passed, real life slowly distracted us from these impulses. House buying stopped us thinking about chickens on buses. Car loans, stopped us thinking about the shower dance. Our great friends in Melbourne made the faces of the people we'd met travelling, fade.

However, whatever you call it, dromomania, wanderlust, itchy feet, or being spoilt brats. We've been infected with something there is no cure for.

Something is building.

The lobster will return…….

THE STATS

THE JOURNEY

Australia
Melbourne to Darwin (Flight) 3,140km

Indonesia
Darwin to Bali (Flight) 1,643km
Bali to Yogyakarta (Flight) 542km

Singapore
Yogyakarta to Singapore (Flight) 1,255km

Malaysia
Singapore to Kuala Lumpur (Train) to KL 370km
Kuala Lumpur to Cameron Highlands (Bus) 200km
Cameron Highlands to Ipoh (Bus) 94km
Ipoh to Georgetown (Bus) 158km
Georgetown to Langkawi (Ferry) 93km

Thailand
Langkawi to Koh Lipe (Ferry) 30km
Koh Lipe to Koh Lanta (Ferry) 175km
Koh Lanta to Krabi (Bus) 90km
Krabi to Bangkok (Bus) 820km

Burma
Bangkok to Yangon (Flight) 586km
Yangon to Bagan (Flight) 513km
Bagan to Mandalay (Ferry) 190km

Mandalay to Inle Lake (Flight) 177km
Inle Lake to Mandalay (Flight) 177km

Thailand

Mandalay to Bangkok (Flight) 1025km
Bangkok to Sukhothai (Bus) 430km
Sukhothai to Phitsanulok (Bus) 57km
Phitsanulok to Chaing Mai (Train) 270km
Chiang Mai to Chaing Rai (Bus) 187km
Chiang Rai to Chiang Khong (Car) 134km

Laos

Chiang Khong to Pakbeng (Ferry) 153km
Pakbeng to Luang Prabang (Ferry) 152km
Luang Prabang to Vientiane (Minibus) 388km
Vientiane to Thakhek (Bus) 350km
Thakhek to Pakse (Bus) 333km
Pakse to Don Khon (Minibus) 130km

Cambodia

Don Khon to Kratie (Bus) 240km
Kratie to Siem Reap (Bus) 510km
Siem Reap to Phnom Penh (Bus) 314km
Phnom Penh to Sihanoukville (Bus) 226km
Sihanoukville to Kampot (Minibus) 100km
Kampot to Ha Tien (Minibus) 70km
Ha Tien to Phu Quoc (Ferry) 30km

Vietnam

Phu Quoc to Ho Chi Minh City (Flight) 301km
Ho Chi Minh City to Da Lat (Bus) 311km
Da Lat to Nha Trang (Bus) 140km
Nha Trang to Hoi An (Bus) 516km
Hoi An to Hue (Bus) 130km
Hue to Hanoi (Bus) 674km
Hanoi to Lao Cai (Train) 296km
Lao Cai to Sapa (Minibus) 38km
Sapa to Lao Cai (Minibus) 38km
Lao Cai to Hanoi (Train) 296km
Hanoi to Halong City (Bus) 146km
Halong Bay Cruise (Boat) 20km
Halong City to Hanoi (Bus) 146km

China
Hanoi to Hong Kong (Flight) 870km
Hong Kong to Shanghai (Train) 1991km
Shanghai to Beijing (Train) 1350km

Mongolia
Beijing to Ulaanbaatar (Train) 1356km
Ulaanbaatar to Elstei (Bus) 60km
Elstei to Ulaanbaatar (Bus) 60km

Russia
Ulaanbaatar to Irkutsk (Train) 1113km
Irkutsk to Listvyanka (Bus) 70km
Listvyanka to Irkutsk (Bus) 70km
Irkutsk to Moscow (Train) 5153km
Moscow to St Petersburg (Train) 650km

Finland
St Petersburg to Helsinki (Train) 415km

Sweden
Helsinki to Stockholm (Ferry) 470km

Denmark
Stockholm to Copenhagen (Train) 600km

UK
Copenhagen to Liverpool (Flight) 1030km
Liverpool to Birkenhead (Ferry) 8km

England, Wales, Scotland
Pootling around the UK (Car) 604km

France, Switzerland, Italy, UK
MJ the Camper through Europe 5575km

Czech Republic
Milan to Prague (Flight) 871km

Germany
Prague to Berlin (Bus) 351km

Italy
Berlin to Milan (Flight) 840km

Holland
Liverpool to Amsterdam return (Flight) 1040km

UK
Birkenhead to Leek (MJ) 116km
Leek to London (Train) 214km
London to Southampton (Bus) 129km

USA
Southampton to New York (Liner) 5920km
New York to Boston (Bus) 340km
Boston to Southington (Bus) 223km
Southington to New York (Bus) 189km

Canada
New York to Montreal (Train) 590km
Montreal to Quebec (Train) 250km
Quebec to Ottawa (Train) 450km
Ottawa to Toronto (Train) 450km
Toronto to Jasper (Train) 3555km
Jasper to Vancouver (Train) 869km
Vancouver to Victoria (Bus/Ferry) 115km

USA
Victoria to Seattle (Ferry) 150km
Seattle to Honolulu (Flight) 4310km
Honolulu to Kona (Flight) 260km
Kono to Maui (Flight) 130km
Maui to Honolulu (Flight) 150km

Japan
Honolulu to Narita (Flight) 3818km
Narita to Tokyo (Train) 81km
Tokyo to Kyoto (Train) 513km
Kyoto to Kanai (Train) 97km

Malaysia
Kanai to Kuala Lumpur (Flight) 4915km

Australia
Kuala Lumpur to Adelaide (Flight) 5700km
Adelaide to Melbourne (Flight) 655km

DOMESTIC BEERS

Australia
XXXX Gold

Indonesia
Bintang, Bali-Hai, Ankor

Singapore
Tiger, Raffles Export

Thailand
Chang, Singha, Leo

Myanmar
Dagon Green, Myanmar Beer, Andaman Gold, ABC Stout, Mandalay Beer

Thailand
Archa

Laos
BeerLao, BeerLao Dark, Namkhong, BeerLao Gold

Cambodia
Angkor, Cambodia Beer, Bayon, Phnom Penh, Crown Gold, Kingdom,
Anchor

Vietnam
Bia Saigon Special, 333, La Rue, Bia Hoi (home brew "Fresh Beer"), Huda,
Festival, Hue Beer, Hanoi Beer, Zorok, Thang Long, Halinda

China
Tsingtao, Suntory , Yanying, Pabst Blue Ribbon Beer

Mongolia
Borgio (since 1927), Golden Gobi, Szngur, Zhaam Khar, Niislzl

Russia
Baikal Beer, Baltika, Okhota, Stary Melnik, Burkhan, Kainsko, Kulyer,
Kamchatka, Zhiguli , Bouka, Baltika Draft Premium, Zatcky Gus, Mead
(Honey Beer)

Finland
Lapin Kulta, Karhu Tumma I, Keisari, Koff, Marsalkka, Karjala III, Lapin
Kulta IV

Sweden
Pripps Bla, Spendrups, Mariestads

Denmark
Carlsberg Dark Draft, Jacobsen Weissbier, Carlsberg

England
Bumble Bee Honey Beer, Pedigree, Tanglefoot, Green King IPA, Thwaits
Wainwright, Marstons Burton Bitter, Marstons Double Drop, Adnams
Broadside, Directors, Badger Fursty Ferret, Fullers ESB, Lancaster Bomber,
London Pride, Elbow Beer, Tetley Huntsman Ale, Badger Blandford Flyer,
York Guzzler, Old Golden Hen, Fillers Bengal Lancer
Abbot Ale, Timothy Taylors Landlord, Old Hooky, Marston's Old Empire,
Badger Golden Glory, Newcastle Brown, Old Peculiar, Black Sheep Brewery
Black Cat, Co-op Organic Ale, Co-op GoldMiner, Adams, Southwold
Bitter, Theakston Masham Glory, Tribute Cornish Pale Ale, Brakspear
Oxford Gold, Wychwood Scarecrow, Wychwood Hobgoblin, Wychwood
Wychcraft, Wychwood Goliath, Shepherd Neame Master Brew, Whitstable
Bay Organic Ale, Shepherd Neame Spitfire, Batemans Dark Lord, Royal Air
Force Collection Battle of Britain, Woodfordes Wherry, Adnams Gunhill,
Ringwood Old Thumper, Adnams Explorer, Marstons EPA, Adnams Spin-
drift, Brains The Rev James, Thwaites Double Century, Cains Bitter, Brains
SA, Brains Original Bitter, Brains Dark, Robinsons Old Bob, Theakston XB,
Green King IPA Gold, Joseph Holt Humdinger, Ruddles County, Lancaster
Red, Wells Bombardier, Wells Bombardier The Colonels Choice, Weetwood
Cheshire Cat, Salopian Oracle, Woodlands Oak Beauty, Badger Poachers
Choice, Kentish Ale, Theakston Hogshead Bitter, Greene King Twisted
Wheel, Black Sheep Ale, Ghastly Ghoul, Robinsons Dizzy Blonde, Jennings
Cumberland Ale, Burton Union IPA, Sharps Doom Bar, St Edmunds,
Green King XX Mild, Wentworth WPA , Hackney Brewery 2114, London
Fields Brewery Love Not War, Hackney Hopster, Admans Topaz Gold,
Youngs Special, Youngs Bitter, Wells Bombardier Gold, Brains Barry Island
IPA, Brains SA Gold, Brains Boiler Maker

France
Les Bourgeoises de Calais Ambree, Kronenbourg, Monaco, CHTI, Gwiniz
Du, Dremmwe Rousse Bio, Jenlan Blonde, Pelforth Radler, Fischer Traditio-
nell, Pelforth Brune, Kronenbourg Rose, La Gravelinoise

Switzerland
Schwinger Bugel

Czech Republic
Pilsner Urquell, Staropramen, Staropramen Nefiltrovany, Master Dark,
Krusovice Musketyr, Kozel, Greslak, Budweiser Budvar, Lobkowicz, Cerna
Hora

Germany

Schoffenbier, Berliner Black Beer, Neuzeller Schwarzer, Berliner Kindl,
Bitburger, Kostritzer, Georg Pils, Georg Dark

Italy

Ichnusa, Nastro Azzurro, Peroni Grand Premium, Peroni, Moretti, Sans
Souci

Dutch

Heinken, Wieckse Witte, Rudi Marzen de Prael, Chateau Neubourge Pils
Gulpener, Bock <somethingorother>, Skuumkoppe Dunken Weizen texels,
Witte Trappist La Trappe, Bock Budels

USA

Weyerbacher Last Chance IPA, Founders Centennial IPA, Samuel Adams
Winter Lager, Samuel Adams Brick Red, Budweiser, Clown Shoes Clem-
entine White Ale, Green Dragon Brew, Wachusett Green Monsta IPA,
Wachusett Winter, Newcastle Red Ale, Harpoon IPA, Goose Island IPA,
Pumpkin Pie, Smutty Nose IPA, Georgetown Brewing, Manny's Pale Ale,
Georgetown Brewing Lucille IPA, Rock Bottom Kolsch, Rock Bottom
White Ale, Jolly Rodger Christmas Ale, Leavenworth Squealing Pig, Kona
Longboard, Duke's Pale Ale, Big Wave Golden Ale, Kona Pipeline Porter,
Kona FireRock Pale Ale, Maui Brewing Co Bikini Blonde, Hapa Brown
Ale, Asahi Super Dry, Saporo

Canada

Moose Head, Sleeman Honey Beer, Sleeman Red, Alexander Keith's Red,
Rickards White, Rickards Red, Archibald Chipie, Kichesippi Wychak Black
IPA, Sleeman Black, Mill Street Original Organic Lager, Mill Street Tank
House Ale, Mill Street Weizenbock, Mill Street Vanilla Porter, Steamwhistle
Pilsner, Jasper Park Lodge Brown Ale , Granville Island Brewing English
Bay Pale Ale, Granville Island Brewing Cypress Honey Lager, Fort Garry
Dark Ale, Fort Garry IPA, Labatts Blue, Steamworks Kolsh, Steamworks
Pale Ale, Steamworks Blitzen, Steamworks Heff, Steamworks Stout,
Steamworks Pilsner, Kokanee, Vancouver Island Brewing Hermann's Dark
Ale, Driftwood Fat Tug IPA, Green Leaf Pale Ale

Japan

Kirin, Asahi Black, Kirin Green Label, Asahi Original, Yebiscu, Asahi Clear,
Suntory Rich Malt, Yona Yona, Kirin Classic

The UNESCO Sites

Indonesia
Borobudur Temple Compounds
Prambanan Temple Compounds

Thailand
Historic Town of Sukhothai and Associated Historic Towns

Laos
Town of Luang Prabang
Vat Phou and Associated Ancient Settlements within the Champasak
Cultural Landscape\

Cambodia
Angkor

Vietnam
Ha Long Bay
Hoi An Ancient Town
My Son Sanctuary
Central Sector of the Imperial Citadel of Thang Long, Hanoi

China
The Great Wall
Imperial Palaces of the Ming and Qing Dynasties in Beijing and Shenyang

Russia
Lake Bakail
Kremlin and Red Square, Moscow
Historic Centre of Saint Petersburg and Related Groups of Monuments

Finland
Fortress of Suomenlinna

Denmark
Kronberg Castle

England
Maritime Mercantile City, Liverpool
Ironbridge Gorge
Frontiers of the Roman Empire (Hadrians Wall)
Palace of Westminster and Westminster Abbey including Saint Margaret's
Church

France
Amiens Cathedral

Paris, Banks of the Seine
Versailles
Cathedral of Notre-Dame, Former Abbey of Saint-Rémi and Palace of Tau,
Reims

Czech Republic

Historic Centre of Prague

Germany

Museumsinsel (Museum Island), Berlin

Italy

Venice and its Lagoon
City of Verona

Netherlands

Amsterdam Singelgracht

USA

Statue of Liberty
Hawaii Volcanoes National Park

Canada

Historic District of Old Québec
Rideau Canal
Canadian Rocky Mountain Parks

Japan

Historic Monuments of Ancient Kyoto

28281472R00222

Printed in Great Britain
by Amazon